From Cultural Deprivation to Cultural Security

This important book considers how youth of color and other marginalized youth experience socio-cultural deprivation from the repetition of traumatic socio-historic experiences as well as from the institutions they interact with such as schools, mental health organizations, and social services agencies. Focusing on the importance of connection to cultural heritage, the book shows how young people's cognitive development can be mediated in educational settings through humanizing and culturally sustaining rituals that build rapport and facilitate learning and healing.

The authors define socio-cultural deprivation and locate its origins for marginalized youth in post-traumatic slave syndrome, post-apocalyptic stress syndrome and similar socio-historic trauma, epigenetic trauma, and contemporary trauma. They weave theory and research, autobiography, and professional anecdotes to identify and elaborate upon socio-cultural deprivation and to provide rituals for rapport-building that can be applied to classrooms, group counselling, social work practices, and other human-centred work. Rituals include those acknowledging indigeneity; exploring personal ancestry and alternative forms for those who have no connection to their biological family; healing experiences through yoga, meditation, progressive relaxation, and visualization practices; and explicit relationship-building activities.

From Cultural Deprivation to Cultural Security will be a crucial text for training and practising psychologists, educators, social workers, youth workers and counsellors, concerned with the positive development of children, adolescents, and young adults.

Dale Allender, PhD, is an associate professor at Sacramento State University in the Teaching Credentials and Doctorate in Educational Leadership departments. Dr Allender has worked to disrupt anti-Black racism and to promote cultural security since 1995 at schools, treatment centers, universities, and museums throughout the United States, in Dakar, Jerusalem, and Vancouver.

Arya Allender-West, MA, is a Ronald E. McNair fellow at CSUS, conducting research identifying Black female college students' successful navigation of micro-aggression to illuminate the unique obstacles the population faces and provide best practices in advising, as well as to advance goals of non-biased teaching and counselling.

Applying Child and Adolescent Development in the Professions Series

Editor Kimberly A. Gordon Biddle
Emeritus Professor of Child and Adolescent Development, Sacramento State, California, USA

The field of Child and Adolescent Development is being recognized and legitimized more and more as good preparation for a variety of careers in various fields such as psychology, education, allied health, non-profits, and social work. As more theories are created and research is conducted, more attention and recognition is given to the field of Child and Adolescent Development.

This series takes core and current topics in the field of Child and Adolescent Development, defines the topics, describes the topics as they develop in children from infancy to age 25 or describes how the topic impacts children from infancy to age 25, and then applies them to careers in five main fields, psychology, education, allied health, non-profits, and social work. Various application strategies and techniques are shared. The core topics addressed in this series of books are as follows: attachment, motivation, social and emotional competence, executive function, and multilingual and multicultural development. The current niche topics represented in the series are these; transformative frames for antiracism, socio-cultural deprivation, and growth mindset for transformative thinking. The writing level is accessible and engaging for students in high school and the first or second year of college. However, the information may be useful for graduate students, too. These books are excellent for early-, mid-, and late career professionals, too. Employee training and professional development can be enriched with the books of this series.

It is the intention of the book authors that the volumes are helpful to all people who work with and care for children. Indeed, the topics explored in Applying Child and Adolescent Development in the Professions Series move the field forward.

Inspiring Motivation in Children and Youth
How to Nurture Environments for Learning
David A. Bergin

Promoting Regulation and Flexibility in Thinking
Development of Executive Function
Kristen M. Weede Alexander and Karen M. Davis O'Hara

From Cultural Deprivation to Cultural Security
Tackling Socio-Cultural Deprivation with Children and Young People
Dale Allender and Arya Allender-West

For more information about this series, please visit: www.routledge.com/Applying-Child-and-Adolescent-Development-in-the-Professions-Series/book-series/ACADP

From Cultural Deprivation to Cultural Security

Tackling Socio-Cultural Deprivation
with Children and Young People

Dale Allender and Arya Allender-West

Routledge
Taylor & Francis Group

NEW YORK AND LONDON

Designed cover image: monkeybusinessimages via Getty Images

First published 2024
by Routledge
605 Third Avenue, New York, NY 10158

and by Routledge
4 Park Square, Milton Park, Abingdon, Oxon, OX14 4RN

Routledge is an imprint of the Taylor & Francis Group, an informa business

Library of Congress Cataloging-in-Publication Data
Names: Allender, Dale, author. | Allender-West, Arya, author.
Title: From cultural deprivation to cultural security : tackling socio-cultural deprivation with children and young people / Dale Allender and Arya Allender-West.
Description: New York, NY : Routledge, 2025. | Includes bibliographical references and index. |
Identifiers: LCCN 2024006886 (print) | LCCN 2024006887 (ebook) | ISBN 9781032011677 (hardback) | ISBN 9781032011707 (paperback) | ISBN 9781003177500 (ebook)
Subjects: LCSH: Youth with social disabilities. | Minority youth--Social conditions. | Minority youth--Psychology. | Minority youth--Mental health.
Classification: LCC HV1569.3.Y68 A45 2025 (print) | LCC HV1569.3.Y68 (ebook) | DDC 362.7/78008--dc23/eng/20240319
LC record available at https://lccn.loc.gov/2024006886
LC ebook record available at https://lccn.loc.gov/2024006887

ISBN: 978-1-032-01167-7 (hbk)
ISBN: 978-1-032-01170-7 (pbk)
ISBN: 978-1-003-17750-0 (ebk)

DOI: 10.4324/9781003177500

Typeset in Times New Roman
by MPS Limited, Dehradun

"When I first read the writings of Franz Fanon, I was stymied by them. Perhaps fifteen years old, I couldn't grasp its nuances; its careful mastery or its psychological projections and analyses. What came through this teenager's mind was its intense anti-colonialism. And the determination of the Algerian nationalists and the Algerian people to fight the foreigners, the colon; the settlers' unbridled cruelty; unchecked racism and an exploitative spirit, that sought to crush, not just the people, but their very culture, history, religion, and their sense of nationhood."

Mumia Abul Jamal
Franz Fanon Foundation Award Acceptance Speech
Recorded from Death Row by Noelle Hanrahan of Prison Radio
February 26, 2012

Contents

SERIES EDITOR FOREWORD

The field of Child and Adolescent Development is in the infant stages of development, but it is steadily maturing. It is time for it be recognized and legitimized. As the theorizing and conduction of research in the field become more solid, complex, and applicable to life; recognition comes that the field is for people in a variety of professions. The traditional education and psychology fields are enriched with the knowledge obtained from the field of Child and Adolescent Development. Additionally, allied health, social work, and non-profit fields are improved with knowledge of how to apply Child and Adolescent Development in the workplace setting. Everyone who works with or cares for children from birth to 25 years will benefit from reading and applying the information from the books in this series. Collectively, the authors have created books rich with foundational information and application techniques and strategies. Thematic boxes of interviews, case studies, and research and theory into practice run throughout all the books. These books help to answer some of the most important questions concerning children and their development. All who love and care about children should read every book in the series.

The knowledgeable and experienced writing team of Dr. Dale Allender and his daughter Arya have completed a deep, moving, and worthy textbook about Cultural Deprivation. A very impactful occurrence that is written into United States history and the histories of others all over the globe. Dr. Dale and Arya give us solutions to Cultural Deprivation in the professional, evidence-based, and sensitive textbook. How do you heal those who have experienced Cultural Deprivation? After defining it and relaying personal and professional experiences with Cultural Deprivation, the authors provide solutions and strategies. Professional Standards, rituals, indigeneity, mind/body connections and relationship building are solutions and strategies put forth in the textbook for healing. This book is necessary reading for all adults in all settings that interact with children from birth to age 25, from classrooms to therapeutic and medical settings. It is especially enlightening for parents and all Child and Adolescent professionals.

Introduction

We often look to anthropologists to tell us what culture looks like, what culture is, and how to define culture. Edward Burnett Tylor offered one of the earliest and most influential definitions of culture for many decades (Baldwin et al., 2006). Tylor asserted in his text, *Primitive Culture,* that "Culture, or civilization, taken in its broad, ethnographic sense, is that complex whole which includes knowledge, belief, art, morals, law, custom, and any other capabilities and habits acquired by man as a member of society" (Tylor, 1889). Hierarchical framing ran rampant among other anthropologists. Structuralist thinker Claude Levi Strauss used similar frames 60 or so odd years later with books such as *The Savage Mind* and *The Raw and the Cooked.*

Fast forward about 100 years later, Richard Geertz defines culture as "... an historically transmitted pattern of meanings embodied in symbols, a system of inherited conceptions expressed in symbolic forms by means of which men communicate, perpetuate, and develop their knowledge about and attitudes toward life" (Geertz, 1973, p. 89). Gabriel Idang (2015), professor of African philosophy from the University of Uyo in Nigeria, shares:

> The culture of a people is what marks them out distinctively from other human societies in the family of humanity. The full study of culture in all its vastness and dimensions belongs to the discipline known as anthropology, which studies human beings and takes time to examine their characteristics and their relationship to their environments. Culture, as it is usually understood, entails a totality of traits and characters that are peculiar to a people to the extent that it marks them out from other peoples or societies. These peculiar traits go on to include the people's language, dressing, music, work, arts, religion, dancing and so on. It also goes on to include a people's social norms, taboos and values.

DOI: 10.4324/9781003177500-1

While anthropological definitions can be helpful in parsing out cultural elements, contours, and expressions, Baldwin et al. (2006) notes that getting ahold of the concept of culture can be slippery. So we sometimes turn to poets, artists, and activists to help us gather our thoughts about ourselves.

This book is less about how culture is defined and more about the vital access to participation in cultural transmission experiences, one's own culture, and the culture of the dominant society.

Anti-Black racism, settler colonialism, and similar projects are exercises in cultural deprivation. All of these assaults on humanity through particular individuals and their communities present devastating physical, biological, economic, and other life-threatening consequences. Why focus on culture as opposed to, say, state violence like the work of Attorney Ben Crump (2019) or Michelle Alexander (2020) or economic exploitation? The truth is that this is not a new conversation. But it is a recurring need. Disrupting the cultural transmission process can impact cognitive and social processes and can threaten our livelihoods and our very lives.

I am most often in conversations with educators at different levels of instruction. In fact, some of the ideas in this book began during my study with cognitive psychologists Yvette Jackson and Eric Cooper. I worked with and learned from Jackson and Cooper in translating theories of Rueven Feuerstein, Asa Hilliard, and Pauolo Freire to classroom practice in school districts with schools with largely African American and African diaspora student populations. We were trying to change instructional practices from the school that prevented these students from accessing the dominant culture's educational norms. Also, we were simultaneously trying to change practices that were preventing students from accessing their own culture in these formal spaces.

This book provides an opportunity for me to share insights and practices gleaned through that work, and other sources of learning and experience about cultural security that can be helpful beyond the education profession and into the allied health professions. The specific rituals I describe are not new. I did not invent them. In fact, I did not necessarily order these rituals in the way they are presented in this book. To illustrate, I experienced different versions of some of these rituals at critical education events in California recently. During a preliminary fundraising presentation for Malcolm X Academy featuring Cornel West, hosted by the Sacramento Neighbor Program, school founder Jordan McGowan led a land acknowledgment and ancestral veneration to open the event. A week or so before the event, I saw it at a teacher professional development event exploring recent prohibitions to the ethnic studies curriculum. The event was hosted by Liberated Ethnic Studies Model Curriculum

Consortium. However, my goal is not to represent these organizations and individuals. I am sharing insights into these practices based on 35 years as a teacher, mentor, trainer, organizer, and advisor at schools, community colleges, universities, treatment centers, and advocacy organizations.

Narrative Inquiry

I am offering narratives of my personal and professional experiences of conceptualizing and enacting rituals. My inquiry combines several narrative genres, such as critical race counter stories (Solorzano and Yosso 2002), personal narrative, and critical family history (CFH) (Sleeter 2016; 2020). While personal narrative offers reverie that helps bind the grand narrative; critical race counter stories illuminate the role of racism and racialized trauma involved with individual instances of cultural deprivation; CFH frames each chapter. CFH draws on genealogy, DNA, and the historic record to tell a critical tale about place and encounter. CFH asks, "How do your stories situate the actors within the history of settler colonial and other exploitive actions?" I am writing from a U.S.-based African American perspective, so the bulk of my narratives and examples will be based here. I also acknowledge diaspora and interdependence and thus some of the narratives and examples will extend beyond my geography and ethnicity. I will always strive to give specific details and contexts. In my own narratives, I refer specifically to myself and, where possible, I use information that is in the public domain. When including others in my narrative without public domain information, I have largely used pseudonyms.

Chapters

The chapters in this book depart from the aforementioned conversation about culture to an exploration of cultural deprivation. The goal of Chapter 1 is to provide a robust description of cultural deprivation significantly based on a critical review of the term as it is defined by the American Psychological Association's Dictionary of Psychology online.

Chapter 2 adds additional dimensions of the definition and then briefly explores the impact of cultural deprivation and the goal of cultural security. In this chapter, the concept of cultural security is discussed largely from the point of view of Black psychology, highlighting the works of Wade Nobles, Resmaa Menakem, and Joy De Gruys, and Pan African Studies scholars, such as Cheik Anta Diop and Edward Bruce Bynum.

Chapter 3 acts as the first transition into addressing cultural deprivation in classrooms and communities. Whereas Chapters 1 and 2 analyze cultural deprivation on a variety of personal and political levels, Chapter 3 first presents an overview of three professional practice standards documents that address cultural deprivation: NASW Standards for Cultural Competence in Social Work, The American Medical Association's Strategic Plan to embed antiracism in their practices and policies, and the Board of Professional Teaching Standards principles. The rituals introduced in this chapter and explored in greater detail in the chapters that follow include indigeneity, ancestry, mindfulness, and relationship-building. I will assert repeatedly: I am not the originator of these rituals. This book is not an assertion of originality. Rather, it is a personal and professional exploration of my understanding and integration of these rituals into my professional practice.

Part 1

Context

Chapter 1

What Is Cultural Deprivation?

Part I

Introduction

This chapter has three basic sections: the first offers critical family history to illuminate different kinds of cultural deprivation as defined by the APA. I begin here in order to not only introduce my readers to who I am but also to introduce actions over time causing cultural deprivation and to describe rituals fostering cultural security to be discussed in later chapters.

Next, it provides a detailed look at the definition of cultural deprivation. The exploration utilizes the American Psychological Association's three-part definition. The focus of this section is on establishing concrete examples of cultural deprivation in the various categories offered by APA scholars. While the examples are not exhaustive, they provide in-depth exploration on individual, social, and societal levels from throughout history up to the present.

This book's examples and narratives focus mostly on the United States and will frequently say so explicitly. Sometimes specific locations within the United States will also be referenced. Occasionally there will be a reference to locations outside of the United States and outside of North and South America. Narratives and examples will also span time from very immediate, somewhat current, and historic.

Critical Family History: Origins and Migrations

My paternal grandmother, Eloise Garnett Adams, descends directly from enslaved Africans, Thomas and Caty Gumby, through her mother, Arley Adams, and her mother's mother, Mary Burke. The Gumbys were trafficked from somewhere in Gambia or Senegal and enslaved first in England, and later on the Nomini and Leo Hall Plantations in Westmoreland County, Virginia. Their enslaver, Robert Carter,

DOI: 10.4324/9781003177500-3

sometimes referred to as King Carter, became one of the wealthiest men in British Colonial Virginia. King Carter kept detailed records of his vast property. He built bunk beds for his enslaved and gave them pork parts not eaten by his family.

The Carters enslaved the Gumby family for generations before Robert Carter III manumitted them, just after the American Revolutionary War. During their enslavement, his father, Robert Carter II, impregnated Thomas and Caty's daughter, Mary, at least four times. Sometimes databases place Mary and Carter II together as husband and wife, but the legal record shows that Carter was married to Priscila Churchill of Christchurch, Virginia. It is more likely that Carter raped Mary repeatedly, "… as the rape and sexual assault of Black women and girls [during enslavement] has been well documented by the historical record" (Foster, 2011). Further, under the conditions of enslavement, no such thing as consent is possible.

After their manumission, over the next several generations, my grandmother's ancestral family, including Mary Harris, Baptist Billy, Frank Burke, and Winny, slowly migrated West from the Virginia plantations into what became West Virginia (Finley 2010; Levy 2005). During the 1800s, Joseph Burke, who was born after the manumission, migrated into Ohio. They joined Appalachian communities made up of other free people of color, and Irish and Scottish servants, newly freed of their indenture along their migratory paths. The communities came together and apart, trading trauma responses inherited since before the arrival of some to North America, and to others continuing long after their arrival (Menakem, 2017). They hunted rabbits and squirrels and made moonshine in the backwoods. They endured during Reconstruction, Post-reconstruction, Jim Crow, and *Brown v Board*.

In spite of my grandmother's light skin, in the 1950s, she and my father and his darker-skinned brother were harassed for crossing the community-living color line in Canton, Ohio. Eventually, the wielded weight of multiplied hate forced them to move out of the White neighborhood where they tried to settle. The move, or the terror of being forced to move, likely ended my father's basketball playing at McKinnley High School; and perhaps also his desire to become a lawyer.

In the midst of that mob-induced terror of forced flight, the three of them also navigated physical abuse from a husband/step-father. Although his demons were his own to wrestle, they overruled and roamed freely amongst his new family. When my grandmother, father, and uncle made plans to move again, their travel was interrupted by his bullet. My grandmother stepped, but my father stepped first, catching the shot meant for her in his right side rib cage. The event did not stop their departure from the Appalachian region of Northeastern Ohio.

After a brief hospital stay, with the weight of shrapnel in his body, they moved to Cleveland.

A year later, my father met my mother–the granddaughter of administrators from two different HBCUs, who nonetheless decided to drop out of college. She left the historically White university in the far North, which she attended during her first semester. My mother never returned to school thereafter. My mother and father married in 1959, very soon after meeting at the department store where they were both working. My mother left her parents' politics of negro respectability and ties to Tuskegee and Wilberforce Universities for my father's flight-oriented trauma. Pigs' feet, pig ears, chitterlings, and rabbit stew sometimes surfaced from her new mother-in-law's kitchen. But while she heartily took up my father's "flight-rather-than-fight posture," my mother was careful to keep her children away from some of the food offered by her husband's family. And my father similarly steered clear of employment offers from his new wife's uncle, a three-term member of the Ohio State Assembly, former president of Cleveland's chapter of the NAACP, and member of the Ohio Board of Education.

In 1972, my father was arrested. He was arrested again in 1973, and a third time in 1974. All three times he escaped from police custody. The first time he left town clandestinely and relocated to Milwaukee without repaying the bail bondsmen who put up money for his release, pending trial. When he escaped the second time, handcuffed to a sick bed, through a series of tunnels beneath Milwaukee County Hospital, he left the Midwest for Los Angeles in my grandmother's purple Dodge Charger. The third escape was by train to gambling houses in Portland, Oregon, and Greyhound buses to boarding houses in Seattle, Washington, while contemplating further flight to Vancouver, British Columbia, located across Washington State's northern border in Canada.

After hearing of his pre-Christmas escape every quarter hour in news flashes broadcast on my mother's cube-shaped, portable radio one evening, and assisting his flight from our apartment building, we waited. Eventually, my mother and her four children traveled by train from Milwaukee to Chicago, Chicago to Salt Lake City, and Salt Lake to Los Angeles to join my father at his two-room apartment on Alvarado Street.

During this second escape from jail, my parents settled into a false ethnicity that more closely matched our ascribed phenotype. They moved into a Mexican American community a few blocks from the barrio. He changed his name to José. And he forced out a false accent when he said, "I don't speak-a Spanish" in response to the countless West Coast city strangers who randomly spoke to us in Spanish.

My father's arrest, flight, and eventual imprisonment ruptured and nearly decimated our family's cultural production processes. My siblings and I were intermittently cut off from our maternal grandparents, often with hostility. We missed months of third and fourth grade during that time, hiding across three different states; and we missed months of school in the years after my father's release, trying to regain stability while teetering between poverty and recidification. My paternal grandmother, who often took care of our entire family as we traveled about, was cut off from her local community. And so was her new husband, who followed her.

All of my siblings have been in different degrees of therapy to different degrees of impact. We have been incarcerated, institutionalized, hospitalized, and dead. With each tragedy, the presence and impact of cultural deprivation in one form or another has surfaced. Sometimes as a primary trigger, other times as a complicating factor.

This is not a book about what my father and mother did or did not do and whether or not it was legal or illegal or ethical, etc. It is not even necessarily a book about the systemic factors that led marginalized Black Indigenous People of Color (BIPOC) individuals and families to behave one way or another. This book explores a pervasive practice with myriad manifestations enacted against marginalized and colonized communities. The chapters in this book also describe some rapport-building rituals and reflections that can help blunt and transform the negative impacts of that phenomena.

It is a book that uses narrative contexts or case studies and research studies to illuminate this theoretical concept—cultural deprivation—and to apply research-based pedagogical, therapeutic, and medical practices to address the negative impacts of the phenomena.

Understanding Cultural Deprivation Part I

This book is about cultural deprivation as a colonial act. That is cultural deprivation that is designed to systematically extract value from individuals and communities while keeping that same value from them. Cultural deprivation has a holistically negative impact on its victims. Thus, this book is about practices that promote cultural security (Nobles) for the victims of cultural deprivation that can be facilitated within instructional, therapeutic, and medical relationships between BIPOC clients, patients, and students, and their professional guides.

Although this book is written with BIPOC communities in mind most specifically, all people can find the information and exercises beneficial and useful, including other marginalized communities and intersectional identities. Similarly, while this book may be of particular interest to BIPOC professionals working with BIPOC communities, White professionals working with BIPOC communities will also find the framing and activities helpful in their educational and healing practices.

Before exploring practices or exercises for cultural security, let's begin with a thorough exploration and understanding of cultural deprivation as a phenomena and colonizing set of practices.

The American Psychological Association's online dictionary, "a collection of more than 25,000 authoritative entries across 90 subfields of psychology," offers three definitions of cultural deprivation. Each definition requires some unpacking and critical processing and some specific examples to appreciate the widespread presence and varied processes of cultural deprivation among BIPOC communities.

Definitions of Cultural Deprivation

1 Lack of opportunity to participate in the cultural offerings of the larger society due to such factors as economic deprivation, substandard living conditions, or discrimination.
2 Loss of identification with one's cultural heritage as a result of assimilation into a larger or dominant culture. See deculturation.
3 Lack of culturally stimulating phenomena in one's environment.

Source: American Psychological Association (n.d.). Online Dictionary of Psychology retrieved on March, 12, 2022, from https://dictionary.apa.org/cultural-deprivation

---

APA Definition 1

The first definition describes cultural deprivation as a lack of opportunity to participate in the offerings of the larger society due to some malady or marginalized condition. This definition lists economic deprivation, substandard living conditions, or discrimination as examples of sources of cultural deprivation. APA's first definition has more than a nod to Bourdoieau's cultural capital and the field of sociology. Looking at this definition through the lens of Tara Yosso's (2005) critique of Bourdoiean theory, taken together, the first two sources listed: economic deprivation and substandard living conditions can conceivably be "victim-blaming" or naming the victim of deprivation as the source of the trouble. The emphasis on hostile economic conditions in both sources make it easy to conclude "if one does not have the money or other economic means, one cannot participate in cultural activities! It's that simple." If a person simply cannot afford to purchase a ticket to a show, take music lessons, collect geodes, etc.—or anything the larger society has to offer that will transmit some cultural experience for the participant to process and construct understanding to be integrated into cognitive and emotional frames for later application in future lived experiences for a price—that person or those people can be considered culturally deprived.

This definition has also been wielded in a derogatory manner. In this instance, the BIPOC communities are considered culturally deprived because they have not been and perhaps cannot be "properly" acculturated—to the linguistic, behavioral, or aesthetic norms of the dominant culture. There is a slippery shift from identifying differences in cultural norms among people with an understanding that some difference is due to lack of background knowledge about a particular cultural norm or institutional process, to ignoring the fact that sometimes the lack of background knowledge is due to marginalization and resulting deprivation, and then labeling the marginalized group or individual that has been blocked from access as somehow being inherently deficient or culturally deprived. This usually leads to a deprivation cycle. For example, stigmatized language referring to BIPOC in doctor's notes can lead other medical professionals from depriving them of access to sufficient doses of pain medication.

Ibram X Kendi (2017) explains that when associated with people of African descent, racist ideas such as this were created and propagated to justify the economic marginalization and cultural deprivation. Further, when these ideas are consumed by the broader public, not only does the economic and cultural exploitation continue, but the abuses against humanity are also reframed, and/or framed and instantiated in society as normal and natural.

However, the first and third sources taken together add to this understanding. Economic deprivation is now associated with discrimination—an opposing, marginalizing force is directly or indirectly preventing the marginalized person or people from having access to the larger society's offerings. Again, offerings that allow for cognitive, emotional, and sometimes physical processing result in potential intellectual, social, and bodily growth and advancement in the larger society. The presence of the marginalizing force will nearly always be a major factor in contemporary cultural deprivation experiences and their legacies.

Power and Dominance

The phrase "the larger society" in this first definition is structural. "Larger" indicates that something has more size, mass, or components than something else: in this case, a society. The definite article indicates a singular larger society over a subgroup or subgroups which are, as stated, afflicted either with economic deprivation, substandard living conditions, or discrimination. Because these non-dominant subgroup's afflictions can be, and most often are, caused by actions or inactions executed by the hands of the larger society, it is more appropriate to refer to this entity as the dominant society or dominant culture, rather than the "larger" society.

In some instances, cultural deprivation as described in definition 1 happens even when the larger society numerically is, in fact, subordinated or marginalized. For example, in parts of the Southern United States during the antebellum period, enslaved Africans, free people of color, and Indigenous communities outnumbered the dominant, subordinating class. "South Carolina had a clear black majority from about 1708 through most of the eighteenth century" (Tinkley, 2022). And yet, BIPOC individuals and communities were not considered human by numerical minorities in that region of the world. And at various times, globally there has been a dominant Western culture, even while the numerically larger were non-White and non-Western in orientation.

There are other more contemporary instances where similar perceptual imbalance exists to the detriment of BIPOC communities. The 2020 U.S. Census faced enormous political challenges to its practice of gathering data, leading scholars, and advocates to believe and later confirm that BIPOC numbers would in fact be undercounted. After reviewing the 2020 Census, The Urban Institute asserted: "No race or ethnic group constitutes a majority of California's population: 39% of state residents are Latino, 35% are white, 15% are Asian American or Pacific Islander, 5% are Black, 4% are multiracial, and fewer than 1% are Native American or Alaska Natives" (Elliott et al., 2021). And yet, with likely even more numerical equality among different ethnic and racial communities in California, the percentage of Black home buyers who could afford to purchase a median-priced, existing single-family home in California in 2020 was 19%, compared to 38% for White households. Housing affordability was similarly low for Latinx households, with 20% earning the minimum income needed to purchase a median-priced home (California Association of Realtors, 2021). Further, according to the Census Bureau's American Community Survey, the 2019 homeownership rate in California was 63.2% for Whites, 60.2% for Asians, 44.1% for Latinx, and 36.8% for Blacks. Home ownership is a key indicator of generational stability and wealth in the United States. Home ownership is land possession. While it may be true that no clear majority exists, the Latinx community outpaced Whites in 2020—and this is likely with some Latinx respondents choosing a White racial identity on the census but home ownership is far below. Combining the Latinx numbers with that of any other BIPOC community will demonstrate similar inequities. Finally, in October 2022, *Realtor Magazine* reported that the California Realtors Association issued a formal apology for supporting housing discrimination through racial covenants and red-lining practices (Tracey, 2022). Thus, the larger society numerically does not always determine dominance.

Having clarified the idea of "larger" as "dominant," we can understand that cultural deprivation is a process that is enacted upon subordinated communities by dominant cultural forces from a dominant group in society. However, when philanthropists, foundations, education institutions seek to address cultural deprivation as described in definition 1, they often do so with a focus on the "missing" experiences and set about establishing various cultural transmission experiences, such as tickets to the opera or ballet, museum passes, free concerts in the park, etc.

In the United States, cultural deprivation has often been attributed to BIPOC communities, some immigrants, displaced or refugee communities, victims of genocide, and other atrocities intrinsically and conditionally (Yosso, 2005). While this definition has been maliciously wielded as a judgment of the intrinsic worth of another class of people, it can be turned on its head, and instead seen as a description of

1 The different dehumanizing events and processes enacted by dominant groups in formal and informal spaces with partial or total impact on cultural transmission processes of marginalized and colonized people; or
2 The description of the impact of dehumanizing events and processes enacted by dominant groups in formal and informal spaces with partial or total impact on cultural transmission processes of marginalized and colonized people.

At one time or another, all BIPOC communities in the United States have been partly or completely blocked from accessing one or more cultural institutions, or prevented from participating in practices constructed by the dominant society as necessary for or descriptive of full citizenship status. For example, access to the products of and participation in civic culture through voting (Epperly et al., 2020), union membership (Spievak, 2019), academic societies, etc. unfolded over time, unevenly, even recursively, for different racial and ethnic groups. Below, specific events and processes across time and location that disrupt cultural transmission of dominant cultural offerings in government services, education, safety, and medical care are considered.

Mathematical Erasure

There is more to say about the 2020 Census, referenced above with regard to cultural deprivation as constructed by APA definition 1. Previously, the 2020 Census was referenced to look carefully at the idea of "larger" and "dominant." We can also look at how the 2020 Census became an active cultural deprivation endeavor that the Donald Trump presidential team committed. Doing so, though, would require that we also note that historically the census actively kept portions of the population out of its count, or partially counted. The census is supposed to be an instrument for providing an accurate accounting of the people living in the United States at a given time. The three-fifths compromise of 1787 codified the United States' understanding that people could not only be officially counted as less than a person, but also that this "less than human" condition justified depriving them of access to cultural transmission experiences operating in the dominant society at that time.

Fast forward nearly 250 years later, on March 10, 2022, the Census Bureau (2022) reported:

> The results show that the 2020 Census undercounted the Black or African American population, the American Indian or Alaska Native population living on a reservation, the Hispanic or Latino population, and people who reported being of Some Other Race.
>
> On the other hand, the 2020 Census overcounted the Non-Hispanic White population and the Asian population. The Native Hawaiian or Other Pacific Islander population was neither overcounted nor undercounted according to the findings. (Paras 6–7)

An undercount in and of itself is not cultural deprivation in the sense that we are laying out here; however, other elements beyond the simple undercounting that interfered with the process does in fact make this an act of cultural deprivation. Prior to the 2020 Census, the Government Accounting Office (2019) reported over 300 risk factors that could potentially influence the census. Among the significant factors the report reads: "Due to factors including hiring freezes, budgetary constraints, and staff eligible for retirement before 2020, the Bureau may be unable to hire and retain staff with the appropriate skill sets at sufficient levels. As a result, **it may be difficult to achieve the goals and objectives of the 2020 Census**" (emphasis mine).

In addition to the landscape described by the Government Accounting Office, the Trump administration threw additional challenges into the process.

In the midst of understaffed preparations for the 2020 Census count, the Department of Commerce and the Census administration representing the Trump administration sought to add a question of citizenship to the questionnaire used for counting. According to the Lawyers Committee for Civil Rights Under Law, a non-profit whose mission is to secure equal justice for all through the rule of law, targeting in particular the inequities confronting African Americans and other racial and ethnic minorities: In March 2018, the secretary of commerce announced that he directed the agency to add a citizenship question to the 2020 Census. Various groups protested that this would cause an undercount. The Lawyers Committee filed a lawsuit on several legal grounds. Others followed with related lawsuits. Courts found in favor of the Lawyers Committee, but the Trump administration won the right to include the question on appeal. An appeal to the U.S. Supreme Court ruled that the citizenship question could not be included. The Department of Justice later confirmed the ruling and that it would not add the citizenship question.

These challenges were, in fact, cases in point. They illustrate this definition of cultural deprivation: The federal government, represented by the Donald Trump administration, sought to limit the categories of people counted in the 2020 U.S. Census. That administration also sought to limit the amount of staffing the U.S. Census Department could hire for collecting the data about the people living in the United States (Government Accounting Office, 2019); and to limit the time available staff working for the Census Department had for counting the population, and for then processing those counts (U.S. Government Accountability Office, 2020).

After the Government Affairs Office's many warnings of risk factors signaling data collection challenges and impediments, and the actual counting under enormous and varied challenges, on April 26, 2021, the U.S. Census Department reported their first estimates of the total population counts for apportionment. Apportionment is the process of dividing the 435 seats in the U.S. House of Representatives among the 50 states. Apportionment is the constitutionally established reason for conducting a national census.

Four months prior to the release of the U.S. Census population estimates for apportionment, the Census Department released the first data sets from the demographic analysis, one of two studies conducted independently to determine the difference in counts and actual populations by age, sex, and race. Rather than draw on data gathered during the census, the data are gathered from completely independent sources and methods. Population estimates developed from the demographic analysis were derived from current and historic birth and death records, data on immigration and emigration, and Medicare records. The estimates were calculated for age groups 0–74 using the demographic balancing equation:

birth number − death number + immigration number

− emigration number

Medicare enrollment records were used for individuals 75 and older on April 1, 2020, with adjustments for delayed enrollment, ineligible non-enrollment, or other non-enrollment rather than birth records, because birth records are not as complete for this age group. Nearly all of the vital records and Medicare enrollment numbers for the 2020 demographic analysis were dated before April 1, 2020, and thus were not impacted by the COVID-19 pandemic. Vital records totals were then combined with Medicare records for a total population estimate.

Vital Records (By Birth Cohort) + Medicare Enrollment

Additional formulas using the 2020 U.S. Census numbers and the demographic analysis are further calculated to derive a net coverage error. Net coverage error is the difference between the U.S. Census count and the demographic analysis population estimates. A positive net coverage error number indicates an overcount; and a negative net coverage error number identifies an undercount. Net coverage error is also applied to the population estimates from the Post-Enumeration Survey.

The Census Department shared the new population estimates and net coverage error results from the Post-Enumeration Survey along with additional data from the demographic analysis during the 2020 Census Data Quality News Conference on March 10, 2022. The Post-Enumeration Survey, a second independent study commissioned to determine the total population; the difference in counts and actual populations by age, sex, and race; and the quality of the census data was administered after the census. The Census Bureau identifies 161,000 housing units on approximately 10,000 sample blocks. Individuals in these housing units are surveyed using the exact same questions administered in the census. After individuals complete the Post-Enumeration Surveys, researchers search for the survey respondents by name in the census data to determine who was missed from the census or counted in error. Population estimates resulting from the two independent studies are compared to the U.S. Census counts for this evaluation.

During the March 10 news conference, census officials also explained that the additional population estimates have been undertaken for the last 60 years for transparency about the quality of the U.S. Census population estimates. They explained that, while the census faced many unprecedented obstacles, such as the pandemic, wildfires, and hurricanes, the population estimates are robust and consistent with past census counts. They proclaimed that, while all censuses are flawed, the data from the U.S. Census population estimates were fit for policy-making purposes.

Census officials followed the pronouncements with data represented in tables demonstrating undercounts of African American, Native American, and non-White Hispanic populations and an overcount of White and

Asian American populations. The data also demonstrated an undercount of children ages 0–4. In addition to the 2020 undercounts, officials showed how the undercount of BIPOC in the United States has occurred consistently since the introduction of the post-enumeration survey and demographic analysis was introduced into the census data quality checks.

Subsequent Journalist, Scholarly and Political Analysis

While many mainstream and alternative news sources reported on the undercount of BIPOC communities, Roland Martin (2022), an innovative journalist, discussed the short circuited community education process as a factor in the undercount on his live-streaming alternative daily "Roland Martin Unfiltered." He explained that advertising agencies, such as Young and Rubicam that receive government contracts for census participation promotion, ignored smaller BIPOC media companies in favor of companies with a distribution of 50,000 or more. He explained that while these companies largely focus on running ads, smaller BIPOC media companies were "educating people walking them through saying 'this is what it means for your city, your school, your state, your road.'" The agencies are essentially limiting the cultural transmission process in favor of mass marketing. In contrast, he noted how Carol H. Williams agency acted adeptly when COVID struck, quickly shifting their communication campaigns from in-person BIPOC events to digital platforms where BIPOC communities gathered.

Economist Julian Malveaux, appearing as a guest commentator on Martin's program, highlighted that millions of dollars in the form of civic and infrastructural resources were lost to BIPOC communities due to the undercount. First, the undercounted lose representation in the federal government. The role of the local representatives is to broker local cultural norms into policy positions that distribute a wide variety of goods and services. Undercounts disrupt this process. In concert with Malveaux, economists on National Public Radio's podcast entitled *The Indicator*, sponsored by their program *Sound Money*, listed:

- Congressional seats
- Electoral college votes
- Voting districts
- Federal funding for

  - Medicaid
  - Medicare
  - Education

and other public services at risk to the undercounted BIPOC communities; further, they assert that long-term civic planning questions, such as where to build supermarkets or new homes, are answered with census data. Drilling down even further, they explain that if a community is undercounted, they will not get a fair share of tax dollars for roads. If roads are more clogged up, drivers in or through that community will have a harder time getting around. Even Nielsen ratings of audience estimates are impacted by undercounts and overcounts; and consequently, BIPOC cultural media and BIPOC targeted media from traditional television platforms can be erroneously seen as in less demand in those communities. If audience estimates are undercounted, BIPOC cultural media productions are funded less often and receive less advertising dollars. Many of the major news outlets published similar stories with similar examples.

A Tale of Two Cities

When Detroit Mayor Mike Duggan reviewed the 2020 Census count for his city and compared numbers just a year before taken on their own, he found a nearly 30,000 drop in the population (Click on Detroit, 2021). Officials in Detroit concurred with the Mayor and asserted that they were undercounted. To further corroborate, he commissioned the University of Michigan to audit the 2020 Census for the city. UM's Poverty Solutions undertook the work by analyzing three sets of data.

Poverty Solutions analyzed a group of ten block groups, including one set of five block groups with relatively high rates of residential stability and one set of five block groups with higher vacancy rates. They compared the 2020 Census count of those same block groups with postal data from June 2020, the month and year in which the Census Department took their counts. Poverty Solutions also compared the census count from one set of five block groups with data from a canvass conducted by Wayne State University in September and October of 2021. The Executive Summary of the report on these comparison counts reads: "In sum, after conducting an audit of the Census counts of residential units and occupied units in a selection of both more stable and less stable Detroit block groups, we find that the 2020 Census appears to have undercounted the number of occupied residential units across these 10 block groups by 8.1%, missing an estimated 964 Detroit residents." They further conclude that if the census has conducted similar undercounts across the some 600 blocks across the remainder of Detroit, they would have missed potentially tens of thousands of Detroit residents.

With this data in hand, Mayor Duggan fired "the United States government has inflicted an inequity of monumental proportions." Later, the state of Michigan as whole was determined to have been undercounted.

This matters in part because Detroit has long been a geo-political source of Black culture and cultural transmission in the United States. From the Underground Railroad to Joe Louis; Motown originals, remakes, remixes, and hip-hop samples. And Detroit has not only been a liberal Democrat city, the state of Michigan is similarly situated.

While Detroit and others in city and state governments processed what to do about their undercounts, some states like Rhode Island had an overcount. Officials reportedly believed that going into the decennial census they had lost population and would likely lose one of their congressional seats (WPRI, 2022). After the Remuneration Study and resulting Apportionment, Rhode Island retained both of their seats. Officials then acknowledged that, according to the census study, they had been overcounted by about 5%, or nearly 55,000 people. The state's largely White population was reported as 61% White—up from 54% in the census.

Regardless of Detroit's discontent and Rhode Island's measured acceptance, these numbers will not be addressed by the census until 2030. In the Remuneration Study press conference, the official count does not change. Remuneration research and demographic analysis are for reflection and future census training and planning, not redress.

Finally, while the Podcasts Code Switch, also from National Public Radio and In the Thick, from Futuro Media, discussed the complexity of the construct of race as represented in the U.S. Census in 2020 and in previous iterations, they ultimately take a dive into explanations and explorations of the deprivation of capital, services, infrastructure, civic representation, other abstract intangibles, and specific dollar amounts in lost federal funding due to the undercount.

Thus, in spite of the census counts demonstrating an overall increase in BIPOC populations across the United States, if not for these efforts at preventing BIPOC from participating in this cultural practice of the dominant society, and the unprecedented health emergency and natural disasters, the percentage of BIPOC people living in the United States would likely have had an even higher count. Instead, this long-standing practice of undercounting BIPOC populations has limited access to other cultural institutions that host or facilitate vital cultural practices governed by the dominant society.

Education

The census undercounts document an ongoing and contemporary practice of cultural deprivation. Every ten years, BIPOC undercounts act as a mechanism that triggers shutting doors, closing windows, lights out, and other barriers from varying agencies; a decennial deprivation cycle. The education policy blog "Ed Note" explains that census numbers are used to help determine federal funding allocated for special education, school nutrition, after-school programming, classroom technology, maternal and child health programs, and Head Start (McDole & Brixey, 2020). But while the census sets up deprivation in education at a macro level based on allocations, and there is a history of undercounting BIPOC communities, there is also a history of deprivation policy and practice within education and schooling institutions and agencies within the United States.

Moving backward in time, from the initial dispossession of Native American land and the early incarnations of enslavement of Africans, education broadly speaking and education from formal schooling in educational institutions set up by the dominant society was always in service of larger deprivation purposes: either for servitude or further erasure. This understanding comes from Wade Nobles' broader assertions about white supremacy and its "need to force people of color, particularly people with the most color, African folk, to serve the interest, obey the will and satisfy the needs of white people" (Nobles, 2006, p. 64). Where schooling for BIPOC did not serve the dominant society, it was violently prohibited. Where BIPOC schooling served the mission of erasure in service of the dominant society, it was violently enforced.

After the Civil War, through the Reconstruction, Post-reconstruction, Jim Crow, and Desegregation eras and up through the present day, federal, state, and local education entities establish prohibitions on BIPOC access to education and schooling.

In the case of newly emancipated Africans, when state-sponsored schools were made available, they were segregated and funded at lower rates than schools for White students. Further, used and outdated textbooks and curriculum resources were distributed to these schools. Schools separated, in this case by race and unequally resourced are designs of deprivation. Clearly, this deprivation was resisted in different ways by individuals who had developed culturally sustaining teaching. These conditions were also resisted by the development of Black schools and historically Black colleges and universities. However, many of these schools had to contend with arson or the threat of arson by White mobs or other stealthy domestic terrorists. Thus, even with resistance, the force and condition of cultural deprivation was a constant.

After *Brown v Board* struck down segregation in schools, Southern and Northern states alike created new ways to reinforce their cultural deprivation practices in schools. Prince Edward County, Virginia, stands out as a particularly egregious example. Schools designed to inhibit Black people from obtaining formal education existed in this area for decades. So, the condition of deprivation already existed. Rather than follow the new ruling, on May 1, 1959, in response to the order to integrate its schools, officials closed the entire public school system in the county. The dominant community may not have perceived their refusal to integrate as an explicit effort to maintain cultural deprivation through inferior public schools by race, but that was the end result: inferior public schools or no public schools at all.

The school system remained closed for the next five years. Archival footage partially dramatizing this event includes interviews with Black students deemed "The Lost Generation." In the interviews, students explain the gaps in their education and the cognitive struggle they experienced from losing so much schooling (Youtube, 2018, August 11).

During the time the schools were closed, lawyers for the Prince Edward County School District explained that while segregation may be outlawed by *Brown v Board*, integration cannot be compelled. White parents did not want to integrate. In fact, White parents raised money and established private schooling for their children. They also offered to assist Black parents in setting up private segregated schools for Black children. Black lawyers and parents declined the offer, reasoning that they were fighting against public segregation due to unequal schooling. Why would they then turn toward private schools that were segregated? When the Supreme Court ordered the schools be reopened, less than half the White students returned to public schools in the county. And of those who did established separate proms and commencement events.

The closure prevented BIPOC access to the cultural transmission practices in the dominant society's education institutions and formal schooling practices. Schools have been charged with socialization into the norms and expectations of society repeatedly throughout history. While we can and will critique cultural transmission and construction practices in U.S. schools, and the impact they have had on BIPOC psyche over time—particularly in terms of the second definition of cultural deprivation whereby BIPOC communities are kept away from their own culture—there are still important and necessary cognitive and social frames provided at school. Transmission of cultural practices related to formal numeracy and literacy cut across a wide range of other cultural institutions and related practices. Blocking access to the schools blocks access to this socialization institution.

Prince Edwards County school closures represent one example of the APA's first definition of deprivation through blocking access to public schools. Other examples of blocking access to schools occurred in different communities during that time and in the decades that followed. In the 1972 Minnesota lawsuit *Booker v Special School District No. 1*, U.S. District Court Judge Larson ruled against Minneapolis Public Schools for non-compliance of *Brown v Board.* Larson ruled that Minneapolis Public Schools were illegally segregated. The decision further stated that the district had violated the Equal Protection Clause of the Fourteenth Amendment, and concluded that such segregation resulted from the following maneuvers (Hielman, 1994):

- The construction, size, and location of Bethune School
- The addition of seven new classrooms to Field Elementary School in 1964
- The 1967 construction of an addition to Washburn High School
- The location of portable classrooms
- Decisions over school size
- The 1968 change in boundaries between Washburn and Southwest High Schools
- The policy of allowing special transfers of students
- The creation of optional attendance zones along the perimeters of racial minority neighborhoods
- The practice of assigning and transferring teachers and administrators

The district court found that through the above acts, Minneapolis Public Schools had intentionally segregated the schools; had intended the segregation of not only students but also teachers and administrators; and had several policies that promoted segregation, including building facilities in strategic sizes and locations.

The school district was ordered to take affirmative action to de-establish school segregation and eliminate the effects of its prior unlawful activities by implementing its own plan for desegregation/integration, limiting the maximum percent of any school's BIPOC population to 35%; increasing faculty integration; not allowing any student transfers that increase the segregated nature of either school; submitting any plans for new schools or additions to old schools to the court for prior approval; submitting any changes to the desegregation/integration plan to the court for prior approval; and to submitting semi-annual reports to the court.

The district never achieved compliance. Instead, they repeatedly sought modifications of the order from the court, citing a range of challenges to their efforts to comply. Judge Larson often consented to the district's requests, acknowledging their challenges. Eventually, the district sought a termination of the court's oversight. While Judge Larson initially refused, in 1983—ten years after the initial lawsuit—the court acknowledged the cities' efforts and the plaintiff's pursuit toward integration and soon after terminated its jurisdiction over the district.

In the ten years that followed the court's termination, Minneapolis schools were re-segregated. Further, newly elected state legislatures placed limits on the definition of segregation, decreasing the legal requirement for seeking racial balance in the schools. Choice and voluntary consent became the guiding discourse instead. The resegregation led to a new lawsuit in 2018: *Cruz-Guzman v. Minnesota* (Education Law Center, 2021). The plaintiffs in this new suit identified a range of state-level policies and practices that caused this segregation this time around, including:

- boundary decisions for school districts and school attendance areas;
- the formation of segregated charter schools;
- the decision to exempt charter schools from desegregation plans;
- the use of federal and state desegregation funds for other purposes;
- the failure to implement effective desegregation remedies; and
- the inequitable allocation of resources.

Policies and practices named in the 2018 lawsuit are similar to those in the 1972 lawsuit. And the strategies in both are also similar to maneuvers by Prince Edward County in the 1950s. Historic acts of cultural deprivation create the neurobiological templates for future deprivation (DeGruy 2017; Menakem 2017). And they give rise to all manner of new deprivation strategies, such as tracking, high stakes testing, over-representation of BIPOC in special education, and under enrollment of BIPOC in honors and AP courses all represent practices that limit access to transmission of the dominant culture in schools.

Contemporary examples of cultural deprivation by blocking access to schools can occur through what has been called the school-to-prison pipeline: "The practice of pushing kids out of school and toward the juvenile and criminal justice systems" (Flannery, 2015). Clearly there are many aspects of this practice that are not only traumatic culturally, but also psychologically damaging, physically dangerous, and in the extreme also lethal. However, this book focuses on culture and occasionally notes the overlap or intersection between cultural deprivation and other elements of subjugation, marginalization, or erasure.

Ben-Jochannan Revisited

Asiyah, an African American student in a Northern California university who was awarded a Ronald E. McNair fellowship during her junior year of college. The McNair Scholars Program is a federal TRIO program funded at 151 institutions across the United States and Puerto Rico by the U.S. Department of Education. It is designed to prepare undergraduate students for doctoral studies through involvement in research and other scholarly activities.

As part of the fellowship, Asiyah selected a mentor from the College of Education who had a strong grasp of both quantitative and qualitative research methods. He was a Greek American who referenced his ethnicity over his White race. He had a warm demeanor. He told low-key, self-effacing jokes; he affirmed Asiyah frequently. He had poor health and frequently needed to be in dispose. Nonetheless, he was a supportive mentor from start to finish.

The director of the McNair program at the university where Asiyah attended was a full professor in the Criminal Justice Department. She was a White woman. Her two program support staff were African American females. Asiyah's McNair cohort was an all-female mix of different ethnicities who kept in loose contact via chat message groups.

The cohort began the summer when the first COVID-19 surge was easing up, and before the Delta and Omicron variant surges sent everyone scrambling back inside. Although there was a momentary easing of restrictions that summer, all McNair's work was conducted online via Zoom. From the start, Asiyah experienced unclear communication from the program director. Information was given incrementally with no clear objective or culminating end point; information was changed suddenly and frequently; and class documents and slides included dates from previous years.

In addition to the pandemic and quarantine, California experienced heatwaves reaching 115 degrees in some places, further limiting outside activity. Soon after the heatwave, California wildfires caused the air quality to fluctuate between ratings of "unhealthy" and "very unhealthy" by the National Weather Service. Stress levels were high. Asiyah became ill and was soon diagnosed with an autoimmune condition.

When she became ill, she had to shift her research plan. She felt that at that time communication from the McNair program director became hostile. Her grades fell. And McNair events with presentation, networking, and scholarship opportunities were not shared in a timely way.

Asiyah recalled reading Yosef Ben-Jochannan (2004) in her ethnic studies class. She thought about his question: Who is presiding over the education of progressive programs intent on the advancement or liberation of marginalized communities?

The label "school-to-prison pipeline" can also cause an over-identification of this phenomena and the practice of depriving BIPOC youth access to educational institutions. School-to-prison pipeline practices deprive victims of access to school, but policing practices can block BIPOC youth and adult access to all types of cultural institutions, dominant and marginalized alike.

Policing as Cultural Deprivation

Disproportionate minority contact (DMC)—a related phrase to school-to-prison pipeline—de-emphasizes school as the sole location, or even the most important location where cultural deprivation occurs by way of policing. The term DMC instead zeroes in on "contact" between BIPOC youth and law enforcement, generally speaking. "The Office of Juvenile Justice and Delinquency Prevention (OJJDP) (2014) refers to racial and ethnic disparities in the juvenile justice system as *disproportionate minority contact.*" DMC used to stand for *disproportionate minority confinement.* The word *confinement* was changed to *contact* in 2002 because of disproportionality throughout all stages of the juvenile justice system (e.g., school suspension, school expulsion, police stops in public or private locations outside such as parks or street corners, inside public or private locations such as businesses, agencies or institutions, questioning, interrogating, arresting, diversion, probation, recidivism, etc. through capital punishment), and not only at confinement (OJJDP, 2014).

I am emphasizing in this definition the fact that this report identifies BIPOC youth as subjected to DMC. BIPOC youth are just beginning to act with agency within the dominant society's cultural institutions as they are being disproportionately removed from those spaces by law enforcement, often at the request of individuals of authority within cultural transmission and construction institutions, and often during cultural transmission and construction experiences.

The following instances illustrate the way in which DMC can prohibit access to the dominant culture: In 2018, two African American men were arrested in a Philadelphia Starbucks coffee shop while waiting for a third man to discuss their civic and socio-cultural work together (Stewart, 2018). Starbucks' staff asked the men to order coffee or leave. The men replied that they were waiting for their associate, and that many people use that Starbucks for meetings, often without ordering. The Starbucks' staff called the police to intervene. They appeared to have called the police based on fear and stereotypes about their racial identity. The employees' call and the police acquiescence was an attempted effort to prevent them from participating in "café culture," where social, entrepreneurial, and creative pursuits are incubated. This example became part of a catalog of incidents where everyday living and attempting to access the dominant cultural institutions, agencies, and businesses were blocked in one form or another by everyday White people and the police acting in concert with each other in a synergistically stereotypic manner.

This effort was only interrupted when cyber activism amplified knowledge and outrage about the incident. After video footage of the arrest went viral, Starbucks' agreed to a settlement outlined by the victims: $1.00 and Starbucks' investment in a youth entrepreneur program. The solution for restitution for having been deprived access to dominant cultural experiences was to force the perpetrators to invest in greater access to the dominant culture.

Two additional examples of BIPOC experiences with the cultural deprivation-character of DMC not only go beyond schools, but occur in international contexts. In the first, after record-setting track and field sprinter Sha'Carri Richardson broke the collegiate record at the NCAA championships in 2019, and after winning the 100 meter at the 2021 U.S. Olympic trials, she was trending as a shoo-in for a medal at the Tokyo Olympics. However, the U.S. Anti-Doping Agency suspended her when they detected THC in a urine sample she submitted. The suspension overlapped with the 100-meter race at the Tokyo Olympics, causing her to miss the event. While she might have run a different race at the Olympics when the suspension ended, the U.S. Olympic Team did not select her to compete.

The prevention of her playing by way of suspension in and of itself is an instance of cultural deprivation, regardless of the legal or policy basis for the deprivation. However, multiple factors compound the experience. The initial suspension occurred due to a substance that was not perform-ance enhancing. Second, after the suspension was lifted, the act of deprivation was suspended. Lastly, the deprivation was disproportionate: the International Olympic Committee ruled that another athlete, Kamila Vaviela, who tested positive for a drug that was actually performance enhancing, should be permitted to compete in the Beijing Olympics (Chappell, 2022). After the Olympics, Richardson's subsequent perform-ances were mediocre, raising concerns that the stress of her experiences with the U.S. Anti-Doping Agency and subsequently the U.S. Olympic team further distanced her from the sport.

Even in the tragic case of the 2022 Russian invasion of Ukraine, as Ukrainians fled persecution, while the Polish government and citizens demonstrated humanity toward their neighbors, they still managed to establish hierarchies of care, blocking access to transportation, hospitality, and security to BIPOC from Nigeria, Jamaica, Tanzania, and the United States and as they struggled to flee the bombs blowing up hospitals, apartment complexes, and other infrastructures of civil society.

The latter two contemporary examples of policing as cultural deprivation are based in anti-blackness, on an international platform. The first involves multiple agencies. And so does the second. But the second example, occurring during an active genocide represents a more complicated, seemingly coordinated commitment to anti-black racism resulting in cultural deprivation. Not only are Black people from across the diaspora lumped into one negative category and prevented from fleeing by police within Ukraine, when able to finally cross into Poland, many were denied transportation or other humanitarian aid. While some Ukrainians were allowed direct entry into the United States, others passed through the U.S. - Mexico border as asylum seekers, bypassing Central Americans, Haitians, and Mexicans also seeking asylum. Further, they have been forced into new rules while the world witnesses the flaunting of these rules in order to allow them entry.

Medical Education and Health Care

Moving away from examples of cultural deprivation through government accounting, schools, and policing, we can also see cultural deprivation historically and in the present regarding BIPOC access to medical care.

Medical care is a cultural practice. Medical care has practices and protocols, artifacts, belief systems, and assumptions about health; care for the body; preparation for birth and death, etc. Many of these elements may seem as though they are cross-cultural or a-cultural, and therefore can be seen in different locations around the world. Or they may appear to transcend culture because they are scientific. There are also many cultural variations among medical beliefs and practices. As a broad example, we can consider Ayurvedic medicine versus traditional Chinese medicine (TCM) versus Western medicine as dispensed in many hospitals and clinics in the United States. While there are regional and ethnic cultural variations within these approaches to health, some general contrasts can quickly be observed. Ayurveda considers bodily health of illness based on dominant elements making up our constitution (Sattva-calm, Pita-agitated, Kapha-lethargic), and their imbalance in diagnosis and treatment (Frawley, 2001). Treatments can consist of massage, mantras, dietary adjustments, herbs for ingestion or application in baths or massage, and yoga postures. Ayurvedic medicine is holistic.

Dr. Maryam Amanpour (2019) of Five Branches University notes that in both TCM and Ayurvedic medicine more healing modalities are made available to doctors and patients than in Western medicine. For example, U.S.-based Western medical care is increasingly delivered through technological devices to determine the body's health and pharmaceuticals to treat ailments as opposed to more natural, less mechanically processed herbs. In contrast, Ayurvedic and TCM treatment modalities include dispensing herbs, prescribing cleansing practices, dietary shifts, meditation, sound therapies, or color therapies. In addition, specific exercises that work directly with qi or prana, such as chi gong, tai chi, and yoga, etc. are also prescribed. TCM adds acupuncture to its treatment regimen because this treatment also works directly with chi.

Thus, blocking or depriving individuals or groups access to the dominant society's medical care is not only detrimental to the individual or group for obvious reasons of physical and mental health, quality of life, and longevity, it is also a form of cultural deprivation.

Health disparities statistics among BIPOC present an enticing body of evidence for exploring cultural deprivation, especially since the COVID-19 pandemic and resulting quarantine. However, it is worth stepping back, and considering how cultural deprivation precedes treatment disparities and disproportionately negative health outcomes for BIPOC. For example, in January 2022, Cable News Network journalist Amachari Orie reported on the culture of medical textbook illustration. Orie began by sharing that a series of medical illustrations featuring Black fetuses, drawn by a Nigerian medical school student studying in Ukraine had gone viral. Chidiebere Ibe, the medical school student-artist, touched a cultural nerve with these images. Apparently, medical school students are not frequently exposed to BIPOC bodies in their textbooks. Ibe said, even in Nigeria, White skin images dominate the medical literature.

Amachari Orie's (2022) article curates a series of other specific instances surfacing this pattern in medical illustration culture, alongside Ibe's story. Orie identifies Dr. Jenna Lester, assistant professor of the Department of Dermatology and director of the department's Skin Color Program at the University of California San Francisco, whose research (Lester et al., 2020) in the *British Journal of Dermatology* documented similar disparities in medical illustration. Orie next includes a Food and Drug Administration (2021) warning about limitations of the effectiveness of pulse oximeters—medical devices that measure blood oxygen levels—for people with darker skin tones. Essentially, these devices that measure a patient's oxygen level by using light and a sensor to detect the color of the blood have been found to provide less accurate readings on darker skin. Finally, the article cites another study (Parker et al., 2017) looking at the existence and representation of gender bias in the major anatomy textbooks used at Australian medical schools. The authors conducted a systematic visual content analysis of 6,044 images in which sex/gender could be identified, sourced from 17 major anatomy textbooks published from 2008 to 2013. The study not only found the persistence of underrepresentation of images of women in these books, it also revealed "a lack of visual ethnic, age, body type and sex/gender diversity."

The omission of Black bodies in medical illustration books intended for teaching medical care practices has sweeping implications. For example, the Parker et al. (2017) study first cited empirical research linking gender bias in medical education with negative attitudes and behaviors in healthcare providers. Health disparities among BIPOC have already been alluded to above. Understanding the role of medical textbook illustration in Black and Brown body erasure in health disparities is complex. What might medical treatment for BIPOC look and feel like when the educational resources used to train medical professionals have erased or ignored their existence? How might this early erasure contribute to cultural deprivation later? Could erasure-oriented stereotypes influence the culture of pain treatment and management in medical care where BIPOC patients often experience deprivation? Kaplan Medical took up this conversation in a series of webinars on racial inequality in medicine.

Kaplan is an international test and professional licensure exam preparation company. Kaplan focuses on a wide range of professional endeavors, namely a range of medical licensure examinations. Their training includes in person, virtual, face to face, group, private, on demand, and live. During their October 15, 2020, webinar entitled "Black Pain Matters: How Historical Medical Assumptions about Black Pain Thresholds Impact Care," panelists shared thoughts and personal experiences about being Black female medical students and being patients receiving medical care. The panel included three African American female medical students, the director of Kaplan Education Foundation—a female BIPOC, and an African American female moderator. The panelists collectively defined the term "Black pain" as pain that is real physically, but exacerbated by the medical establishment's lack of engagement with or disbelief in their Black patient's level of discomfort. Medical professionals' lack of treatment and/or disbelief in Black patients' pain can cause their Black patients to have to defend their need for pain medication or other treatment of the source of their pain.

Medical professionals in the United States have blocked BIPOC access to medical treatment and to pain medication throughout history. Examples include James Marion Sims and his predecessors, who conducted gynecological experiments on unanesthetized and unmedicated, enslaved Black women in the 1800s (Holland, 2018). Some scholars note that anesthesia was not widespread at the time (Wall, 2006). Others note that, when Sims "perfected" his surgery after hundreds of attempts on Black women, he expanded his work to anesthetized White women (Owens, 2017). Further research also notes that Sims participated in an intellectual tradition of describing Black people in medical journals as less sensitive to pain, due to thicker nerve endings and other non-sensical, racist ideas (Ownes, 2017). Thus, the decision to not introduce interventions to mediate pain appears more ideological, and less circumstantial. It is also important to note that the reason for the surgery was less about healing the enslaved women and more about returning the enslaved women to their role as breeders for their enslaver (Ownes, 2017).

This lack of intervention phenomena is embedded deep into medical research and treatment. During the University of New Hampshire's third and final talk of the three-part lecture series entitled "Medical Ethics and Human Subject Research in the Shadow of the Holocaust," Dr. James Jones explained that during the Tuskegee experiment, a non-therapeutic experiment conducted on African American men against their will between 1932 and 1972 involved withholding of treatment for syphilis. The first time the patients could have been treated was in 1937 when the Surgeon General organized a new round of mobile clinics to isolate cases and provide treatment; the next opportunity was the draft during World War II, where men would have been examined and provided treatment; the third time was in 1943 when the Henderson Act passed and required the testing and treatment of venereal disease. The discovery of penicillin was the fourth opportunity for treatment. In all four cases, the public Health Department intervened to block the men in Macon County and others from receiving treatment.

Susan Moore's death is another important instance. Susan Moore was a Black medical doctor Moore—who died of COVID-19 after advocating for professional her own care, and subsequently being released from the hospital. Dr. Moore documented her lack of treatment and death on social media. This brave act—not unlike that of Philando Castille's girlfriend who live-streamed her fiancé's murder at the hands of Brooklyn Park, Minnesota, police—laid bare one uniquely positioned Black patient's experiences of cultural deprivation. Dr. Susan Moore was being denied access to pain management culture of which she had a professional knowledge.

This is not the same as the culture of addiction, whereby medical and pharmaceutical professionals collaborated to over-prescribe addictive pain medications, mostly to White patients. Within the culture of pain management, there are an array of pharmaceuticals to treat pain from over-the-counter medicine to prescription, to medication administered only by medical professionals. There is research and training to understand how pain medication works upon the human body and when and where it is best to dispense and consume pain medication. There are also belief systems about how much and when it is appropriate to consume the medication. And there are protocols or rituals for ascertaining a patient's pain levels.

Giving and receiving medical care is a cultural experience that extends beyond the event where the cultural acts are practiced and performed. The novelty or repetition of the experience, or elements of the experience impact relevant thinking, communication. These experiences of cultural transmission and construction in medical care help shape the future beliefs, understandings, and experiences about medical culture.

The American Psychological Association's first definition of cultural deprivation describes the blocking of access to the dominant society's culture. The medical students on this Kaplan panel shared that they have experienced their attendants and resident doctors emoting in frustration when seeing Black patients, and then not giving that Black patient adequate or proper amounts of pain medication. The latter is closely related to DMC. Medical facilities are institutions where Black bodies are often policed or removed by security guards or brought in by the police. Mental health professionals and doctors have also been accused of policing Black bodies for control and compliance.

The panelists identified two categories of stereotyping that lead to disproportionate health outcomes for Black patients: beliefs about Black physiology, and beliefs about the need for control and compliance from Black bodies when dispensing medical treatment. Both beliefs and the behavior they manifest cause cultural deprivation. In addition, they note that as medical students there are gaps in the training they receive about practicing medicine with White patients versus training about treatment for Black and Brown patients (2020). They note skin color and difficulty to detect bruising or skin yellowing from jaundice or from gums that are pink.

Kaplan panelists identified several sources for these stereotypes about BIPOC bodies. They explain that beliefs about Black physiology stem from false claims in early pseudoscience about nerve endings in Black bodies being thicker (Hoffman et al., 2016), damaged or primitive, resulting in greater pain tolerance.

Kaplan's webinar series was prompted by the summer of 2020 uprisings in protest of the mounting visual evidence of police murder of Black people. Most notable were the murders of George Floyd in Minneapolis, Minnesota, and Breonna Taylor in Louisville, Kentucky. Another video with similar message posted on Dr. Eseosa Ighodaro's YouTube channel around the same time as the Kaplan video was prompted by the death of Dr. Moore while hospitalized with COVID. During the webinar, the doctors experienced repeated attempts at Zoom bombing until they shut off audience participation features altogether. This too was an act of cultural deprivation. The doctors who organized the webinar were calling the public's attention to an all-too-common lethal example of cultural deprivation. In this instance, the doctors doing the reporting and reflecting were also deprived of access to the technology necessary to amplify their open exchange of ideas and information.

Tales of Blood and Spirit

Asiyah is an African American female college student who was diagnosed with lupus in her early twenties. Lupus is an autoimmune disease where the immune system attacks the body because it does not believe it belongs. Overall 90% of lupus patients are female. In some places Black women's rates of lupus are more than three times higher than their white counterparts, and the severity and progression rates are higher (Chae et al., 2019). Frequent blood and urine tests are required by doctors in order to diagnose and manage lupus. In the year Asiyah was officially diagnosed, she had nearly 40 vials of blood drawn.

Asiayh interacts with many different technicians. She says that generally the African American technicians are direct and pleasant; and many others are as well. She noticed that as the pandemic dragged on, technicians were generally more fatigued looking and less patient. Asiyah does not like having to go to the lab all the time. She must psych herself up with pep talks. Many times, she breaks down and cries before going in.

She feels this way partly because of the needles. She explains that she was receiving acupuncture treatments prior to the diagnosis, but the experience of having to be poked so frequently after her diagnosis became a real turn-off emotionally. And it was painful to have to be poked so frequently.

When I asked her to explain further, she said that nearly every time the technicians say that they have a hard time finding her vein. They often stab her several times. They move the needle in multiple directions before taking it out and trying another spot on her arm. And then maybe a third. Sometimes the technician will have to ask another technician or a supervisor to come over and assist in finding the veins. Sometimes they will not look at her at all during the procedure. Other times they will make comments as if it is her fault that they cannot find the vein. A few times they made hurtful remarks.

Asiyah no longer goes to acupuncture for treatment. And she still has a difficult time having to go to the hospital for labs.

Summary

Chapter 1 begins with a critical family history illustrating intergenerational cultural deprivation. It provides an overall definition of cultural deprivation. Cultural deprivation is complex and uneven in communities and societies. The American Psychological Association defines cultural deprivation as (1) not having access to the dominant society, (2) not having access to one's own culture, (3) and not having access to cultural stimulation at all. An exploration of the 2020 U.S. Census undercounts of BIPOC communities and children demonstrates historic and systemic cultural deprivation practices. Undercounts result in less funding and political representation for BIPOC. Chapter 1 describes additional examples of APA's first definition of cultural deprivation in health care, policing, and education further illustration.

Activities

Activities include media produced by BIPOC professionals narrating and processing historic and contemporary experiences of cultural deprivation, and who are working toward cultural security.

1   The webinars below, referenced in the chapter, discuss lack of access to medical care and medical education. Listen to webinars with people who make you feel safe. Pause the audio as needed and work through the content cognitively and emotionally. Listen for pathways toward cultural security in both webinars.

Moore, Z. Netsanet, A., Pilai, A., Sanchez, N., and Smith, N. (2020). Black Pain Matters: How Historical Medical Assumptions about Black Pain Thresholds Impact Care. Kaplan Medical. Retrieved from https://www.youtube.com/watch?v=4IaiD11JJxM&list=PLbsXPZPls2m-5LPmbxqYMPlXXKMX4130u&index=18&t=352s on December 17, 2023.

Ighodaro, E. Tragedy: The Story of Dr. Susan Moore & Black Medical Disparities. Retrieved from https://www.youtube.com/watch?v=dkGkLVgDfnw&list=PLbsXPZPls2m-5LPmbxqYMPlXXKMX4130u&index=11&t=3s on December 16, 2023.

Moderators: Dr. Eseosa Ighodaro, MD, PhD; Neurologist, Neuroscientist, Activist; and Dr. Taaka Cash, DNP, MPH, PMHNP-BC

Panelists: Dr. Ima Ebong, MD; Epilepsy neurologist; Dr. Darlinda Minor, MD; adult and forensic psychiatrist; Dr. Jessica Isom, MD MPH; community psychiatrist and medical educator; Nofisat Almaroof,

MD Board Certified Family Physician T/IG/FB/IN Dr. Linelle Campbell, 4th year Emergency Medicine Chief Resident; Dr. Magdala Chery MD, @drmagdalachery, Board Certified Internist, Founder of the #NotJustABlackBody Campaign Dr. Erica Littlejohn, PhD; neurophysiologist; Alema Jackson, MS Nurse & Pre-med Student, Co-Founder of Aspiring MDs and Black Women in Medicine Clubs; Kassa Kassahun University of Texas at Austin Graduate/Prospective Medical Student; Edoghogo Ighodaro B.S, Pre-med student

2   The Story of Us: Episode 34 Part One of Intersectionality Matters, https://podcasts.apple.com/us/podcast/34-the-story-of-us-part-1/id1441-348908?i=1000514132373

In the aforementioned listed episode of the podcast, "Intersectionality Matters," Kimberlè Crenshaw holds a discussion with Bryan Stevenson, David Blight, Viet Than Ngyuen, and Ruha Benjamin at the Sundance Film Festival about how stories we tell each other, especially national stories amplified in media platforms, such as movies and television shows can reproduce or transform racial hostility, inequality, marginalization, and oppression.

During the discussion, they challenge ideas about American innocence, American heroism, and American progress; and the role of media technologies from Hollywood and Silicon Valley in amplifying stories that produce and reproduce these ideas. They also describe different ways to root out this narrative reproduction and replace it with more honest, redemptive, and humane stories.

Podcast Elements

Speaker	Biography	Quotes
Kimberle Crenshaw	Host	
Bryan Stevenson	Founder and executive director of the Equal Justice Initiative. Author of *Just Mercy: A Story of Justice and Redemption*	"We live in a genocidal society"
David Blight	Professor of American Studies Yale University. Author of *Fredrick Douglass: Prophet of Freedom*	"Reconciliation always comes with costs." "Harmonious forgetfulness ... just think about what that means" "[President Woodrow Wilson] he calls the Civil

(Continued)

Speaker	Biography	Quotes
		War the quarrel forgotten" "Our history tells us to be careful about how much healing you promote without real justice to go with it."
Viet Than Nguyen	Professor of American studies at University of Southern California. Author of *The Sympathizer*.	
Ruha Benjamin	Professor of American studies at Princeton University. Author of *Race After Technology*.	"Media technologies are just one niche of technologies that reflect and reproduce the racial status quo" "If we think of storytelling as the DNA of humanity then so much of this legacy of white supremacy is being baked into technologies that are having an impact on every area of our lives." "The public wasn't just watchful; everyday were storytellers" "people aren't just consuming, but also producing stories through social media."

Podcast Structure

Intro to Intersectional Matters Podcast (0:00–0:39)

Intro to episode: The Story of Us Part 1 (0:39–7:08)

In the first segment (7:08–21:11), Kimberleè, Bryan, and David Blight open the discussion.

In the second segment (21:12–31:16), Krenshaw, Viet Than Nguyen, and Ruha Benjamin discuss specific prevailing myths about America that enable continuity of racist action.

In the third segment (31:17–38:35), Krenshaw, David Blight, and Bryan Stevenson conclude with Crenshaw's summary.

Closing segment (38:36–40:14), Krenshaw connects Hollywood to Washington and challenges us to create new ways of receiving stories.

Podcast Listening Prompts

After working your way through the different elements above, review the prompts below. Discuss the pre-listening prompts with others. Respond to the listening prompts in writing as you listen. Finally, discuss the post-listening prompts with others after listening to the podcast.

a Pre-listening prompts
   The following questions below can help surface thoughts related to the content discussed in the podcast, promoting deeper processing. Answer the question in writing then discuss them with others before listening.

   i What are some family stories that are told frequently? How far did these stories go back?
   ii What are some of your family's favorite media programs or experiences?

b Listening prompts

   i What is the role of stories and storytelling in families, communities, and countries?
   ii What are some common stories discussed in the podcast?
   iii What are some counter stories discussed in the podcast?

c Post-listening prompts

   i Inventory your media and explore some of the themes and messages you are exposing yourself to on a regular basis.
   ii Identify media with counter-narratives—narratives that counter white supremacy that you know about or watch/listen to regularly.

3. 52. Democracy at Stake - Fighting for the Freedom to Learn, https://podcasts.apple.com/us/podcast/52-democracy-at-stake-fighting-for-the-freedom-to-learn/id1441348908?i=1000611484970

In the aforementioned listed episode of the podcast "Intersectionality Matters," Kimberlè Crenshaw holds a discussion with Cheryl Harris, Robin D. G. Kelly, and Janai Nelson.

During the discussion, they connect the contemporary cultural deprivation trends exemplified most notably with the governor.

Podcast Elements

Speaker	Biography	Quotes
Kimberle Crenshaw	Host	We at the African American Policy Forum are joining thousands of academics, artists, policy makers, students, and concerned community members from around the world to form a counter tide against this mounting backlash. This group is called the freed to learn network.
Robin DG Kelly	Gary B. Nash professor of American history at UCLA	The social movements of the last 30–40 years may be the most militant movements in U.S. history.
Cheryl Harris	Rosalinde and Arthur Gilbert Foundation Chair in Civil Rights and Civil Liberties at UCLA School of Law	We can see the relationship between [the reaction to the AP Black Studies course] and the actual book censorship; the removal of books and these works from libraries.
Janai Nelson	President and director-counsel of the NAACP Legal Defense Fund (LDF)	That Executive Order was a blueprint for many states that literally borrowed the same language from that Executive Order; that language of victimization; that language of division; that language of censorship and suppression proliferated across states.
Kenneth Nunn	Professor of law emeritus University of Florida	
Sophia De la Cruz	3rd-year undergraduate political science major at University of Florida	
Kristen Andersen	4th-year undergraduate anthropology major at University of Florida	

Podcast Structure

Intro to Intersectional Matters Podcast (0:00–0:39)

Intro to episode: Democracy at Stake: Fighting for the Freedom to Learn (0:39–5:28). A montage of Professor Nunn and De Santis' press conference talking about the AP course. Professor Nunn again, Sophia De la Cruz, Kristen Anderson, and Crenshaw about the attack on AP African American History and its larger attack on Black thought and our ability to teach history accurately.

In the first segment (5:28–19:24), Kimberleè Crenshaw provides a timeline of the College Board's development of an AP African American History course. The timeline begins with the inception of the course after the rebellions of summer 2020 continues through the announcement and subsequent editing of the course to omit topics such as intersectionality, and through to the identification of evidence that the College Board was developing the course with advising of the Florida government.

In the second segment (19:25–100:50), a conversation among Kimberleè Crenshaw, Robin D.G. Kelly, Cheryl Harris, and Janai Nelson. The discussion identifies Executive Order … as the source of not only Florida's legislation influencing the College Board's AP Black History course, but many states throughout the country also discusses the Critical Race Theory Tracking Project.

Cheryl Harris presents a discussion about how normal or neutral processes can produce racial harm. Robin Kelly talks about how primary and secondary sources materials for the proposed AP Black Studies course are impacted by the broader cultural deprivation efforts facing the class.

In the closing segment (100:50–110:00), the panelists discuss current efforts to push back on the College Board and policy makers crafting policy that causes cultural deprivation.

Podcast Listening Prompts

After working your way through the different elements above, review the prompts below. Discuss the pre-listening prompts with others. Respond to the listening prompts in writing as you listen. Finally, discuss the post-listening prompts with others after listening to the podcast.

d. Pre-listening prompts
    The following questions below can help surface thoughts related to the content discussed in the podcast, promoting deeper processing. Answer the questions in writing and then discuss them with others before listening.

    i   What Black studies courses did you take if any in high school or college?
    ii Did you celebrate Black History Month in school? If so, how? What were some of the elements of the celebration? What historical information about Black people can you recall from the celebrations?

e. Listening prompts

  i   What prompted the College Board to create an AP Black History course?
  ii What happened when the course was released? Who responded to it, and in what ways?

f. Post-listening prompts

  i   What specific strategies are each of the presenters working on to document and resist cultural deprivation practices around the AP Black Studies course?

Suggestions for Further Study

1   Levy, A. (2005). *The First Emancipator: The Forgotten Story of Robert Carter, the Founder Who Freed His Slaves.* Randomhouse: New York.
2   U.S. Census Bureau (2022, March 10). 2020 Census Data Quality Results News Conference. (Video). YouTube. https://www.youtube.com/live/tl73H8JBuPU?si=r9RyeW70ZpS-oIqz.
3   The National Center for Truth and Reconciliation University of Manitoba, https://nctr.ca

     The National Center for Truth and Reconciliation serves indigenous survivors of the traumas of the boarding school phenomena in Canada. The center also educates all Canadians about the horrors of the boarding school phenomena. From the center's website: "We preserve the record of these human rights abuses, and promote continued research and learning on the legacy of residential schools. Our goal is to honor Survivors and to foster reconciliation and healing on the foundation of truth telling."

4   Truth and Reconciliation Commission, https://www.youtube.com/channel/UCohv4CbqR6qcqHknSZ1yRVA/featured

     The full event marking the Final Report of the Truth and Reconciliation Commission is archived in the videos below. The first video presents the English version and the second video is in French. Various indigenous languages are woven throughout both videos. Both videos are over three hours long.

  a   Truth and Reconciliation Final Report (English Version), https://www.youtube.com/watch?v=mZoLgdzrw7c
  b   Rapport final de la Commission de vérité et de réconciliation, https://www.youtube.com/watch?v=V5nVvMcFeQE

Chapter 2

What Is Cultural Deprivation?

Part II

Introduction

This chapter explores the impact of cultural deprivation. This chapter locates its origins for marginalized youth in post-traumatic slave syndrome, post-apocalyptic stress syndrome, and similar socio-historic trauma, alongside contemporary trauma.

Finally, this chapter explores the concept of cultural security. This chapter was initially intended to be a brief of cultural deprivation. As I wrote, two things happened. The first was a feeling that a brief overview was not enough to substantiate or ground the activities in subsequent chapters. The second was a seeming flood of blatant contemporary examples of different types of cultural deprivation across all areas of endeavor.

Critical Family History: A Story within a Story

Reading Is Fundamental

In 2010, I served as the keynote speaker for the Annual Reading Is Fundamental (RIF) fundraising gala in Washington, DC. RIF is a children's literacy non-profit that, among other things, gives away books to students in low-income and BIPOC communities. I was a "RIF Kid" in fourth grade. I received a children's encyclopedia of mythology when RIF came to Cass Street Elementary School in Milwaukee. During my talk, I explained that book inspired me so much that I wrote my PhD dissertation about approaches to teaching mythology in high school classrooms. And it inspires me now to collect books about myths from all over the world.

I offered to do the presentation because I wanted to show appreciation for the role of that powerful gift in shaping my life trajectory. I also wanted to convey the power of these kinds of cultural transmission programs

DOI: 10.4324/9781003177500-4

generally. Often, the effort of one program inspires others like the literacy programs where books are given away at birth by country music icon Dolly Parton's foundation or Kaiser hospital in Oakland, California.

The book I received inspired me at the time to look for mythology books in all of the school libraries where I attended during my family's transience. I saw so many mythology books during that time that I noticed patterns. For example, sometimes the books were called *Mythology* and sometimes they were called *Greek Mythology* or *Greek and Roman Mythology*. Other times they used the words *Classical Mythology*. However, the stories were always the same: Zeus frees his siblings from their Titan father; Apollo's son Phaeton begs to ride his father's sun chariot through the sky; Cupid and Psyche have a secret love life. I puzzled over the synonymous and hierarchical use of terms in the book titles.

Occasionally there would be a book about Norse mythology where only stories of the Norse gods would appear. And every once and a while the Norse myths would appear in a collection with some of the Greek myths, and maybe even one or two tales from one of the Native American nations. Once there was a collection of stories from India. And next to it a copy of *1001 Nights,* often called *The Arabian Nights*. I began to wonder where my stories were. I didn't know that John Henry, whom I would become obsessed with as an adult, was more culturally connected to my family's Black Appalachian heritage (Nelson, 2006) than Hercules, Hermes, or Helen of Troy.

Carter G. Woodson Vs. Thor—The Norwegian God of Thunder

In 1930, Carter G. Woodson explained in his groundbreaking *The Miseducation of the Negro* that the problem with education for Blacks at the time is that teachers in Black schools and White schools teach the Black people to hate themselves and to love all things European. Woodson asserts, "The educated negroes have the attitude of contempt toward their own people because they are taught to admire the Hebrew, the Greek, and the Latin and the Teuton, and to despise the African" (23). Woodson was writing about the instructional, social, legal, and policy contexts of Black education. And as Jarvis Givens (2021) points out in his study of Woodson and Black teaching practices during his time, legal and extra-legal consequences could be reigned down upon Black educators who were caught teaching culturally affirming content.

Although written almost 100 years prior, my fourth-grade experience falling in love with mythology during the 1970s illustrates the tenacity and continuity of the impact of cultural deprivation. My family's transience gave me the vantage point of visiting multiple school libraries in

Ohio, Wisconsin, California, and Illinois. I was specifically looking for mythology books. I almost always only found books about Greek mythology and Norse mythology whose titles were either tools for teaching hierarchy or erasure. The books provided access to dominant cultural motifs that served me well while studying Shakespeare in preparation to be an English teacher. But they kept me searching for the literary and spiritual antecedents of my own cultural narratives.

While I studied mythology, my older brother read Marvel comic books. The hero he most enjoyed reading was Thor, a new representation of the Norse god of thunder. While I was asking questions about the missing stories from my own heritage, my older brother told his friends he was from Asgard—the mythological home of this blonde-haired, blue-eyed deity. He never learned to look at his own thick, black, course, wavy hair or full lips as heroic. The transformation from Peter Parker to Miles Morales, or the emergence of T'Challa as the Black Panther is an important step toward representation of BIPOC stories from the industry. Introducing new and classic superheroes, especially when created by BIPOC artists and writers, can help support cultural security.

High John Conquers the Classroom

I was a guest teacher for a classroom in a suburban Minnesota high school right outside the Twin Cities several years before the murders of Philando Castille, George Floyd, and Daunte Wright. The school was ethnically diverse, but the African diaspora students (Nigerians, Ethiopians, Somalians, and African Americans) made up the bulk of the student body. I chose to do a dramatized retelling of a High John folktale. When I returned to the school one month later, one of the students said to me: "I told my mom what you taught us the last time you were here. She was mad. She said how come this is the first time you get to study your ancestral stories?"

Understanding Cultural Deprivation Part II

APA Definition 2

The second definition offered by the APA website explains cultural deprivation as a lack of identification with one's own culture due to assimilation. APA relates this term to "deculturation," which nods to the processes by which cultural deprivation might occur: by force or coercion or some other means. This definition ought to be the first. Whereas the first definition begins with the subordinated position—the malady or the marginalization that has blocked access to the larger—or dominant group's culture, the second definition names the origin of the malady or marginalization: assimilation, deculturation, force, and coercion.

Definition of Deculturation

n. the processes, intentional or unintentional, by which traditional cultural beliefs or practices are suppressed or otherwise eliminated as a result of contact with a different, dominant culture. Compare acculturation. —deculturate *vb.*

Source: American Psychological Association (n.d.). Online Dictionary of Psychology. Retrieved March, 12, 2022, from https://dictionary.apa.org/deculturation

---

For marginalized communities, assimilation is not access to the dominant society. Assimilation is an acceptance of dominant cultural norms which include the subjugation of BIPOC communities. Therefore, this second definition acts as a ground zero for cultural deprivation. Having been deprived of one's own culture, assimilated the dominant cultural values of self-subordination, one is then blocked from access to the dominant culture described in the first definition.

Cultural deprivation is not cultural drift, which the APA defines as change in the culture that is gradual and uncontrollable. cultural deprivation is an intentional effort by a dominant society's individuals, groups, or institutions to prohibit access, destroy, or exploit culture. Just as in the first definition, cultural deprivation is an active occurrence, whereby a dominant force—the dominant society—actively seeks to prevent marginalized communities from accessing the dominant culture; and, similarly in this second definition, a dominant force actively seeks to prevent marginalized communities from identifying with or participating in their own culture. cultural deprivation of this sort happens through cultural prohibition, cultural exploitation, and cultural destruction. Examples of each subset of APA's definition two for cultural deprivation follow under each subheading.

Cultural Prohibition

Cultural deprivation that occurs by way of prohibition interrupts the transmission and co-construction process by preventing BIPOC individuals and communities from engaging in cultural production; and also, by preventing BIPOC access to their cultural production, in formal, informal, and intimate spaces. Cultural prohibition practices in formal spaces, such as schools, hospitals, and therapeutic settings, is often reinforced through legislation, legal systems, and institutional or agency policy. When cultural prohibition is reinforced in multiple formal spaces, it becomes systemic.

While the opening paragraph on cultural prohibition has a decidedly critical race theory grounding, Uri Bronfenbrenner's (Rosa & Tudge, 2013) bio-ecological systems theory of human development is a helpful model for understanding this process as well. Bronfenbrenner's meso-system represents the interaction among his microsystems (home, school, church, playground, corner store, etc.). At a most simplistic level, if home, school, church, and work express a similar discourse, and the discourse is engaged repeatedly, and in novel circumstances, its influence is likely to produce reflexivity over time. If the meso-system represents discord among the microsystems, influences may be less automatic.

Songs of Freedom

Laws have been established and enacted to prohibit transmission of BIPOC culture for hundreds of years. Amir Whitaker and Iya Janina Walter's (2023) book *Forbidden Afro Unidad: Culture and Rebellion across the Diaspora* documents laws forbidding enslaved Africans and others in their company from playing drums, singing and dancing beginning in 1688 in Barbados. The law was established to prevent enslaved Africans from communicating with each other, gathering, and plotting rebellion. Similar laws were created wherever Africans were enslaved using the others as models, such as New York in 1692, Jamaica in 1696, Antigua in 1723, South Carolina in 1736, Georgina in 1755, etc. These laws not only demonstrate enslavers' and colonists' knowledge of the coercive nature of their enslaving practices; the laws demonstrate their knowledge of the importance of cultural production and transmission for cultural security.

Dr. Whitaker surfaced the contemporary salience of these laws during a 2022 Los Angeles Unified School District Board meeting. At the meeting, Whitaker and students illustrated parallels between the centuries-old legislation prohibiting drumming across the Caribbean, the United States, and several countries in South America and current school district policies allowing school resource officers to confiscate cultural items from students, such as Afro pics (Leung et al., 2018).

Similarly, laws have been established to limit the practice of indigenous religion (Deloria, Jr.). Two specific examples from history include Tenskwatawa's religious movement in the 1810s and Wovoka's Ghost Dance movement of the 1890s (Dunbar-Ortiz, 2014). Later, the American Indian Church faced restrictions (Lawson, 1986), even after laws overturning the outlawing of Indigenous religions, access to lands sacred to some tribes, necessary to complete various religious rituals are often in effect.

Another example occurs with the book *David Walker's Appeal* (1829). Walker's book, which called for the abolition of slavery by way of abandonment and rebellion, was outlawed in North Carolina in the 1830s. Soon after, an assortment of laws was established in that state, and eventually throughout the South, to limit teaching and preaching, especially by Free People of Color to enslaved Africans. To be sure, these laws were resisted in all manor, and a "fugitive" literacy culture developed. But generations of laws followed, similarly limiting and disrupting educational engagement and attainment not only for enslaved and emancipated Africans but also their descendants.

Forced School Attendance

One of the most noteworthy examples of cultural deprivation occurred at the institutional level across the United States and into Canada from the mid-1800s up through the early 1980s. During this time, the Canadian and U.S. governments worked with churches to coerce or forcibly remove Indigenous children from their families in a wide variety of tribal communities, to attend boarding schools. While at the boarding school, the children were prevented from speaking their languages, practicing their religions, wearing their traditional clothing, etc.

The boarding school phenomena was in fact both a form of cultural prohibition and cultural destruction. The latter we will take up below. Of the former, Ron Reed, Karuk Ceremonial Leader, says,

> When modern contact happened, we had to forget about all of our relationships; we had to forget about all of the sciences; and we had to forget about all of the philosophies; we had to forget about everything that was ingrained in us for thousands of years. (2019)

This description of cultural prohibition can be applied generally, but it was said in specific reference to the boarding school experience.

Curriculum Clashes over Culture

Contemporary examples of cultural deprivation occurring when culturally based curriculum or teaching approaches are prohibited are on the rise. In the now infamous case of Arizona creating a law banning the Mexican American Studies program at Tucson Unified School District, a federal judge ruled that the legislation showed racial animus—it was racist—for targeting Mexican Americans and limiting their constitutional right to free speech (*Arce v. Douglass*). Despite this 2016 ruling, and increased legislation requiring ethnic studies in several states, such as California, Oregon, and Washington, in 2022, Arizona legislators have introduced HB 2112 which limits discussion about race and ethnicity. And the year before, a similar bill was introduced and passed, but later declared unconstitutional by the Arizona State Supreme Court. At the time of this writing, Chalkbeat, a progressive educational news service, documents some 32 states with laws in various stages of development.

Cultural deprivation occurs through legal maneuvering and lawsuits, as well. For example, the California Department of Education recently settled out of court with The Californians for Equal Rights Protection. Ed Source reported that

> the California Department of Education and the State Board of Education said in a statement that it would delete them "out of an abundance of caution and in order to avoid prolonged and costly litigation." However, the state agreed to pay $100,000 of the plaintiffs' legal expenses; it would also send a letter to school districts informing them of the deletions. The curriculum included several unity chants. The two that will be removed are the In Lak Ech Affirmation, which focuses on the Nahui Ollin (pages 9–12), and the Ashé Affirmation, whose origin is Nigerian (page 14). (Fensterwald, 2021)

The state established an ethnic studies model curriculum and graduation requirement to foster greater cultural security for their students. The settlement altering educational policy became an instance of cultural deprivation. Further, the state—meaning taxpayers—is required to pay for this prohibition act.

Cultural Appropriation

Cultural appropriation is said to occur when dominant societies initially denigrate cultural practices or products from marginalized and subjugated communities, but then later take up those same practices or products that were previously denigrated in their original or authentic forms. Conversely, appropriation involves engaging cultural practices and products out of context for which they were intended or conceived of by the source communities. Further, this kind of appropriation can garner social gain for the appropriators when BIPOC tradition and innovation is seen as trendy or innovative and the appropriate becomes identified as a trendsetter, or simply a fashionable participant in a new trend.

For example, a series of interviews on cultural appropriation conducted by BBC reporters begins with a Black British woman and an Indian British woman describing instances of harassment and ridicule, one for wearing her hair in braids and the other for wearing a Bindi—a traditional Hindu symbol associated with accessing intuition and wisdom. A follow-up series of interviews with White British men and women at a park wearing "festival" clothing—bohemian, Indigenous aesthetics—expressed indignance at having to answer for wearing bindis. Shuvi Jha (2018) of the Hindu America Foundation offers a conceptual response:

> My belief is this: if you turn up to Coachella with a jeweled Bindi on your forehead along with a profound knowledge about the religious and cultural meaning behind the ornament, then by all means, go flaunt that bindi! But if you do not know the symbolism behind the dot or don't care to learn about it, then there's no reason for you to wear it. As proven, the Bindi is more than just a red dot.

Cultural appropriation becomes even more egregious when others, especially members of the dominant society, monetize their engagement with the practices or products of others, especially when BIPOC communities are discouraged, blocked, or prevented from earning a living or receiving financial compensation for their cultural production because the dominant society monetizes BIPOC.

Cultural Appropriation Becomes Cultural Prohibition

Cultural appropriation becomes cultural prohibition when the appropriation no longer becomes associated with the specific community, when the community decreases its engagement in the cultural expression or product; It can also be when the cultural community can no longer earn a living by engaging in their cultural arts, because the cultural practice has become affiliated with the dominant culture. Any time communities are limited or prevented from engaging in cultural practices, expressions, or products this definition is at play. It is a widespread and layered phenomena that affects most marginalized communities, but in different ways.

Broken Bones and Artifacts

While economic appropriation is an egregious form of cultural prohibition, we can describe a far more devastating cultural deprivation practice. In May 2021, Dr. Marc Lamont Hill reported on Penn Museum's apology letter for housing the world's largest collection of human skulls. The skulls had been pillaged from graves of enslaved Africans, mostly from Cuba. Some of the skulls had also come from enslaved Africans' graves in Philadelphia, where Hill reported the story from. The report noted the role of catalysts, such as Black Lives Matter in producing the letter of apology, and the museum's reorganization of the African section toward a decolonized presentation.

Two weeks later, Hill (2021) followed with a story about a second apology letter from Penn Museum. The story explained that since the previous story broke, additional unique human remains were found at the museum. Further, not only were these bones being housed at Penn, but they were also being used in an online forensics course taught by a Princeton professor online using the MOOK platform provided by Coursera.

This set of remains belonged to one or two young African American girls, named Katricia, or Tri Africa and Delisha Africa. They died in 1985 during a police raid on their home located on Osage Avenue in West Philadelphia, Pennsylvania. The 1985 raid was the second police raid on the Africa family and the Ona' Move headquarters. During this raid, police helicopters dropped two 1.5-pound (0.75-kg) bombs on the building causing the death of these children and eleven other Africa family members. Penn museum acquired the bones from the City of Philadelphia Medical Examiner's office. As most members of the Africa family were in prison, they were not able to refuse consent to the collecting, housing, and use of the remains.

The trafficking of human remains is a thriving endeavor: Harvard Peabody (Hudetz & Ngu 2023); Smithsonian (Lee, 2020); UC Berkeley, UC Davis, and UCLA (Howle, 2020); and UT Austin (Roldan, 2020) have all experienced challenges from Indigenous communities for housing human remains of their ancestors. These cases suggest that even when there is federal legislation (i.e., NAGPRA) and precedent for the application of that legislation, entities will still enact cultural deprivation. In the case of the University of California, State Auditor Elaine M. Howle, CPA, noted in her report that "the university's inadequate policies and oversight have resulted in inconsistent practices for returning Native American remains and artifacts among the university campuses we reviewed at Berkeley, Davis, and Los Angeles" (Howle, 2020).

Redman (2016) explains how widespread the practice of collecting, displaying, and/or otherwise desecrating human remains from BIPOC and other marginalized communities goes back for hundreds of years as part of the settler colonial project. While the above examples focus largely on the United States, Kennewick Man (Raja, 2016) is a case in point among aboriginal Australians. Trafficking of BIPOC human remains is an enduring part of Western culture. It is a collective cultural experience in many locations over an extended period. And there is a related collective experience of going to see these remains over time (Monteiro, 2023). As such, this phenomenon is ripe for producing epigenetic trauma (Monteiro, 2023).

These instances of cultural deprivation can also be considered cultural destruction, as we will see in the next section. However, they are also acts of cultural appropriation in that individuals and institutions used the human remains from subjugated people unable to ethically consent to their use by virtue of their subjugation. Human remains of BIPOC people were used as entertainment trends, out of context, and for social gain and for economic gain. They are acts of cultural deprivation because they prevent specific individuals and family members from engaging in funerary rites, specific honorific rites, and specific ancestral healing rituals. Malidoma Patrice Somé (1993) asserts that the psychic problems of modern-day humans are related to our loss of ritual. Ancestral rituals sustain individuals and communities. These acts of desecration requires new individual and community rituals that have never before been contemplated in many cases.

Cultural Destruction

Cultural deprivation by way of prohibition can be linked to cultural genocide or culturcide: Complete annihilation, not only of cultural artifacts and practices, but also of the very spaces for and sources of cultural transmission, as well as the cultural transmission relationships.

Destruction of Real Property—The Place of Cultural Transmission

Apart from family separations, cultural destruction of BIPOC communities has happened historically through violence and the threat of violence to BIPOC institutions. As noted in definition number one, rich cultures and cultural institutions have been developed and grown parallel to and even in conversation with dominant cultures who have enforced segregation from their institutions. History shows us that most often the dominant culture does not allow subgroups, such as BIPOC communities to flourish. History shows us that the dominant culture often disrupts and deprives this cultural transmission, described in the second definition.

Many Indigenous hunting and burial grounds, seasonal camp sites, and other important geographic spaces—locations of cultural transmission and co-construction—have been destroyed by settler colonial development for many years, including railroads, pipelines, roads, mining, farming, allotment, etc. Often the development leaves the land permanently altered from its natural and cultural condition.

For example, the Black Hills in South Dakota have been permanently altered by the Mount Rushmore sculptures and Lake Tahoe in California/Nevada, which was not only the Washoe summer campsite and fishing source, but also an important spiritual location has become a ski resort and summer vacation town. The hot springs and burial mounds in Xenia, Ohio, had been inhabited by indigenous communities for 1,000 or more years. During the 1700s, the Miami and Shawnee tribes lived in this area for hunting, trading, and plotting resistance against the newly formed United States and their colonial settler citizens. After the war of 1812 and the defeat of pan Indigenous cultural renaissance efforts led by Tenskwatawa, these communities were forcibly removed. The hot springs were turned into the Twana Resort, a spa retreat for Southern enslavers and enslaved women they took with them, and eventually the site of Wilberforce University, the first private historically Black college owned and operated by African Americans.

In some instances, where African Americans established communities and institutions such as the above, property has been partly or completely, destroyed by dominant cultural forces. Black Wall Street in Oklahoma and Rosewood, Florida, are instance of communities and multiple institutions destroyed. For examples of individual property destruction, we can list the 16th Street Baptist Church in Birmingham, Alabama; the Black Panther Headquarters in Chicago or Sacramento; or the MOVE headquarters in Philadelphia. These examples are complex and often fit many different categories of cultural deprivation. The bombing of the MOVE headquarters may have begun as an act of cultural destruction of real property, but it became an act of destruction of humanity—the sources of cultural transmission and construction—in the death that ensued and the exploitation of the bones of the children after the second bombing.

Mobile Property—The Articles of Cultural Transmission

Humans use tools, instruments, and devices for all our secular and spiritual activity—formal, informal, and official. We sign our names. We walk with walking sticks and talk with talking sticks. We count prayers with beads. We light candles. We adorn our hair with combs and picks; we read books; shoot pool with cues; whisk eggs; strum guitars; send text messages, take pics, and talk on mobile phones. These represent our articles of cultural transmission.

We transmit and co-construct culture through them. They regulate or extend our thoughts, words, and behavior. We personalize our objects. We decorate them. We label them. We display them or we keep them secret. We use them for special occasions, or we use them every day and often. We wrap them in sentiments. We put our memories in them, to be retrieved later. We hold on to them. We bequeath them.

And because we infuse different objects with different degrees of cultural significance, when they are destroyed and no longer available for our use, we can experience cultural loss. If our books are burned, phones confiscated, our instruments broken, etc. we can no longer process culture through them in the same way.

Humanity—The Sources and Subjects of Cultural Transmission

Murder is often related to destruction of real property. In all the cases listed above, Black people were living on that land and in those buildings when the destruction occurred and some died because of simply being there. People are involved in various cultural transmission activities, such as teaching and learning, preaching and praying, organizing, advising, and demonstrating craft and techniques. Indiscriminate and targeted murder has become a significant act of cultural destruction in contemporary times.

Family Separation–The Apparatus of Cultural Transmission

Family separations have been a major mechanism of this deprivation and destruction. African families were separated for hundreds of years during enslavement. And African American families continue to be separated today by over-policing. Policing is a major mechanism for cultural deprivation in and of itself, and it also contributes to the family separation mechanism through arrests and homicide.

In addition, the Page Act of 1875 effectively created family separations among Chinese immigrant families. The act prohibited women from entering the United States who were suspected of prostitution. Chinese women were stereotyped as prostitutes and subsequently prohibited their entry into the country. In many cases, this act of steretyping separated them from their husbands and brothers, and sometimes children from their fathers, as children are much more likely to stay with their mothers.

Indigenous families were separated up into the late twentieth century through boarding schools. Latinx families were separated early in the twenty-first century at the U.S.-Mexico border. Family separation has occurred consistently for hundreds of years for BIPOC communities, but especially African American men and women during disproportionate incarceration.

As referenced above, DMC acts not only as a mechanism to prohibit access to the dominant society's culture; it also acts as a mechanism to disrupt access to one's own culture. While youth are certainly producers of culture, they are also the receivers of cultural heritage transmitted by mentors, elders, parents, and other family and community members. DMC prevents this from happening, which can lead to cultural destruction. DMC enacts cultural destruction not only by preventing others from participating in cultural expression, production and consumption, but also because they cause family institutions to erode.

Family separation is defined as genocide by the United Nations article on the "Prevention and Punishment of the Crime of Genocide."

Kidnappers and Jailers

Additionally, between 2016 and 2020, journalists from all major and many independent news outlets began documenting the Donald Trump administration's family separations. Migrant parents arriving at the U.S. Southern border from Central America and Mexico were detained and housed in separate facilities from their children. Soon thereafter, medical and mental health professionals began documenting the impact of this practice.

In all three instances—forced boarding school attendance; disproportionate removal from police activity, and immigration enforcement—federal, state, and local agencies engage in the practice of cultural deprivation and destruction through family separation. The agencies disrupt the cultural transmission process within families.

APA Definition 3

Finally, APA's third definition briefly notes that cultural deprivation occurs when there is no cultural stimulation at all. This definition most likely occurs in institutions or other extreme dysfunctional settings. This definition sometimes acts in service of the second when large members of a population are incarcerated. This book is most interested in the second definition, but there will be instances where this final definition will also be addressed.

Impact of Cultural Deprivation

As previously stated, cultural deprivation enacted against BIPOC individuals and communities is often preceded by or accompanied with other forms of subjugation, racial oppression, or colonization. Because these other forms of subjugation often include gross assaults requiring immediate redress, such as physical violence, malnourishment, wage-theft, impoverishment, etc. it's easy to lose sight of the cultural concerns. However, research-based theories, such as post-traumatic slave syndrome (DeGruy, 2017), post-apocalyptic stress syndrome (Martinez-Alire & Borunda, 2017), complex trauma (Kwenele, 2020), and racialized trauma (Menakem, 2017) identify the impact of socio-historic disruptions in the development of cultural frames of reference apart from, and in relation to, the seriousness of physical and economic oppression.

Joy DeGruy's (2017) groundbreaking theory, post-traumatic slave syndrome (PTSS), draws on clinical records, interviews, first-person slave narratives, and primary source documents dating back over several centuries to explain the impact of multigenerational trauma associated with the transatlantic slave trade on many enslaved Africans' descendants. PTSS not only conceptualizes traumatic experiences resulting from centuries of slavery but also includes experiences of ongoing oppression and institutionalized racism. This, of course includes bodily harm, threat of bodily harm, and often subsequent psychic injury. This is the primary means of BIPOC subjugation and exploitation. Additionally, PTSS includes the adaptive and survival behaviors and attitudes socialized within communities over time.

DeGruy adds that PTSS includes "a belief (real or imagined) that the benefits of the society in which they live are not available to them" (p. 105). DeGruy's addition is an important identifier of cultural deprivation as both an individual element of PTSS with its own impact; and an element associated with the assaults from enslavement and white supremacy. Early classification sciences and other forms of dis-information about Black people served as a basis for justifying human trafficking practices (DeGruy, 2017; Kendi, 2017). Thus, the historic instances of literal physical and emotional violence; historic and ongoing explicit cultural prohibition, appropriation, and destruction that occurs in policy and practices among the professions has resulted in widespread and varied conditions of cultural deprivation.

DeGruy discusses challenging family relationships as another impact of PTSS. This should not be surprising given the ongoing assault on BIPOC family's ability to transmit and co-construct culture. Families are instruments and places of cultural development and corresponding neuro-biological development. The preceding sections have provided examples of family disruption, most notably in the section on cultural appropriation and cultural destruction.

Finally, in addition to these broader considerations of belief in one's own cultural marginalization and disrupted family culture; DeGruy identifies vacant esteem, persistent anger, and racist socialization as impacts of PTSS. The latter two can be correlated with cultural deprivation most closely. Frustration and anger of over-persistent blocking access to cultural engagement and learning to adopt racist behavior seems quite ordinary as an impact of this ongoing conditioning. We can retain value in ourselves and feel constant resentment about being block from dominant cultural resources and our own cultural production; or we might grow to resent the thing we think is the reason or source of our marginalization and minortization: our own cultural, racial, or ethnic heritage.

PTSS is not a blanket diagnosis for all BIPOC. It is persistent partly due to epigenetics and partly to ongoing conditions of assault and cultural deprivation. Still, persistence does not equate to universals. Not all BIPOC are impacted by cultural deprivation in equal measure. Further, when the impact presents itself in the conditions outlined above, it is instructive to read trauma-informed therapist Resmaa Menakem (2017) reminder that this is a form of racialized trauma. Menakem reminds as he affirms that this does not mean BIPOC are defective, and readers should not infer this in any way. In as much as this book is instructive, some readers will need to read this explicitly. Readers are to understand from these impacts that something has happened to BIPOC and continues to happen, as outlined in the preceding sections of this chapter. And as all human beings vary in psychic temperament, cultural deprivation experiences will impact BIPOC differently.

Cognitive psychologist Reuven Feuerstein's definition of cultural deprivation is a synthesis of the second and third offered by APA. However, Feuerstein elaborates on the impact of this condition in his synthesis definition. Reuven Feuerstein defines cultural deprivation as a reduced capacity on the part of individuals to modify their intellectual structures in response to direct exposure to external sources of stimulation (Rand et al., 1979). The source of this inability, or reduced capacity, to organize and elaborate information is a lack of "mediated learning experiences ... by mediating agents (e.g., parents, teachers, and siblings) according to their intentions, culture, and emotional commitment" (Fuerestein, 1979). The implication is that something has occurred which has interrupted and prevented this transmission.

Elsewhere he elaborates that cultural deprivation refers to a condition that exists in individuals who have not had the opportunity to learn the knowledge passed down by their cultural heritage in an active, personal, participatory, and engaging way. Thus, it is not simply the presence of parents or teachers or other keepers of culture in communities. The quality and consistency of this process is equally important. BIPOC communities have been subjected to innumerable instances of interruption and disruption of this active, personal, participatory, and engaging cultural transmission.

Context, Difference, and Deprivation

Several important contexts about Feuerstein's work can help further illuminate his ideas about cultural deprivation. First, Feuerstein distinguished between cultural difference and cultural deprivation. He asserted that someone who has had cultural transmission can navigate new cultural learning experiences more readily than someone who has not. Those who have been deprived of mediated learning experiences in their own culture show a reduced potential for learning, and this makes the transition to each new life experience problematic. In situations of cultural deprivation, it is possible to identify a certain kind of difficulty in relating to others, being able to listen to different opinions and seeing different points of view. When children lack educational experiences that relate well to their learned cultural frame of reference, new learning is limited.

Feuerstein explains that the mediation or the transmission process itself is what is important. Regardless of the cultural content. With cultural mediation and transmission, one builds the mechanism–the frames (Lakeoff 2008), metaphors (Lakeoff and Johnson 2003), labels, etc., and the corresponding cognitive capacity to navigate new experiences. One implication, which he has pointed out, is that whereas deficit perspectives label BIPOC community cultures disparagingly for the challenges members face from cultural deprivation, it is the deprivation that is the culprit, not BIPOC cultures.

Second, Feuerestein's intellectual context shaping the language of his theory comes from his work with development theorist Jean Piaget. Piaget's work concerned stages of development. Piaget believed that certain behaviors were not possible until the brain developed and reached maturation at a given stage. Fuerestein believed that this theory did not account for variation in development. He further believed that this variation can be attributed to cultural mediation and trauma or oppression. He believed that Piaget's theory did not account for these occurrences.

Feuerstein and DeGruy have identified specific impacts of cultural deprivation. Whereas Feuerstein identifies mediation practices to address cognitive injury resulting from cultural deprivation, DeGruy first notes the importance of the removal of harm and other social justice measures supporting safety and security as a precondition to therapeutic intervention. Feuerstein writes from a post-holocaust perspective. DeGruy is informed by the ongoing conditions of cultural marginalization.

Understanding Cultural Security

Cultural security is an emergent interdisciplinary field of study broadly concerned with role of cultural property in international, colonial, neo-colonial, conflict, and post-conflict relations. Culture is always under threat. Erik Nemmeth, an early proponent of this field, argues that the international threat to cultural property and by extension cultural heritage is not just ever-present, it continues to increase. This new field of study is a response to the evolving threat. To help understand the perimeters, Nemmeth offers that "the concept of cultural security encompasses research, analyses, and strategies aimed at mitigating exploitation of cultural property as a pawn in foreign relations and as a tool in acts of political violence and terrorism" (2015, p. 2). While working through his initial ideas at The Gray Area Festival, Nemmeth identifies economics; the protection of indigenous artifacts; and international security in contemporary, historic, and changing times as the main areas of study. Nemmeth roots his discussion in cultural property whether antiquities, contemporary collectables, and all other aesthetic manner in between; even as he admits that there is a need to do something about cultural security more broadly, beyond artwork and artifact. "While fine art, antiquities, and monuments represent only one aspect of cultural identity, an examination of exploitation of such cultural property provides insight into the increasing relevance of cultural heritage to international security" (p. 1). Nemmeth's work in this new field provides insight into the processes and impact of cultural prohibition, appropriation, and destruction of objects of cultural transmission and co-construction.

The previous section on understanding cultural deprivation identified instances of cultural deprivation enacted across a wide range of professions. Educators and medical and mental health professionals in local communities need to understand their role in promoting cultural security. Their role may or may not include addressing the impact of the economic and political relationships between nations regarding the appropriation or destruction of cultural property. Their role will more likely be to address the psychic, social, and physical impact of these broader activities on individuals, families, and communities. The professions should also be processing how to shift away from the ongoing practices causing disruptions in cultural transmission and co-construction among marginalized and minoritized communities stemming from their work with their students, clients, and patients.

A paradigm for understanding BIPOC cultural security can help build new professional practices to address and transform cultural deprivation's impacts. Black safety (Ohito & Brown, 2021) helps us think not only about physical safety, but also cultural security, because it highlights the need to prevent harm among Black people living their daily lives engaged in all manner of cultural activity. Black safety is a condition where one is protected from danger, risk, and injury. And it is the precondition of getting ahead of the thing that would cause the harm in the first place. Thus, we can also think about emotional and mental safety.

In the foundational writings on Black psychology, Wade Nobles takes up the idea of cultural security from the vantage point of liberating the

African consciousness. The need for liberation references the condition of cultural deprivation. Nobles asserts: "We fail to see that part of the confusion results from ... the white power elite trying to paint a particular image of the African-centered movement that frightens and divides our community" (p. 264). And again, he adds, "European contact with Africa has always been driven by the desire to transform or rearrange things African into fundamental European constructs" (p. 265). Once again, the first section in this chapter outlined ways in which the professions participate in cultural deprivation practices. These practices transform and rearrange BIPOC access to culture.

What does a liberated African consciousness look like? Better still, what are its components? What is it made up of? Nobles answers these questions in part by referencing Cheik Anta Diop's cultural identity and cultural security.

History

Diop explains that the strongest shield we can create against cultural aggression comes from knowing our history. Knowing what actions we have taken with, for, or against others and knowing what actions have been taken by others with, for, or against us can be profoundly clarifying. Working through historical accounts supports cultural security because the work attempts to not only answer such questions as: What happened? How did it happen? But the process links the responses to these questions, with new questions, such as: What is my role? What actions have I taken—or can I take to create value in society? Constructing personal, social histories fills narrative gaps, and facilitates correlative neurobiological connections (Lakoff, 2008). Narrative gaps are the result and the intention of cultural deprivation.

Addressing gaps in our personal and social history can help address distortions from mis, dis, or mal information by fostering inquiry- and evidence-based epistemologies. Diop says *rediscover* the *thread that connects* us to our most remote ancestral past. This is an active process in search of tangible evidence, even as it implies something mythic. Diop's scholarship spans many different disciplines in order that he might take a deep dive into that remote African past. This is a lifelong effort of listening to stories, examining the historic artifacts, and considering rich contexts. Culturally secure individuals and communities are not easy prey to information disorder. They are fortified by narrative cohesion and continuity.

Language

Diop says that the development of historical conscience is the safest way toward cultural security, but he is hard pressed to value history over language or vice versa in this regard. As a historic subject of French colonial rule, he notes that linguistic unification is elusive unless we dig deep into the past of proto languages. He calls for more research on classical African languages and a re-orientation of education for Africans that has a linguistic lineage rooted in Egypto-Nubian languages, in the same way that Western education has a Greco-Latin base.

Linguistic cultural deprivation includes blocking access to the dominant language and other, more diverse language resources present in our multi-ethnic communities; blocking marginalized and minoritized individuals and groups access to their own language; and blocking access to language resources altogether. Culturally secure individuals and groups not only have multiple levels of proficiency and opportunity to speak in their primary language, they know how to access resources for developing proficiency in other languages. Linguistic cultural security would not involve a dominant language at all. Thus, our professions should always be places that facilitate robust, helpful experiences with language related to their specific vocations.

Psychology

Diop considers this third factor to be less important than the first two. To identify the psychic character of a given African people, he suggests examining various African revolutionary movements and look for the cultural elements that were left intact as invariants in their new paradigms and practices for the people. Wade Nobles' presentation of Diop shifts his third factor from a vaguely impactful element contributing to cultural security to the most important.

He explains that we are first and foremost a spiritual being. This spiritual psychic being is housed in a physical container, and this is in a human form. And that human form lives in a social or historic world that constructs racial hierarchies. African psyche knows the knowable and the unknowable.

In a world arranged by colonial might and global white supremacy, cultural security is not a static concept. Cultural security is a deliberate practice. It is a verb rather than a noun. It is what we do for ourselves and others in our personal lives, certainly. But as professionals in health and healing vocations, our instructional and therapeutic rituals can also be a practice of cultural security.

Summary

Chapter 2 begins with a critical family history vignette to illustrate APA's second definition of cultural deprivation: not having access to one's own culture. The second definition is further divided into three categories: cultural prohibition where BIPOC are prevented from participating in cultural production and accessing cultural production; cultural appropriation where engaging cultural practices and products out of context, and benefits socially or financially. And cultural destruction. Cultural destruction is further divided into the 1) destruction of real property (the place of cultural production), mobile property (the objects of cultural production) and human "property" (the instruments of cultural production). Cultural deprivation impacts people on social, emotional, and cognitive levels.

Cultural security is an emergent discipline focused on the economic, indigenous, and international political relationships. Cultural security is also wholistic term concerned with cultural identity, history, language, and psychology.

Activities

Seven scenarios or case studies below represent official communication and oral narratives that demonstrate different instances of cultural deprivation. Pair up with another student and review two of the cases. After reading, review the cases with your partner. Discuss: What is significant? What made it significant? What can you do with this information in your personal and professional life?

1   Source: The letter was retrieved from the Penn Museum website on 3/3/ 22. https://www.penn.museum/towards-respectful-resolution/

A Message to the Community

April 28, 2021

From Wendell Pritchett, Provost

and

Christopher Woods, Ph.D., Williams Director

University of Pennsylvania Museum of Archaeology and Anthropology

Towards a Respectful Resolution: An Apology to the Africa Family

(Content Warning: contains discussion of human remains.)

The Penn Museum and the University of Pennsylvania apologize to the Africa family and the members of our community for allowing human remains recovered from the MOVE house to be used for research and teaching, and for retaining the remains for far too long.

The Africa family and our community have experienced profound emotional distress as a result of the news that human remains from the horrific 1985 bombing of the MOVE house were at the Penn Museum and this fact has urgently raised serious questions: Why were the remains at the Museum in the first place? Why were they used for teaching purposes? And, most importantly, what are we going to do to resolve this situation?

In 1985, the Philadelphia Medical Examiner's Office asked Penn physical anthropologists to assist with the efforts to identify some of the remains from the MOVE house. It is common for physical anthropologists to assist in forensic cases where individual identity is uncertain, and over the years our experts revisited this question, driven by new science and technology. But despite these efforts, we, unfortunately, are still unable to provide conclusive confirmation of identity.

Chris Woods personally learned on April 16 that these remains were in our Museum and that they had been used in a forensic anthropology class, having assumed his role as director on April 1. The important topic of returning human remains to descendants was very much on the minds of Museum staff as there had just been a public announcement of plans regarding the Morton Cranial Collection, and the issue of the MOVE victim's remains was raised in this context. In the April 12 announcement of the plans for the Morton Collection, we vowed to work with local communities to learn their wishes and to return individuals to their ancestors, wherever possible, as a step toward atonement and repair for the racist and colonial practices that were integral to the formation of these collections.

While the remains recovered from the MOVE house were not part of the Museum collection, it could not be clearer that this same standard should be applied here as well—these remains should be returned to the Africa family as soon as possible. The research of our physical anthropologists was done in the interests of serving our community, but by any measure 36 years is far too long to have waited.

We understand the importance of reuniting these remains with the family. This is our goal. And we are committed to a respectful, consultative resolution.

For many, one of the most traumatic parts of this narrative is that some of these remains were used in a forensic anthropology class that was offered by Princeton University and taught by a member of the Penn Museum staff. This course has now been suspended.

Classes in forensic science require human remains to teach the next generation of forensic specialists. However, it is an ethical imperative to show the utmost respect to family survivors. Informed consent must be given by the person before death or by the family afterward. Regretfully, this did not happen in this case—and it was a serious error in judgment to use these remains in a class of any kind, especially given the extreme emotional distress in our community surrounding the 1985 bombing of the MOVE house. Unquestionably, the decision to use the remains in this way has torn at old wounds that our city and community have long sought to heal.

The Museum has promised to reassess our practices of collecting, stewarding, displaying, and researching human remains, and we are committed to this promise. It is now obvious, however, that this reassessment must also include how human remains are used in teaching as well as a comprehensive review of the holdings and collection practices of our Physical Anthropology section.

As part of this review, the University of Pennsylvania has hired attorneys Joe Tucker and Carl Singley of the Tucker Law Group to investigate how the remains came into the possession of the Museum and what transpired with them for nearly four decades. This report will be shared with the community and its findings used to help us ensure that nothing of this nature is repeated in the future.

We must constantly bear in mind the fact that human remains were once living people, and we must always strive to treat them with the dignity and respect that they deserve.

2.   The letter was retrieved from the Peabody Museum of Archeology and Ethnology website on 3/3/22. https://peabody.harvard.edu/news/message-peabody-museum-director

Message from the Peabody Museum Director

January 28, 2021

Dear Members of the Peabody Community,

Founded in 1866, the Peabody Museum is intricately linked to 19th-century legacies of settler colonialism and imperialism both in the United States and around the globe. In its development as a premier research and teaching institution, the Peabody directly benefited from collecting practices that we recognize today ignore the wishes and values of families and communities, particularly people considered to be outside of western traditions. We must confront the difficult truth that this legacy is embedded within the entire history of the Museum. Collecting—at the Peabody and elsewhere—drove the removal of human remains and cultural materials from communities of origin, creating, for example, one of the largest collections of American Indian remains in the country. These legacies are with us today, present in the language used to document collections, in past exhibitions, and in the ways collections have been used in teaching and research.

As part of a Museum-wide focus on ethical stewardship and Harvard University's aim to understand and address the historical and enduring connections to the legacy of slavery, we have examined Museum records for individuals who are identified as African American or of African descent and whose associated geographical information places them within the United States. As Harvard University President Larry Bacow announced today, we have identified human remains of fifteen individuals of African descent who were or were likely to have been alive during the period of American enslavement.

This revelation reminds us of the breadth and reach of the legacies of the Museum's history, and of our ethical responsibilities to affected communities, including those focused on the thousands of Native American individuals within the collection and the Museum's work under the Native American Graves Protection and Repatriation Act (NAGPRA). In both size and scope, the Peabody cares for one of the largest collections subject to NAGPRA, which, before the legislation was passed, included remains from more than 10,000 individuals, and still includes 7,000 individuals today. A year ago, Edgerley Family Dean of the Faculty of Arts and Sciences Claudine Gay, appointed an NAGPRA Advisory Committee to support the Museum's long-term commitment to the implementation of NAGPRA and the ethical and moral imperative it represents. This committee, as well as our Faculty Executive Committee, looks forward to joining the work of the University's new steering committee on human remains chaired by Professor Evelynn Hammonds, who is a member of our Faculty Executive Committee.

The Peabody, alongside President Bacow, apologizes without equivocation for not confronting our historic collecting practices and stewardship of all of these human remains and for our failure as an institution to face the ethical and moral issues that undergirded the practices that brought them to our Museum. In 1990, when NAGPRA was passed, our Museum should have issued a formal apology. Today, we take the occasion of this current discovery and this wide-ranging institutional apology, to make a specific and formal apology for the practices that led to the Peabody's large collection of Native American human remains and funerary objects.

We pledge to prioritize the urgent work of understanding and illuminating our history and to begin to make amends. As part of our focus on ethical stewardship, the Museum has begun a new collaborative, multi-year, cross-departmental initiative to critically examine our institutional history. We want to engage, with focus and urgency, our teaching and research mission through collections research, offering a new undergraduate class, and assessing our historic documentation, among other activities.

This effort is only the first step in a much longer and ongoing process of repairing the harm that historic collection practices have perpetrated. The Museum will be an active participant in the University's new steering committee on human remains. With regard to the fifteen individuals named in President Bacow's announcement, the Museum is already engaged in learning more about the history of each person so that ethical and respectful decisions can be made, including transfer to descendant communities, re-interment, and burial.

Facing our history is essential to the Museum's ethical stewardship of the collections in its care. The revelations that such history includes individuals who may have been enslaved, as well as thousands of American Indian individuals, requires a commitment to face that history. We pledge to do exactly that, as we strive to fulfill our responsibility to society and to Indigenous and other communities around the world.

Sincerely,
Jane Pickering
William & Muriel Seabury Howells Director

3. Hair Scares Everywhere

A Tale of Twists Taken Apart and Braids Unbraided

When Asiyah was in elementary school, her father and mother spent time putting their daughter's hair in twists, puffs, and braids before school. Her father had no braiding skill, but he could manage other styles. Asiyah's mother could braid just fine. Both of her parents took time to ensure she was always groomed, even when she wanted to wear t-shirts and sweatpants to school like the other kids.

Asiyah attended St. Peter's Episcopal School in an urban community in Northern California. As with most schools, occasionally the schools would have an outbreak of lice requiring a healthcare professional—often a school nurse—to carefully examine the heads of all the children in school. On those days, Asiyah always came home with her head down. Every time healthcare workers examined her hair, they would undo her braids and twists. Once this happened on picture day.

St. Peter's had a small number of African American students. This happened to all of the girls at one time or another.

Senate Bill No. 188

CHAPTER 58

An act to amend Section 212.1 of the Education Code, and to amend Section 12926 of the Government Code, relating to discrimination.

[Approved by Governor July 3, 2019. Filed with the Secretary of State July 3, 2019.]

legislative counsel's digest

The people of the State of California do enact as follows:

SECTION 1. The Legislature finds and declares all of the following:

a   The history of our nation is riddled with laws and societal norms that equated "blackness," and the associated physical traits, for example, dark skin, kinky and curly hair to a badge of inferiority, sometimes subject to separate and unequal treatment.

b   This idea also permeated societal understanding of professionalism. Professionalism was, and still is, closely linked to European features and mannerisms, which entails that those who do not naturally fall into Eurocentric norms must alter their appearances, sometimes drastically and permanently, in order to be deemed professional.

c   Despite the great strides American society and laws have made to reverse the racist ideology that Black traits are inferior, hair remains a rampant source of racial discrimination with serious economic and health consequences, especially for Black individuals.

d   Workplace dress code and grooming policies that prohibit natural hair, including afros, braids, twists, and locks, have a disparate impact on Black individuals as these policies are more likely to deter Black applicants and burden or punish Black employees than any other group.

e   Federal courts accept that Title VII of the Civil Rights Act of 1964 prohibits discrimination based on race, and therefore protects against discrimination against afros. However, the courts do not understand that afros are not the only natural presentation of Black hair. Black hair can also be naturally presented in braids, twists, and locks.

f   In a society in which hair has historically been one of many determining factors of a person's race, and whether they were a second class citizen, hair today remains a proxy for race. Therefore, hair discrimination targeting hairstyles associated with race is racial discrimination.

g   Acting in accordance with the constitutional values of fairness, equity, and opportunity for all, the Legislature recognizes that continuing to enforce a Eurocentric image of professionalism through purportedly race-neutral grooming policies that disparately impact Black individuals and exclude them from some workplaces is in direct opposition to equity and opportunity for all.

4.   Parkill, M. (2022). Read the full text of the Pope's apology for Canada's residential schools. CTV News. Retrieved on April 4, 2022 from https://www.ctvnews.ca/canada/read-the-full-text-of-the-pope-s-apology-for-canada-s-residential-schools-1.5844874?cache=%3FclipId%3D2097462

In a speech delivered on Friday [Delivered Friday April 1, 2022], Pope Francis apologized for the Catholic Church's role in Canada's residential school system, after Indigenous delegates traveled from Canada to the Vatican to speak with him about the abuses suffered in those schools. Below is the full text of the Pope's apology, translated from Italian:

Dear brothers and sisters,

Good morning and welcome!

I thank Bishop Poisson for his kind words and each of you for your presence here and for the prayers that you have offered. I am grateful that you have come to Rome despite the difficulties caused by the pandemic. Over the past few days, I have listened attentively to your testimonies. I have brought them to my thoughts and prayers, and reflected on the stories you told and the situations you described. I thank you for having opened your hearts to me, and for expressing, by means of this visit, your desire for us to journey together.

I would like to take up a few of the many things that have struck me. Let me start from a saying that is part of your traditional wisdom. It is not only a turn of phrase but also a way of viewing life: "In every deliberation, we must consider the impact on the seventh generation". These are wise words, farsighted and the exact opposite of what often happens in our own day, when we run after practical and immediate goals without thinking of the future and generations yet to come. For the ties that connect the elderly and the young are essential. They must be cherished and protected, lest we lose our historical memory and our very identity. Whenever memory and identity are cherished and protected, we become more human.

These days, a beautiful image keeps coming up. You compared yourselves to the branches of a tree. Like those branches, you have spread in different directions, you have experienced various times and seasons, and you have been buffeted by powerful winds. Yet you have remained solidly anchored to your roots, which you kept strong. In this way, you have continued to bear fruit, for the branches of a tree grow high only if its roots are deep. I would like to speak of some of those fruits, which deserve to be better known and appreciated.

First, your care for the land, which you see not as a resource to be exploited, but as a gift of heaven. For you, the land preserves the memory of your ancestors who rest there; it is a vital setting making it possible to see each individual's life as part of a greater web of relationships, with the Creator, with the human community, with all living species and with the earth, our common home. All this leads you to seek interior and exterior harmony, to show great love for the family and to possess a lively sense of community. Then too, there are the particular riches of your languages, your cultures, your traditions and your forms of art. These represent a patrimony that belongs not only to you, but to all humanity, for they are expressions of our common humanity.

Yet that tree, rich in fruit, has experienced a tragedy that you described to me in these past days: the tragedy of being uprooted. The chain that passed on knowledge and ways of life in union with the land was broken by a colonization that lacked respect for you, tore many of you from your vital milieu and tried to conform you to another mentality. In this way, great harm was done to your identity and your culture, many families were separated, and great numbers of children fell victim to these attempts to impose a uniformity based on the notion that progress occurs through ideological colonization, following programs devised in offices rather than the desire to respect the life of peoples. This is something that, unfortunately, and at various levels, still happens today. How many forms of political, ideological and economic colonization still exist in the world, driven by greed and thirst for profit, with little concern for peoples, their histories and traditions, and the common home of creation! Sadly, this colonial mentality remains widespread. Let us help each other, together, to overcome it.

Listening to your voices, I was able to enter into and be deeply grieved by the stories of the suffering, hardship, discrimination and various forms of abuse that some of you experienced, particularly in the residential schools. It is chilling to think of determined efforts to instil a sense of inferiority, to rob people of their cultural identity, to sever their roots, and to consider all the personal and social effects that this continues to entail: unresolved traumas that have become intergenerational traumas.

All this has made me feel two things very strongly: indignation and shame. Indignation, because it is not right to accept evil and, even worse, to grow accustomed to evil, as if it were an inevitable part of the historical process. No! Without real indignation, without historical memory and without a commitment to learning from past mistakes, problems remain unresolved and keep coming back. We can see this these days in the case of war. The memory of the past must never be sacrificed at the altar of alleged progress.

I also feel shame - sorrow and shame - for the role that a number of Catholics, particularly those with educational responsibilities, have had in all these things that wounded you, in the abuses you suffered and in the lack of respect shown for your identity, your culture and even your spiritual values. All these things are contrary to the Gospel of Jesus Christ. For the deplorable conduct of those members of the Catholic Church, I ask for God's forgiveness and I want to say to you with all my heart: I am very sorry. And I join my brothers, the Canadian bishops, in asking your pardon. Clearly, the content of the faith cannot be transmitted in a way contrary to the faith itself: Jesus taught us to welcome, love, serve and not judge; it is a frightening thing when, precisely in the name of the faith, counter-witness is rendered to the Gospel.

Your experiences have made me ponder anew those ever timely questions that the Creator addresses to mankind in the first pages of the Bible. After the first sin, he asks: "Where are you?" (Gen 4:9). Where are you? Where is your brother? These are questions we should never stop asking. They are essential questions raised by our conscience, lest we ever forget that we are here on this earth as guardians of the sacredness of life, and thus guardians of our brothers and sisters, and of all brother peoples.

At the same time, I think with gratitude of all those good and decent believers who, in the name of the faith, and with respect, love and kindness, have enriched your history with the Gospel. I think with joy, for example, of the great veneration that many of you have for Saint Anne, the grandmother of Jesus. Nowadays we need to re-establish the covenant between grandparents and grandchildren, between the elderly and the young, for this is a fundamental prerequisite for the growth of unity in our human family.

Dear brothers and sisters, it is my hope that our meetings these days will point out new paths to be pursued together, instill courage and strength, and lead to greater commitment on the local level. Any truly effective process of healing requires concrete actions. In a fraternal spirit, I encourage the Bishops and the Catholic community to continue taking steps towards the transparent search for truth and to foster healing and reconciliation. These steps are part of a journey that can favor the rediscovery and revitalization of your culture, while helping the Church to grow in love, respect and specific attention to your authentic traditions. I wish to tell you that the Church stands beside you and wants to continue journeying with you. Dialogue is the key to knowledge and sharing, and the Bishops of Canada have clearly stated their commitment to continue advancing together with you on a renewed, constructive, fruitful path, where encounters and shared projects will be of great help.

Dear friends, I have been enriched by your words and even more by your testimonies. You have brought here, to Rome, a living sense of your communities. I will be happy to benefit again from meeting you when I visit your native lands, where your families live. So I will close by saying "Until we meet again" in Canada, where I will be able to express to you my closeness. In the meantime, I assure you of my prayers, and upon you, your families and your communities I invoke the blessing of the Creator. Thank you

5. Skeletons in Tulsa's Closet

In 1997, I participated in a National Endowment for the Humanities Fellowship for the study of Native American literature at Oklahoma City University, under the direction of Lawana Trout. I studied with English teachers, history social science teachers, and school counselors from sites throughout the United States. Several teachers were also Native American: a Diné woman who taught on the Navajo reservation; a Lakota woman who taught on the Pine Ridge Reservation in South Dakota; a Laguna Pueblo woman and a Cheyenne man. While we were treated with opportunities to read and dialogue with writers, such as Diné poet and essayist Luci Tapahaonso, and Cree musician and poet, Joy Harjo. We also listened to White scholars read sacred poetry which they had translated into English. While a number of the Native American teachers squirmed and even said overtly that the scholars had no idea what they were unleashing with their translations.

During the second or third week of the institute, we attended a museum in Tulsa. The Diné teacher brought her middle-school aged son, and two other members of her family. Part of our tour took us down into the bowels of the museum. Our anthropologist and archeologist guides took us into the "bone room" (Redman, 2016), where the museum housed their human remains collection. At the end of a dark hall, on the outside of the opening door to the bone room, the Dine teacher and her sisters began to shriek and cry. They squeezed her son, all refusing to go any further. They would not set foot into the room. I was confused. One of the sisters explained that there were human remains of Native people in the room we were about to enter. Not only was the theft of indigenous graves a violation of their humanity and ethnic identity–there was evil magic associated with death, and with the desecration. It was a psychic and spiritual violation. It was dangerous to do; and it was dangerous for us to be around the violated remains without the intercession of indigenous elders who could properly repatriate the remains. A Lakota social studies teacher from our group asked how the museum is engaging with NAGPRA—the Native American Graves and Repatriation Act of 1990. I don't recall the response. But I do recall the skulls, femurs, clavicles and other assorted bones.

I recalled this event in spring 2021, after hearing Temple University Professor Dr. Marc Lamont Hill (2021) report on Penn Museum's apology letter for housing the world's largest collection of human skulls.

6. The Murder of James Harriston Gunn

I have a faint recollection of hearing Aunt Martha mentioned in quiet, somber tones. I don't remember hearing that she was my grandfather's sister, or that she lived in Dayton, Ohio. But when

I connected with my mother's first cousin and her sons after a DNA test brought us together; The murder of Martha's husband "Doc" was among the first family stories they shared. I asked my father about the murder. He confirmed the story. He said he thought *Jet* magazine—a weekly publication devoted to Black news, culture, and entertainment-had written about the murder. Martha's life was chronicled in stories from the Zanesville and Dayton newspapers.

Martha was born in Zanesville, Ohio, in 1906. She was mentored by Aunt Mae, a school teacher and member of the Colored Women's Club Movement. At an early age, Martha and her brothers were forced off the side of the road where they were walking, and into a ditch by an unnamed, faceless driver driving recklessly, the *Zanesville Gazette* reported. Martha was hospitalized. When she was a little older, Martha was in a car accident while riding with her Aunt Mae and Uncle Walter Banks, both also teachers. Again, an incident with a reckless driver, the paper reported.

Martha left Zanesville for Zenia where she attended Wilberforce University, the first private historically Black college in the United States. Martha pledged Alpha Kappa Alpha—the first Black sorority—becoming a lifelong member of the her chapter. After graduating, Martha received her teaching credential, and taught diet and nutrition and cooking classes at the original Paul Lawrence Dunbar High. Martha served as trustee at Wayman African Methodist Episcopal Church and participated in civic and service engagement in church, and as a member of the Links and Criterion Clubs, which focused on women and youth.

Martha married physician James Harristown Gunn. Gunn was born in MS. He attended Howard and after medical school, he established a private practice with hundreds of patients. He also established a Black Business Club.

One Sunday evening while he and Martha were watching television, someone crept onto their porch and shot James Gunn in his head, throat, and heart through the living room window. The police did not hold Martha as a suspect. Although they interviewed all of his patients and Martha put up money for a reward for the killer's capture, no concrete leads emerged leading to their capture. Martha's name no longer appeared in the newspaper after the murder.

Suggestions for Further Study

1   Levy, A. (2005). *The First Emancipator: The Forgotten Story of Robert Carter, the Founder Who Freed His Slaves.* Randomhouse: New York.
2   The National Center for Truth and Reconciliation University of Manitoba. https://nctr.ca

    The National Center for Truth and Reconciliation serves indigenous survivors of the traumas of the boarding school phenomena in Canada. The center also educates all Canadians about the horrors of the boarding school phenomena. From the Center website: "We preserve the record of these human rights abuses, and promote continued research and learning on the legacy of residential schools. Our goal is to honor Survivors and to foster reconciliation and healing on the foundation of truth telling."
3   Truth and Reconciliation Commission. https://www.youtube.com/channel/UCohv4CbqR6qcqHknSZ1yRVA/featured

    The full event marking the Final Report of the Truth and Reconciliation Commission is archived in the videos below. The first video presents the English version and the second video is in French. Various indigenous languages are woven throughout both videos. Both videos are over three-hour long.

    a   Truth and Reconciliation Final Report (English Version). https://www.youtube.com/watch?v=mZoLgdzrw7c
    b   Rapport final de la Commission de vérité et de réconciliation. https://www.youtube.com/watch?v=V5nVvMcFeQE

4   Feuerstein, R., Feuerstein, R. S., & Falik, L. H. (2010). *Beyond Smarter: Mediated Learning and the Brain's Capacity for Change.* Teachers College Press: New York.
5   Was this the Last Black History Month? Intersectionality Matters Podcast: Episode 45. https://podcasts.apple.com/us/podcast/45-was-this-the-last-black-history-month/id1441348908?i=1000556571260
6   Ivy League Secret Exposed: Classes Used Bones of Black Children Killed in 1985 MOVE Police Bombing. https://www.youtube.com/watch?v=daHwwPimoE8&t=85s

    This excerpt of the news program *Democracy Now,* aired April 27, 2021, corroborates the story relayed above, reported by Marc Lamont Hill on *Black News Tonight.* The episode includes archival imagery of the Philadelphia Police Department's bombing of the MOVE home for context, as well as evidentiary video of the use of the child's bones for a virtual Coursera class on forensics.

7 Bone Rooms: How Elite Schools and Museums Amassed Black and
   Native Human Remains Without Consent. https://www.youtube.
   com/watch?v=gO-qNds8u_4. This excerpt of the news program
   Democracy Now, aired April 30, 2021, expands on the story above
   detailing the practice of bone collection and display by Western
   museums of all types, including medical museums and private
   collections.

Chapter 3

Addressing Cultural Deprivation in Classrooms and Communities

Introduction

The previous chapters presented a critical exploration of cultural deprivation and cultural security. This chapter will provide an overview and description of culturally sustaining rituals (indigenous orientations, ancestor acknowledgment and veneration, mindfulness, and relationship-building) to address the impact of cultural deprivation and to promote cultural security. These therapeutic, educational, and wellness practices are taken up at length in individual chapters in the remainder of the book. The overview is preceded by highlights from specific professional practice standards that either explicitly reference, or conceptually support the four cultural security ritual practices. The individual standards come from three different professional associations' standards of professional practice documents. Chapter 3 examines *Standards and Indicators for Cultural Competence in Social Work Practice* from the National Association of Social Workers (NASW); the *National Board of Professional Teaching Standards Five Core Propositions* from NBPTS; and the *American Medical Association Strategic Plan to Embed Racial and Social Justice and Advance Health Equity* from the AMA. These professional practice documents address the target professional audiences of this book.

This chapter begins with a critical family history vignette exploring legacies of identity loss and incomplete efforts to seek cultural security through the thread of history. An important takeaway from this chapter should be that professional associations and governmental agencies are both complicit in and also working against cultural deprivation practices in their domains of endeavor. Or, while there has been a history of cultural deprivation practices within many professional associations, many have evolved to incorporate cultural security practices as important standards, and in some cases rules and regulations to live up to. Lastly, there are also ethnic-specific professional associations, such as the Black Nurses Association and National Association of Black School Educators, whose members enact their professional responsibilities as a platform for cultural security.

DOI: 10.4324/9781003177500-5

Critical Family History: My Grandfather's Photographs

I found a picture of Mount Vernon in a plastic grocery-store bag full of pictures that my grandfather photographed. Ralph Turner, my mother's father, memorialized everything with short, handwritten notes with impeccable penmanship. He wrote on the back of photographs, naming the location, event, or activity depicted. He recorded the event he was attending on the back of ticket stubs to the theater or sporting events. The ticket stubs were stored in an old shoebox. And he often wrote his name, address, and the date on the blank page at the start of his many books. He was curating historical artifacts and libraries.

Ralph Turner photographed Mount Vernon in 1954. During the same year, he was reading *Black Power,* Richard Wright's reflections from his trip to the Gold Coast before it became the independent nation of Ghana in 1960. My grandfather had several of Richard Wright's books on his shelf. He was reading Wright's memoir *Black Boy* two years before he read *Black Power* and photographed Mount Vernon. Ralph Turner signed his copy of Wright's 1945 narrative with illustrations by Ashley Bryant in similar fashion: recording the date as 1952 and including the additional note: "2nd Copy".

Also, he was attending plays at the Karamu Theater (Figure 3.1) in Cleveland during the 1950s, and perhaps in the decades prior. The Karamu

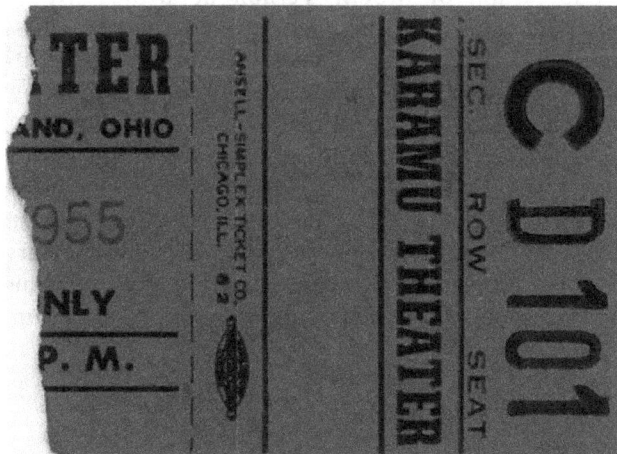

Figure 3.1 Ralph Turner's ticket stub to a play at the Karamu Theater. Karamu means place of joyful gathering in Swahili. It was established by social workers as an interracial arts colony connected to the settlement house movement. In the 1970s, with the rise of Black power, the theater took on an all-Black focus.

Theater was not only a place that staged plays with Black and White actors, but it also began promoting itself to Black and White audiences alike in the 1920s. The Karamu Theater eventually became known as the oldest African American producing theater in the United States, incubating talent that flourished in the Harlem Renaissance.

The Karamu Theater began as Karamu House, a settlement house established in 1917, during the settlement house movement in Cleveland, Ohio. Settlement houses were started by social workers to meet the needs of ethnic communities in specific regions of the city. "Karamu," which means "a place of joyful meeting" in Kiswahili—an East African language spoken mostly in Kenya, Tanzania, and Mozambique—was established by two White social workers from Oberlin University to bring people of different races, ethnicities, religions, and social classes together.

Ralph Turner's artifacts enabled me to learn deeper things than the rich history of the settlement house movement. I hadn't put it together initially—my grandfather's grandfather—born enslaved in 1835, was named George Washington Turner. I didn't even know that was his name or when he was born until a few years ago. I recall my grandfather showing me a picture of a family and telling me something about the people pictured, but exactly what I don't recall. I was barely ten years old. Even after I learned that my second great-grandfather's name George Washington, I never made the connection. On the back of my grandfather's photograph of Mount Vernon he wrote "Mount Vernon. Ancestral home of General George Washington. First President and employer as a slave holder of my great great-grandmother, a native of Africa." I wondered how he would know this precise information in 1954 before all of the networked databases and AI tools for finding genealogical documents—let alone before home DNA kits.

The picture reminded me of an excerpt of archival footage included in the Public Broadcasting Station's series *American Experience* documentary on Malcolm X (1994). The footage shows a panelist asking Malcolm X his name, and Malcolm X responding by describing an example of cultural deprivation:

PANELIST: *What is your real name?*
MALCOLM X: *Malcolm. Malcolm X.*
PANELIST: *Is that your legal name?*
MALCOLM X: *As far as I'm concerned, it's my legal name.*
PANELIST: *Well, would you mind telling me what your father's last name was?*

MALCOLM X: *My father didn't know his last name. My father got his last name from his grandfather and his grandfather got it from his grandfather who got it from the slave master. The real names of our people were destroyed...*

PANELIST: *Well, was there any*

MALCOLM X: *during slavery.*

PANELIST: *Was there any line, any point in the genealogy of your family when you did have to use a last name and if so, what was it?*

MALCOLM X: *The last name of my forefathers*

PANELIST: *Yes?*

MALCOLM X: *was taken from them when they were brought to America and made slaves, and then the name of the slave master was given, which we refuse, we reject that name today and refuse to*

PANELIST: *You mean, you won't even tell me what your father's supposed last name was or gifted last name was?*

MALCOLM X: *I never acknowledge it whatsoever.*

I wonder about my grandfather's inner dialogue around this understanding. I don't have any other documentation to corroborate his writing. In fact, my cousins—Ralph Turner's brother Ed's children and grandchildren—grew up believing our family name "Turner" meant we were related to Nat Turner's lineage. And they have found documents showing that Nat Turner's son once lived in Zanesville—the town where Ralph and Ed, and their brothers and sisters, father, and aunt were born (Figure 3.2).

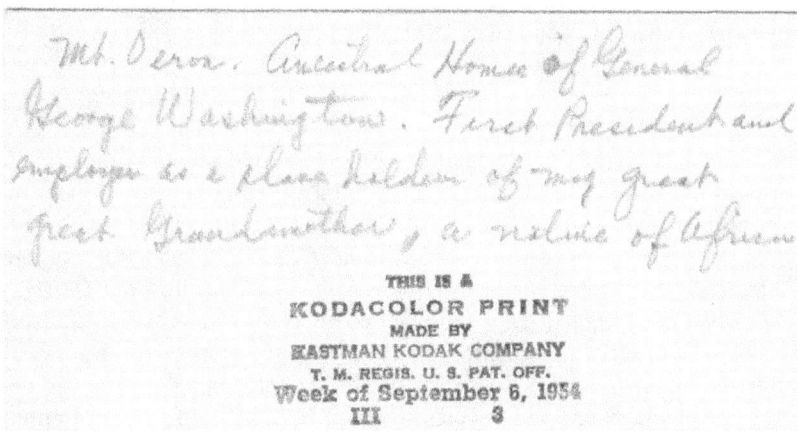

THIS IS A
KODACOLOR PRINT
MADE BY
EASTMAN KODAK COMPANY
T. M. REGIS. U. S. PAT. OFF.
Week of September 6, 1954
III   3

Figure 3.2 Ralph Turner's note at Mt. Vernon.

I did not grow up knowing about George Washington Turner. I only recall his photograph. And I recall my grandfather pointing to the picture and telling me about him. But I don't remember what he said. I reached out to the library at Mount Vernon. I was transferred to several people. They listened and commented with intrigue and amazement. The librarian I needed to reach was not at her desk the day I called. Her voicemail provided an email address, so I sent an inquiry with attachments of the scanned photograph and handwritten note from 1955, but I haven't heard anything back yet.

Professional Practice Standards Promote Cultural Security

NASW Standards and Indicators for Cultural Competence in Social Work Practice

The introduction of this book began with several anthropological and philosophical definitions of culture. But culture is defined in different ways. Although it may seem obvious to assert: culture is not limited to its relationship to race and ethnicity. The NASW's *Standards and Indicators for Cultural Competence in Social Work Practice* includes in their definition of culture ways in which people with disabilities or people from various religious backgrounds or people who are gay, lesbian, or transgender experience the world around them. For NASW, culture includes, but is not limited to, history, traditions, values, family systems, and artistic expressions of client groups served. Cultural production, transmission, and co-construction is influenced by race and ethnicity, and immigration and refugee status, tribal status, religion and spirituality, sexual orientation, gender identity and expression, social class, and abilities. NASW asserts that their members recognize that they work within intercultural contexts that impact service delivery.

NASW's Code of Ethics

The NASW is the largest association of professional social workers in the world. In addition to providing professional development to its membership, and providing standards for social worker professionalism, NASW serves as a policy advocate. The *Standards and Indicators for Cultural Competence* are rooted in the NASW's *Code of Ethics* and *the Universal Declaration of Human Rights.* The Code of Ethics was initially published in 1967. This early document includes two ethical principles speaking implicitly against cultural deprivation practices: "using information in a responsible manner" and "accepting responsibility to protect communities from unethical practices." The document has undergone numerous updates over the years.

The current version, published in 2021, begins with a robust preamble and a statement of core values: service, social justice, dignity and worth of the person, the importance of human relationships, integrity, and competence. An extended processing of the Code of Ethics' purpose follows the list of values. The NASW Code provides education, certification, and clarification for the public and the profession about the standards of behavior during the enactment of the service to humanity. The profession's primary value—service—is most often required during crisis or traumatic experiences. Trauma affects the neurobiology of the client and the professional working with them. Everyone needs to know and expect that the professional social worker will be able to regulate their experiences rather than haphazardly harm the client during service delivery. Harm breaks down the NASW service imperative and runs counter to this primary mission. The Code enculturates this understanding among all stakeholder groups. Further, it is a tool for NASW to investigate the social work profession if public complaints are made.

The seeming gravity of the Code's purpose is balanced by an expectation that the social worker will always seek to grow in knowledge and experiences that will enable them catharsis, reflection, mindfulness, rest etc. to work within the Code of Ethics while serving people in need. This necessary attention to the psychic and social health of the social worker was only added to the Code in the 2021 edition. It is unethical to neglect self-care because repeated exposure to trauma can have a long-term effect on the social workers' neurobiology, negatively impacting their ability to serve others.

The Code then orients the profession to thinking about ethical principles and ethical practices. Ethical principles expound upon and expand thinking about the six values stated above. The second principle, "social workers challenge social injustice," encompasses the most explicit directives to the social worker for interrupting instances of APA's definition one and two of cultural deprivation: By "striving to ensure access to needed information, services, and resources, equality of opportunity; and meaningful participation in decision making for all people" and by seeking to "promote sensitivity to and knowledge about oppression and cultural and ethnic diversity" (NASW, 2021). Sensitivity to cultural and ethnic diversity can contribute to cultural security. The third principle, "dignity and worth of the person," highlights a social worker's dilemma also discussed in the purpose section: managing cultural conflict, disfluencies, or disconnect among individuals or groups and dominant society. Cultural conflict is not the sole focus of the principle. But the principle discusses its inevitability or at least likelihood.

Ethical practices or standards guide the social worker's behavior toward clients, colleagues, workplace, profession, and society. Cultural deprivation is addressed in multiple places, especially regarding ethical practices toward clients.

The Universal Declaration of Human Rights

NASW also lists *the Universal Declaration of Human Rights* (UDHR) as a foundational document for the *Standards and Indicators of Cultural Competence in Social Work.* The UDHR is a post-World War II product. It was written between 1946 and 1948 by a nine-member committee made up of United Nations General Assembly members from China, Lebanon, The United Soviet Socialist Republic, Chile, France, United Kingdom of Great Britain and Northern Ireland, the United States, Australia, and Canada. The Committee was chaired by Eleanor Roosevelt from the United States. The UDHR was ratified on December 10, 1948, in Paris.

The committee drafted the document as an explicit effort to create a framework that would help prevent future genocide and culturicide like that preceding World War II enacted by the Nazi party. The framers believed that, if all governments in the world pledged to uphold a basic set of principles about humanity, they would be less likely to commit atrocities against individuals and groups, especially within their borders. Eleanor Roosevelt, representing the United States on the United Nations General Assembly, led the gathering to vote overwhelmingly to approve the UDHR: 48 nations voted in favor, and no nations voted against, while 8 nations abstained from voting.

The UDHR lists 30 articles describing rights all humans everywhere possess, regardless of race, ethnicity, gender, nationality, or any other identity factor. The first set of articles recognizes the condition of being human and the inherent affordances of life, liberty, and freedom from degradation and enslavement which all of humanity is deserving of. The next set of articles reasserts the rights in relationship with law enforcement and by extension the state. For example, Article 6: "Everyone has the right to recognition everywhere as a person before the law." Article 7: "All are equal before the law and are entitled without any discrimination to equal protection of the law." And article 9: "No one shall be subject to arbitrary arrest, detention, or exile." The remainder of the UDHR articles includes a range of rights to engage in cultural transmission and co-construction practices in family, marriage, schooling, personal expression, choice of employment, assembly, etc. Article 27 reaffirms these rights to cultural participation.

1 Everyone has the right freely to participate in the cultural life of the community, to enjoy the arts and to share in scientific advancement and its benefits.

2 Everyone has the right to the protection of the moral and material interests resulting from any scientific, literary, or artistic production of which he is the author.

Article 27 proclaims the first two forms of cultural deprivation described by the American Psychological Association a violation of human rights.

The UDHR is addressed to professional actors acting on behalf of a state; informing state actors of humanity's basic rights; and charging the state with the responsibility to not only *not* violate those rights but also to protect humanity in the first place by setting up fair and equitable systems for cultural transmission and co-construction practices within and across borders; and to assist specific communities in seeking redress when their human rights are violated.

As noted earlier, although the UDHR was ratified in 1948, not all member nations voted in favor. Forty-eight General Assembly members voted in favor, and none voted against, but eight members abstained from voting altogether. Eleanor Roosevelt speculated that abstentions from the Soviet Union concerned their desire to prohibit movement beyond their borders and into other countries, which runs counter to articles 13 and 14. And she believed Saudi Arabia abstained due to its disagreement with the right to change religion, provided for in article 18. She also thought that South Africa would not sign due to its commitment to apartheid (Glass, 2015), which violates the entire rights in the document.

Two enduring critiques arose concerning the Declaration during this time. The first critique focused on the Western colonial nature of the declaration. During a 75th-year anniversary of the UDHR hosted by the Center for Strategic & International Studies, the United Nations High Commissioner of Human Rights admonished the practice of most often naming the American Revolution and the French Revolution as the strongest influencers of what we know about the human rights movement today. The high commissioner then called attention to the Haitian Revolution, where the enslaved revolted against slavery and colonization as a more noteworthy example of human rights history predating the UDHR (2023). The high commissioner's remarks were followed by Marty Flacks, noting that at the time of the UN General Assembly's ratification of the UDHR, some 60 countries were not present to vote on its ratification.

While this is a contemporary comment, in 1947, one year prior to the UDHR's ratification, The American Anthropological Association published a statement written by famed anthropologist Melville Herskovits wherein he asserts that universal human rights encoded Euro-American notions of the individual and private property; and would ultimately serve imperialist objectives. Hershkovitz wrote his statement in response to a UNESCO survey about universal human rights (2020).

Melville Herskovits established the Program of African Studies at Northwestern University and became its first director. He was a central figure in the organization of the first International Congress of Africanists held in Ghana in 1962. Herskovits authored the impactful *The Myth of the Negro Past* (1990). Of all his research, this one book is credited by many with providing Black Americans that historical thread of cultural security because it demonstrated continuities in cultural practices in Africa and the diaspora, especially the United States (Smith & Brown, 2018). Black power theorists and activists especially found value in this text.

In contrast, Herskovits is also charged with blocking notable Black American scholars, such as W.E.B. DuBois, from receiving the funding needed for their research to establish this thread of cultural security for themselves (Smith & Brown, 2018). Further, he is charged with blocking Black American scholars' access to archives from Africa. Arguably, insights derived from Black scholars would have nuanced Herskovits' assertions at the very least; and perhaps advance our understanding of cultural continuities among the African diaspora all the more. Herskovits practiced *interest convergence* scholarship: insights derived, and cultural knowledge constructed benefiting Black Americans' cultural security broadly speaking could only come from him. In this way, Herskovits receives professional and financial accolades and advancements for this work, and carefully guards their distribution.

Herskovits' somehow balanced complexities and contradictions as an African studies knowledge-producing anthropologist and anti-colonial respondent and commentator on UNESCO's human rights survey. And the American Anthropological Association balanced their acknowledgment of Herskovits' role in shaping their discipline with multiple iterations of a support statement in favor of universal human rights written overtime; most recently during the global demonstrations for Black lives in 2020.

However, digitized meeting records of the UDHR's drafting history reveal that some nations agreed with Herskovits' perspective, regardless of the complexity of his positioning. The meeting record for the 182nd Plenary Meeting held on December 10, 1948—the day of the signing—Sir Mohammed Zafrullah Kuan of the Pakistan delegation explained with great humility that Article 19 can be used for colonial pursuit. According to the record, Pakistan at that time expressed full support for the subject of this article: recognizing everyone's right to choose their religion. In 1948, Sir Mohammed Zafrullah Kuam quoted passages of the Koran affirming this human right. According to the meeting record:

He was glad to pay tribute to the work carried out by Christian missionaries in the East, especially in the fields of education, hygiene and medicine; nevertheless, it was undeniable that their activity had sometimes assumed a political character which had given rise to justifiable objections. In certain cases, the means employed to bring about conversion had made that conversion a worse remedy than the ill it set out to cure.

These comments imply an understanding of the way in which governments sometimes initiate or participate in cultural deprivation practices in concert with religious institutions in order to influence or colonize other governments or their citizens. While Pakistan may be viewed differently in more contemporary United Nations Human Rights discussions, the December 10, 1948, record documents that the Pakistan delegation understood the encoding of the freedom to choose one's own religion as advance establishment of legal conditions for settler colonial practices.

There are many nations with human rights histories throughout the world whose traditions might have influenced this early drafting of the UDHR. While it may not have been conceivable to turn to one's defeated opponent to weigh in on a document of this sort, The Soka Gakkai International, which began in Japan, is an interesting case in point.

According to the UN document *Admission of Japan to Membership the United Nations: Resolution/Adopted by the General Assembly* Japan first joined the United Nations in 1956. Japan's Diplomatic Bluebook 2017—the annual report on Japan's foreign policy and activities published by the Ministry of Foreign Affairs—celebrates the 60-year anniversary of ratifying the UDHR in 1994. The government of Japan was clearly not able to fully participate in the drafting of the UDHR at the close of World War II. However, regardless of the Japanese government's relationship with Germany and Italy's fascism during WWII; and adversarial relationship with the United States during the 1940s, there is a Japanese human rights tradition dating back to the 1300s. This tradition begins with a twelfth-century Buddhist monk enduring repeated exile for preaching absolute pacifism, sanctity of human life and respect for human dignity (Seager, 2006, p. 98); and for challenging state-sponsored Buddhist schools for corruption.

In similar fashion as their founder's exile centuries earlier, Josei Toda and his mentor, Tsunesoboro Makiguchi, who died while incarcerated, were arrested during the war for opposing their government's expanding militarism. Toda and Makiguchi had been teachers and were leaders of the lay Buddhist organization Society for the Creation of Value, or Soka Gakai. They argued for an education emphasizing world peace, human dignity, freedom of expression, and religion. Makiguchi and Toda were imprisoned by the Japanese government as "thought criminals" for refusing to renounce their anti-war stance. After the war, Josei Toda was released from prison in Japan. Josei Toda re-established the organization among the survivors of the atomic bombing of Hiroshima and Nagasaki. Toda worked with his student, Daisaku Ikeda, person to person to re-expand Soka Gakai throughout Japan.

When Daisaku Ikeda became Toda's successor, he further established the organization internationally. For example, Daisaku Ikeda has written a yearly peace proposal to the United Nations since 1983. He has also published a series of dialogues with world leaders on human rights, including with Austregésilo de Athayde, a member of the United Nations Commission for the Universal Declaration of Human Rights. It is worth imagining what this newly re-organizing non-governmental group might have contributed to the UDHR. It is also worth imagining other human rights traditions around the world in 1948 that were not represented in the drafting. Although they did not participate in the drafting of the UDHR, later, culturally specific iterations of the declaration have been crafted by the Office of Islamic Cooperation (1990), African Charter on Human and People's Rights (1981), and the United Nations Declaration of the Rights of Indigenous Peoples (2007).

The second critique addressed the issue of nations signing on to the declaration, who have a history and ongoing practice of human rights abuses within their borders. The USSR identified human rights violations in the United States, as a case in point. Human rights abusers leading each other into the drafting and ratifying of a document about human rights does present a contradiction. The United Nations General Assembly ratified the UDHR on December 10, 1948, at the Paris meeting (UN, 1948). On December 9, 1948, at the same meeting the UN General Assembly adopted *Article II Convention on the Prevention and Punishment of the Crime of Genocide*. Three years later, in 1951 prominent African Americans attending the UN's meeting in Paris presented documents detailing genocidal crimes against Black Americans at the hands of the U.S. government (Patterson, 2017). The document charged the United States with the crime of genocide against Black Americans.

How does the world community reconcile these and similar contradictions at the time of the ratification, such as House Concurrent Resolution 108's effort to terminate tribal communities and the U.S. government's responsibilities to them (HCR 108), or Australia's 1961 Policy of Assimilation against Aboriginal and Torres Strait Islander communities, or labor conditions in French colonial Senegal leading to the strikes of 1946 and 1947?

Despite these abstentions, political challenges, and omissions, considerable evidence documents Eleanor Roosevelt's efforts to disrupt cultural deprivation at every opportunity—with the UDHR and beyond. Eleanor Roosevelt's civic engagement work began decades earlier with the New York Settlement House movement. Roosevelt's involvement with this early, service-oriented movement for economic and cultural access, supporting universal cultural rights ideologies and international policy aligns with her work on the UDHR; her hiring Mary McClead Bethune to work as a journalist in the White House; and by visiting Japanese prison camps. Eleanor Roosevelt seemed to be working to embody the standard of UDHR. She demonstrated that rather than a law, the declaration is something that we all strive toward and hold each other accountable to.

The UDHR has a complex history. It is not a perfect document in that it is not universal, and it is contradictory and even hypocritical, but it is also a catalytic document that produces not only many other formal declarations of human rights from ethnic, regional, and religious organizations. It also became the basis of many different human rights laws, and the foundation for such organizations as the NASW.

We might ask how significantly the UN's *International Covenant on Economic, Social and Cultural Rights* impacted future iterations of the cultural competence. The covenant is a more explicit buffer against cultural deprivation. NASW established the first iteration of the Code of Ethics during the time of the covenant's drafting. Interestingly, both documents were published a short time before the Black Panther Party or Self Defense published their Ten Point Platform and Program, which addressed cultural security needs directly.

Cultural Competence Standards 1–5

While all the standards intersect with the rapport-building practices supportive of cultural security, Standards 1–5 are most noteworthy.

Standards	Definition	Indicator	Cultural Security
Standard 1: Ethics and Values	Social workers shall function in accordance with the values, ethics, and standards of the NASW (2021) *Code of Ethics*. Cultural competence requires self-awareness, cultural humility, and the commitment to understanding and embracing culture as central to effective practice.	Indicator #5 ability to recognize the convergence and disparity between the values and practices of the dominant society and the values and practices of the historically oppressed, underrepresented, and underserved populations.	Standard 1, indicator 5 identifies the critical skill of recognizing how communities navigate cultural deprivation conditions.

(Continued)

Standards	Definition	Indicator	Cultural Security
Standard 2: Self-Awareness	Social workers shall demonstrate an appreciation of their own cultural identities and those of others.	Indicator #5 demonstrate comfort with self- and other-awareness about different cultural customs and views of the world.	Standard 2, indicator 5 describes an attitude of respect and contentment with one's own cultural value such that there is no desire to dominate, possess, or encumber another's cultural expression.
Standard 3: Cross-Cultural Knowledge	Social workers shall possess and continue to develop specialized knowledge and understanding that is inclusive of, but not limited to, the history, traditions, values, family systems, and artistic expressions such as race and ethnicity; immigration and refugee status; tribal groups; religion and spirituality; sexual orientation; gender identity or expression; social class; and mental or physical abilities of various cultural groups.	expand their cultural knowledge, expertise, and humility by studying. • The help-seeking behaviors and pathways of diverse client groups • the historical context of margin-alized communi-ties; AND possess specific knowledge about traditional and nontraditional providers and client groups that they serve, including • understanding historicalexperien-ces, immigration, resettlement pat-terns, individual and group oppression, adjustment styles, socioeconomic backgrounds, and life processes • learning styles, cognitive skills,	Standard 3 describes the need for ongoing learning and critical, reflection about the structures, practices, reinforcement of cultural deprivation that blocking access to dominant culture and one's own culture. Standard 3 also describes the need for developing practices and structures concerning ancestry, indigeneity, mindfulness, and relationship-building.

(Continued)

Standards	Definition	Indicator	Cultural Security
		worldviews, and specific cultural concerns and practices	
Standard 4: Cross-Cultural Skills	Social workers will use a broad range of skills (micro, mezzo, and macro) and techniques that demonstrate an understanding of and respect for the importance of culture in practice, policy, and research.	Indicator #5 select and develop appropriate methods, skills, and techniques that are attuned to their clients' cultural, bicultural, multicultural, or marginal experiences in their environments Indicator #10 effectively engage clients' natural support systems in resolving problems; for example, work with folk healers, indigenous remedies, religious leaders, friends, family, and other community residents and organizations	Standard 4 also describes the need for developing practices and structures concerning ancestry, indigeneity, mindfulness, and relationship-building.
Standard 5: Service Delivery	Social workers shall be knowledgeable about and skillful in the use of services, resources, and institutions and be available to serve multicultural communities. They shall be able to make culturally appropriate	identify the formal and informal resources in the community, describe their strengths and weaknesses, and facilitate referrals as indicated, tailored to the culturally relevant needs of clients and client groups	Standard 3 also describes the need for developing practices and structures concerning ancestry, indigeneity, mindfulness, and relationship-building. This standard is especially

(Continued)

Standards	Definition	Indicator	Cultural Security
	referrals within both formal and informal networks and shall be cognizant of, and work to address, service gaps affecting specific cultural groups.	advocate for and promote efforts to create culturally competent services and programs.	concerned with relationship-building.

National Board of Professional Teaching Standards Five Core Propositions

There are many different local, state, national, and discipline-based standards for pre-k-12 teaching and learning endeavors. For example, there are standards for what students should know and be able to do in sixth-grade art, twelfth-grade English, seventh-grade math, etc. And there are standards for what teachers should know and be able to do to facilitate student learning. In 1987, The National Board of Professional Teaching Standards (NBPTS) was established to identify these professional perimeters for highly accomplished teachers. NBPTS has developed discipline-based standards for many school subjects. In addition to identifying what accomplished teachers should know and know how to do, NBPTS hosts a platform and a process for how teachers can demonstrate and document their professional practices, ultimately leading toward National Board Certification. Educators who have the distinction of being NBPTS certified still need to adhere to their state or local government certification agencies, but they are recognized by their peers and colleagues as having gone through a rigorous, performance-based series of examinations demonstrating and reflecting on expert teaching.

The National Board's Five Core Propositions, developed and revised by practicing educators based on research and practitioner expertise, describe what accomplished teachers should know and be able to do to have a positive impact on student learning. Highly accomplished teaching, as defined in these core propositions, is antithetical to cultural deprivation practices. Educators' actions preventing their students from accessing the dominant culture, actions that disrupt their students' access to their own culture, or actions creating conditions blocking all cultural stimulation from their students are all incompatible with teaching as described by these propositions. The last chapter exploring APA's three-part definition provided examples of all three cultural deprivation categories in and around classrooms and schools. Thus, the propositions are not simply about pedagogy. They are also about the ethics of pedagogy: they differentiate teaching and learning from interactions between teachers and students that cause harm under the guise of instruction.

This importance given to the propositions is conveyed in part when the document's authors compare them to the Hippocratic Oath of medicine. Hippocrates was a Greek philosopher who is often referred to as the father of modern, rational, or scientific medicine, especially in Western, Greco-Roman societies. The Hippocratic Oath is a moral code for physicians. It is also a description of the Greek world's shift from "superstition" toward science in medical practice. The oath is sometimes condensed into the phrase "I shall do no harm."

The oath was written either by Hippocrates or his students sometime around the year 400 BCE. The oath has been rewritten several times over the centuries since its discovery in Germany during the 1500s. Most current versions, especially in the United States are based on the rewritten version published by Louis Lasagna, dean of Tufts University School of Medicine in 1964. The oath is enduring; thus, NBPTS's comparison with their Five Core Propositions reframes the stature of teachers and the nature of teaching. The teaching profession is placed on the level of the medical profession and the ethical commitment to leave the student's psyche unwounded is as great as that of the physician to the patient's body.

Proposition 1 requires a commitment from teachers to students and to their learning, enacted by careful and consistent efforts to get to know them. This means teachers should be listening to and observing students in a variety of classroom and school contexts. This first proposition also directs teachers to study about students' background and history and to integrate students' languages into classroom practices into instruction. The proposition requires teachers to adjust to their students as they learn about them from their observations and interactions. Proposition 1 puts the student, not the content, the teacher, or the institution at the center of teaching and learning in school. Proposition 1 addresses the first and second definitions of cultural deprivation.

Proposition 1 is antithetical to practices identified in Chapter 1, such as the recruitment, kidnapping, and imprisonment practices related to indigenous boarding schools. It is against forced monolingualism, segregation, and tracking. Coercive practices forcing students to acquiesce or adjust to something that goes against their sense of self, or against their community or dominant cultural experiences are harmful to students. The proposition does not consider pedagogies of control and compliance, and similar efforts to engage and transmit content to students accomplished teaching.

Similarly, proposition 1—observing, getting to know, and adjusting to students—takes priority over teachers' academic subject knowledge. In this way, NBPTS calls out long-standing curriculum and instruction practices that prevented BIPOC students from accessing their own experiences of cultural transmission and construction. The importance of beginning where students are, and with who they are, is echoed to varying degrees in many other educational standards (e.g., NCTE/IRA Standards for the English Language Arts and LFJ Social Justice Standards). This stance is most pronounced in contemporary K-12 ethnic studies education.

Proposition 1 also does not suggest that teachers adjust to their classroom's cultural variation randomly, without focus or intent. While the NASW Standards, previously explored are concerned with service delivery for their client's self-sufficient living with dignity; NBPTS's proposition's focus is part of an effort to identify and recognize teachers building their students' academic content: numeracy, literacy, etc. in K-12 classrooms. For NASW, knowing the client enables the social worker to make the right pivot toward the most meaningful services. For NBPTS, knowing the student helps the teacher to make the appropriate bridges connecting, and then integrating, their background knowledge with new learning.

Propositions 2 and 3 move from describing the centrality of knowledge about students to teaching, toward an application of that knowledge in service of student learning. These propositions identify at least three ways of applying knowledge of students to teaching and learning that mute the impact of historic and life-experience levels of cultural deprivation: (1) bridging content knowledge between what students know and school content, (2) creating multiple pathways into the content, and (3) creating or allowing multiple pathways of demonstrating knowledge construction from class content. NBPTS recognizes accomplished teachers enacting these practices wherever they occur, and they advocate for their development among minoritized and marginalized schools where BIPOC students face historic and ongoing personal cultural deprivation.

Propositions 4 and 5 describe how accomplished teachers think beyond the individual students and their discipline to greater contexts, patterns, and macro-level implications. Proposition 4 highlights the teachers' attention to research and feedback. Proposition 5 begins with identifying how accomplished teachers engage with professional learning associations and other professionals. The proposition then describes productive engagement with family, especially when there is disconnect between teacher and family ideology. The document notes that accomplished teachers will seek to learn more about the family and the family culture in seeking creative ways to prioritize student learning. Lastly, examples of community engagement for student learning are offered: from art and architecture, civic engagement, and local ecology. As much as possible, accomplished teachers work with student culture rather than against it. Culture is transmitted and co-constructed in communities and families. NBPTS recognizes that accomplished teachers work directly with culture producers, transmitters, and ambassadors.

American Medical Association Strategic Plan to Embed Racial and Social Justice and Advance Health Equity

During an interview with Todd Unger, MD, MPH, chief experience officer for the American Medical Association, Aletha Maybank, MD, MPH (2021), newly appointed chief health equity officer of the American Medical Association, shared that the advent of the COVID-19 pandemic and the murder of George Floyd presented an opportunity for the AMA to talk about racism more explicitly than ever before. Dr. Maybank also described an earlier, deliberative process formally undertaken by the AMA Board of Trustees through Resolution 601-A-17, also known as the Plan for Continued Progress Toward Health Equity. The resolution asked "that the American Medical Association reinstate the Commission to Eliminate Health Care Disparities, including goals and objectives that are Specific, Measurable, Agreed Upon, Realistic and Time Related (SMART) metrics." The AMA Board of Trustees requested that the resolution be referred for a report back with a more comprehensive and sustainable plan for continued progress toward health equity.

In June 2018, The American Medical Association Board of Trustees recommended the following be taken up in lieu of the earlier resolution.

1 That Health Equity, defined as optimal health for all, is a goal toward which our AMA will work by advocating for health care access, promoting equity in care, increasing health workforce diversity, influencing determinants of health, and voicing and modeling commitment to health equity. (New HOD Policy)
2 That our AMA develop an organizational unit, e.g., a center or its equivalent, to facilitate, coordinate, initiate, and track AMA health equity activities. (Directive to Take Action)
3 That the Board provide an annual report to the House of Delegates regarding AMA's health equity activities and achievements. (Directive to Take Action)

Following the ratification of this recommendation, the AMA Center for Health Equity was established and staffed, and the AMA Strategic Plan to Embed Racial Justice and Establish Health Equity was written.

The strategic plan has five sections with many features relevant to understanding the professional underpinnings facilitating the different types of cultural deprivation that co-occur with other types of racialized trauma and oppression historically and that support or allude to the kinds of practices described in the upcoming chapters that can help assuage some of the effects of cultural deprivation. The introduction sections of the strategic plan include a vision for health equity and justice, a land and labor acknowledgment, a commitment to truth, and an ancestral veneration statement. These opening sentiments represent powerful medical, educational, and therapeutic practices that I am trying to elaborate and amplify in this book. They provide an opportunity for reorientation, a paradigm shift for some, a paradigm affirmation for others. The introductory section is the first place that the Five Strategic Focuses are listed. They are elaborated later in Section 2: Organizational Change Work to Move Us Forward.

Section 1: Background and History focuses on health equity foundations by listing important events in AMA's history of work toward health equity and defining important terms, such as *race, racism, ethnicity,* and *intersectionality*. Concepts related to health equity, such as the social and structural drivers of health, structural violence, and "downstream" and "upstream" are explored in more depth than the definitions. This section is an important educational tool, conversational facilitator, and reference point.

Section 2 introduces the Five Strategic Approaches in depth. Whereas the introduction and Section 1 were educational and orienting, many of the subpoints under each of the approaches provide organizational direction for disrupting cultural deprivation.

The AMA's strategic plan to embed racial justice and advance health equity

Three-year roadmap following five strategic approaches

5   Foster pathways for truth, racial healing, reconciliation, and transformation for AMA's past

- Amplify and integrate often "invisible-ized" narratives of historically marginalized physicians and patients in all that AMA does
- Quantify the effects of AMA policy and process decisions that excluded, discriminated, and harmed
- Repair and cultivate a healing journey for those harms

For example, Strategic Approach 2, line 1, reads "Develop structures and processes to consistently center the experiences and ideas of historically marginalized (women, LGBTQ+, people with disabilities, International Medical Graduates) and minoritized (Black, Indigenous, Latinx, Asian, and other people of color) physicians" and Strategic Focus 4, line 3, "Center, integrate and amplify historically marginalized and Black, Indigenous, Latinx and people of color who are healthcare investors and innovators" and Strategic Focus 1, line 4, "Integrate trauma—informed lens and approaches when developing and implementing policies and practices." These examples address the APA's second definition of cultural deprivation.

All three lines under Strategic Approach 5 directly address the first two APA definitions of cultural deprivation. The first refers to definition 2, where marginalized communities do not have access to their own culture: the "invizibilized narratives." The second line corresponds with one where marginalized communities are blocked from accessing elements of the dominant culture (i.e., medical care culture)—the impacts of exclusion that can be quantified. The final line speaks to a need for institutionalizing supportive practices that facilitate healing.

Section 3 is focused on accountability and concrete deliverables. This section demonstrates the action-orientation, rather than an advisory nature of the plan. The first half of Section 3 lists the AMA's Key Accomplishments from 2019 to March 2021 guided by the Five Strategic Approaches. For example, in order to enact Strategic Approach 5, "amplify invizibilized narratives," in 2021, the AMA produced and launched a 26-part YouTube series entitled "Prioritizing Health Equity." The series explores the experiences of marginalized and minoritized physicians, public health leaders, and medical students during the COVID-19 pandemic. Further, Aletha Maybank, MD, mentioned earlier, joined Oprah Winfrey for an interview during a special presentation of "Oprah Talks COVID-19—The Deadly Impact on Black America." The platforms—a popular social media video sharing site, and a Black woman culture icon—a culture producer, culture curator, and culture constructor.

In addition to amplifying invizibilized narratives, Section Three addresses "quantifying the effects of past AMA policy" through the Center for Health Equity Research Director, Fernando De Maio's publication *Unequal Cities: Structural Racism and the Death Gap in America's Largest Cities* via Johns Hopkins University Press.

The second half lists Proposed Key Actions from April 2021 to 2023, with additional examples of deliverables. The proposed actions include efforts to launch "Restorative Justice dialogues between AMA leadership and Black, Indigenous, Latinx and other physicians of color and their communities and families." These dialogues would likely follow the model set in the document by beginning with rituals of land and labor acknowledgment and ancestral veneration. Professionals can take these cues and begin such practices now.

Section 4 includes a range of appendices to deepen the context of their work, such as timelines and links to primary source documents of past transgressions and future inspirations for eliminating blocks to BIPOC healthcare access and BIPOC healthcare culture.

How Do the Standards of Practice Address Cultural Deprivation and Foster Cultural Security?

The professional practice standards highlighted in Chapter 2 provide direction for professions as a collective and professionals as individuals to offer redress for, and intervention against, the impacts of different categories or incidents of cultural deprivation. They also guide their professional associations toward implicit acknowledgment of widespread cultural deprivation practices in the professions. For example, NBPTS does not cite cases where school districts and systems enact cultural deprivation, as I have done in Chapter 1 when discussing school districts' prohibiting BIPOC families access to quality schools (Heilman, 1994). Instead, they recognized a need to build consensus and identify, codify, and certify exemplary teaching in a variety of contexts. This process not only affirms exemplary teaching and teachers; it distinguishes exemplary teaching from less cognitively demanding and emotionally engaging instruction, and by extension, gives us an indication of education that deprives a student from accessing dominant, personal, and multicultural experiences of varying and increasing complexity.

In contrast, AMA's plan lists specific instances where their organization enacted all three forms of cultural deprivation at different times or at the same time. The plan also lists examples where their members were complicit in some other entity's specific act of cultural deprivation. Appendix 9, entitled "AMA's historical harms—look back (1847–1997) additional insights," provides links from the digital version of these descriptions to PDFs of archived documents providing evidence of these actions. The descriptions and links are categorized by specific marginalized and minoritized groups for further specificity. Of course, the list is not exhaustive. But it is explicit, and it is documented.

It is noteworthy that this history of cultural deprivation practices among the professional associations has caused many BIPOC professional organizations to come into being. The Association for the Study of Negro Life and Culture, established by Carter G. Woodson in 1915, is one of the oldest examples of an African American scholarly organization. Dr. Wade Nobles recounts a story describing the establishment of the Association of

Black Psychologists 53 years later in 1968, during the same time that the Third World Liberation Front strikes at San Francisco State University were advocating for Third World Studies departments. Nobles recounts how he and his colleagues experienced cultural deprivation while attending an American Psychology Association conference. The National Black Social Worker's Association narrates a similar origin story on their website. Two years later, the National Association of Black School Superintendents was established. And two years later, NABSS expanded its membership to all Black school personnel and became the National Association of Black School Educators. These organizations were established to build networks of support, cultural healing, and professional growth. In some cases, they were establishing new disciplines. Dr. Nobels goes on to describe the harm that Western psychology can cause Black people. The disciplinary knowledge produced in these organizations enable advocacy through resolutions, expert witness, and further research.

Appendix 10 identifies efforts to address some forms of cultural deprivation, but admittedly less robustly. The highlighted standards also demonstrate an official consensus among representatives in the professions—often some of the most accomplished—about the harm cultural deprivation practices cause individuals, families, communities, and society as whole. Further, they call the profession to account for their role in causing harm, and for the profession to commit to culturally affirming, and even anti-racist practices in some cases. Lastly, they serve as a contrast to region, state, and local governments; businesses; and institutions that are probably, tenaciously, combatively embracing cultural deprivation practices.

Declarations and Pledges

Sometimes organizations or institutions will make declarations of solidarity with a marginalized community facing some egregious offense. These assertions can be an important rhetorical speech act. The weight of the words can transform a mere utterance of personal or even scholarly opinion into a political endorsement, a release of funds, a redirection of labor, etc. Other times, the declarations are performative, with limited or no concrete assertions or follow through.

For example, during the summer of 2020, communities around the world demonstrated for justice after witnessing Minneapolis police murder George Floyd, compounded by footage or reports of many other cis gender and trans African Americans. The demonstrations were relentless, all-encompassing, and far reaching; they disrupted and transformed urban landscapes and infrastructure. News outlets reported that corporate response to the worldwide cry for racial social justice with pledges of anywhere from $50 billion in the *Washington Post*, $200 billion in *Forbes* magazine, to $340 billion by CNBC (Lindsey et al., 2023). Two years later, *The Washington Post* reported that of the 50 companies making pledges, 37 companies have contributed only $1.7 billion (Jan et al., 2021). Dr. Shaun Harper (2022) from the University of Southern California further reports in *Forbes* that much of the money pledged from companies, such as JPMorgan, Chase, and other financial institutions was announced as loans. Others, such as Bank of America, identified investments in Black communities, which Harper speculates could end up funding gentrification. Declarations need follow-through to be truly impactful.

In contrast to declarations of solidarity and financial pledges that often do not materialize, standards of practice documents are generally more enduring. Often, they are enduring, even if they are updated or responding to trends within the chronosystem (Bronfenbrenner), such as NASW's Code of Ethics, which has been updated multiple times. They are sometimes absolute, such as the Hippocratic Oath, the basis for professional medical practice, and a comparison point for other professions.

Professional Echoes and Progressive Legislation

Lastly, while four of the most relevant professional practice standards documents are reviewed in this chapter, we can list many others, such as the California Realtors Association's (CITE) efforts to acknowledge, eliminate, and repair harm from participation in racial covenants blocking Black people's access from purchasing homes. And many states are establishing legislation protecting communities' cultural knowledge production in formal spaces, such as Minnesota, Washington, and California.

After several years of explicit, malicious acts of cultural deprivation from 2016 to 2020, the federal government turned on itself to formally explore the impacts of institutional and systemic racism with executive orders written by the Biden administration targeting specific communities, such as ED14050: White House Initiative on Advancing Educational Equity, Excellence, and Economic Opportunity for Black Americans; ED14049: White House Initiative on Advancing Educational Equity, Excellence, and Economic Opportunity for Native Americans and Strengthening Tribal Colleges and Universities; ED14045: White House Initiative on Advancing Educational Equity, Excellence, and Economic Opportunity for Hispanics; ED14041: White House Initiative on Advancing Educational Equity, Excellence, and Economic Opportunity Through Historically Black Colleges and Universities; and several executive orders addressing marginalized and minoritized communities as a collective group.

These orders have multiple directives. An important component of each requires all government agencies to establish Equity Action Plans, and to staff those plans and to regularly examine potential barriers that marginalized and minoritized communities often face when trying to access an agency's policies, programs, and activities, including procurement, contracting, and grant opportunities. Thus, while there is a trend toward increasing dictatorships and fascism and predictable patterns of deprivation around the world, voices from the education, and allied health professions can take an official stand in supporting practices to promote cultural security.

Introduction to Rituals for Cultural Security

The following categories of rapport-building rituals to support the development of cultural security among marginalized and oppressed individuals and communities are supported by the standards for professional practices described above. I did not invent these rituals. And I don't own them. They are not copyrighted. They are appropriate for processional practice and have been practiced in different ways at different times for many years. But they are bigger than professional practice, alone.

Each one of the narratives at the front of the chapters explores my experiences describing how I engaged practices or processed ideas related to them personally and professionally to prevent cultural deprivation and promote cultural security for myself and others. I practice many forms of mindfulness meditation and have been doing so since middle school. I received ancestral dreams more than once. I have been thinking about indigeneity actively since childhood, and formally as an adolescent and as an adult. And I have been incorporating relationship development practices in professional, activist, and healing spaces.

Indigeneity

Indigeneity begins with questions such as Where am I? They are meant to help us recognize and honor indigeneity in others and ourselves. They are also meant to honor the history of indigenous practices and Indigenous displacement, and to increase our active care of the earth. Rituals that help us recognize indigeneity also help us establish solidarity and thereby help create a different paradigm for establishing cultural security.

Ancestry

Ancestry begins with questions such as Where do I come from? Ancestry is complex and rich, and there are many levels and ways of veneration.

Personal

Personal ancestors are our forefathers and foremothers; family members by blood, choice or circumstance who have died, even family members who are younger than we are.

Unknown

Because of cultural deprivation, we may not have a relationship with people who can teach us about our personal ancestors. And even when we do, we cannot know everyone going back into time. But we can establish frames for venerating unknown ancestors.

Communal

Communal ancestors are our cultural heroes, such as Gloria Anzuldua or bell hooks.

Historic

Historic ancestors are people from the distant past who made an impact on our lives and those of many others, such as W.E.B. Du Bois, Frederick Douglass, Harriet Tubman, etc.

Mitochondrial Eve

Mitochondrial Eve is the mother of all living human beings who lived from approximately 180,000 to 200,000 years ago. Or, we can say that she is the most recent ancestor of all living human beings.

Nature

Many aspects of nature have ancestral significance. For example, there is an evolutionary connection between humans and trees. For example, Dr. Bruce Alison (2005) explains that the hemoglobin in humans and chlorophyll in trees consist of the same molecular structure and iron is in the center of hemoglobin and magnesium is at the center of chlorophyll. And many have lived longer than humans.

Mindfulness

Mindfulness practices help us get in touch with ourselves and begin answering "Who am I?" I learned mindfulness meditation practices most significantly from the Himalayan Institute under the direction of Nina Johnson in Milwaukee, Wisconsin, and through her, Pandit Usharbudh Arya, D. Litt. At that time, there was still great fear about these practices from the general public. The Himalayan Institute was a pioneer in researching biofeedback, breathing practices, and diet and nutrition. The research in the fields of neurobiology has reaffirmed and replicated earlier claims about the value of mindfulness, and identified new, more sophisticated benefits previously unprovable.

Relationship

Relationship-building activities help us answer questions such as "Where do I belong?" My work with the National Urban Alliance helped me to understand the role of relationship-building in teaching and learning. I learned from educational psychologists whose lineage ran through Feuerstein to Piaget.

I have been taught rituals and therapeutic practices to help strengthen cultural security by scholar mentors and spiritual teachers. I have enacted them and experienced them. The following chapters are narratives and observations and reflections on experiences I have had with these rituals, mostly in formal institutional settings, schools, and treatment centers.

Summary

This chapter outlines three professional practice standards documents and analyzes their content through the lens of the APA definitions of cultural deprivation and for the affordances and opportunities they offer that are supportive of cultural security for marginalized and minoritized people in general; for BIPOC people, more specifically; and from Black studies orientation. The chapter first explored the foundational relationship of NASW's *Standards and Indicators for Cultural Competence in Social Work Practice* to NASW's Ethical Principles and the United Nations' *Universal Declaration of Human Rights*. Next, the chapter identified the human and community-centered teaching principles encoded in NBPTS *Five Core Propositions*. Finally, the chapter examines the *American Medical Association Strategic Plan to Embed Racial and Social Justice and Advance Health Equity* for its explicit use of two of the approaches discussed in the remainder of the book: ancestry and indigeneity. The chapter concludes by introducing approaches to cultural security. An important takeaway from this chapter should be that professional associations and governmental agencies are both complicit in and working against cultural deprivation practices in their domains of endeavor. Or, while there has been a history of cultural deprivation practices within many professional associations, many have evolved to incorporate cultural security practices as important standards, and in some cases rules and regulations to live up to. Lastly, there are also ethnic-specific professional associations, such as the Black Nurses Association and National Association of Black School Educators, whose members enact their professional responsibilities as a platform for cultural security.

Activities

1 Professional Association Membership
   One of the most important follow-up activities of this chapter is for students and professionals to join a progressive professional association, union, and related political voting block that will provide professional development and advocacy supporting BIPOC access to dominant cultural resources and their own cultural resources. Also, to join a related political voting block at all levels of engagement: at work, local, state, and national government. Sample organizations are referenced throughout this chapter, including in the "Suggestions for Further Study" section. When becoming a member, actively work on behalf of BIPOC cultural security.

2 Revisit the Roosevelts
   Many of the allied health professions' humanist dispositions that have been encoded in the professional practice and policy can be linked to Eleanor Roosevelt as a channel or conduit for critical human rights thinking and action. Considerable insight can be gained by reviewing the last two episodes of Ken Burns' documentary series.

   • Burns, K. (2014). S1 E6 The Common cause (1939–1944) The Roosevelts: An intimate history. Corporation for Public Broadcasting. Retrieved from https://www.pbs.org/kenburns/the-roosevelts/episode-6 on December 17, 2023.
   • Burns, K. (2014). S1 E7 The A strong and active faith (1944–1962) The Roosevelts: An intimate history. Corporation for Public Broadcasting. Retrieved from https://www.pbs.org/kenburns/the-roosevelts/episode-7/ on December 17, 2023.

3 CRT Forward
   The anti-critical race theory policies and legislation beginning around 2017 is an explicit act of cultural prohibition. The CRT Forward report and panel presentation help paint a picture of the locations, processes, and impacts of cultural deprivation. What is happening where you live? What new regulations, policies, or laws are being established to limit BIPOC access to dominant and personal culture? What actions are being taken to promote cultural security?

- Alexander, T., Clark, L. B., Reinhard, K., & Zatz, N. (2023). CRT Forward: Tracking the Attacks on Critical Race Theory UCLA Law. Retrieved from https://crtforward.law.ucla.edu/wp-content/uploads/2023/04/UCLA-Law_CRT-Report_Final.pdf on December 17, 2023.
- UCLA Law (April 12, 2023). The Miseducation of CRT: Tracking the Attacks on Critical Race Theory. https://www.youtube.com/watch?v=2bQyYTaUcZI&t=7s

    In this installment of "From the Frontlines, The Miseducation of CRT: Tracking the Attacks on Critical Race Theory and Antiracist Education," panelists discuss a new report produced by CRT Forward, an initiative of the Critical Race Studies Program, which details the first two years of the campaign against CRT.

4   Beyond an Apology

AMA (September 24, 2021). Beyond an Apology to Restorative Justice: Prioritizing Equity Spotlight Series. https://www.youtube.com/watch?v=j3spawSjgjo&t=31s

In this "Prioritizing Equity Spotlight" session, sponsored by the Robert Wood Johnson Foundation and the American Medical Association Foundation, a panel of leaders from the American Medical Association, American Academy of Pediatrics, and American Psychiatric Association discuss with the moderator, Gail Christopher, DN, executive director of the National Collaborative for Health Equity, pathways to health equity both within their organizations and across medicine.

Suggestions for Further Study

Suggestions for further study can seem like "filler." However, the suggested readings for this chapter are extensive and substantive. The reading lists include most of the foundational documents referenced in the chapter, and a few additional readings. They are listed in the references as well, but I make a direct suggestion to the reader or the student in this section to go back to the foundational documents to help understand your profession and professional organizations' current efforts to address the profession's complicity in cultural deprivation practices over time, and the standards for individual professionals to facilitate cultural security.

The first set of readings address a range of consensus documents regarding human rights broadly and culturally contextualized.

1   North, M. (trans.) (2002). *The Hippocratic Oath.* National Library of Medicine. Retrieved from https://www.nlm.nih.gov/hmd/greek/greek_oath.html on December 17, 2023.

2 *Universal Declaration of Human Rights.* https://www.un.org/sites/un2.
un.org/files/2021/03/udhr.pdf The United Nations General Assembly
proclaims the UDHR a milestone agreement in human rights history.
The UDHR was written by representatives for different legal and
cultural backgrounds from all over the globe. The UDHR was ratified
by the United Nations in Paris on December 10, 1948.

3 United Nations General Assembly (2007). United Nations Declaration
of the Rights of Indigenous Peoples. Retrieved from https://www.un.
org/development/desa/indigenouspeoples/wp-content/uploads/sites/19/
2018/11/UNDRIP_E_web.pdf on December 16, 2023.

4 African Union (1981). *African charter on human and peoples rights.*
Retrieved from https://au.int/en/treaties/african-charter-human-and-
peoples-rights on December 16, 2023.

5 Organization of Islamic Cooperation (1990). *The Cairo declaration of
the organization of the Islamic cooperation on human rights.* Retrieved
from   https://www.oic-oci.org/upload/pages/conventions/en/CDHRI_
2021_ENG.pdf on December 16, 2023.

The second set of suggested readings includes several professional
practice standards documents for social workers, including the
NASW's Code of Ethics and cultural competence documents and the
National Association of Black Social Workers Code of Ethics. Although
there are other ethnic-specific social worker organizations, such as
the National Association of Puerto Rican Latino Social Workers,
Association of Latino/Latina Social Worker Educators, Latino Social
Workers Organization, National Association of Social Workers-
California Native American Council, and the Asian Pacific Islanders
Social Work Educators Association, there are very few with Codes
of Ethics or other standards of practice documents.

6 National Association of Social Workers Code of Ethics (2021).
Retrieved from https://www.socialworkers.org/About/Ethics/Code-
of-Ethics/Code-of-Ethics-English#purpose on December 16, 2023.

7 National Association of Social Workers (2015). Standards and
indicators for cultural competence. Retrieved from https://www.
socialworkers.org/LinkClick.aspx?fileticket=7dVckZAYUmk%3d&
portalid=0 on December 17, 2023.

8 National Association of Black Social Workers Code of Ethics.
Retrieved from https://www.nabsw.org/page/CodeofEthics on
December 17, 2023.

9 National Congress of the American Indian Resolution on Cultural
Protection. https://www.ncai.org/policies/cultural-protection

10 Asian Pacific Islanders Social Work Educators Association Joint Statement Social Work's Call to Action Against Pandemic Othering & Anti-Asian Racism. Retrieved from https://apiswea.weebly.com/ social-workrsquos-call-to-action-against-pandemic-othering–anti-asian-racism.html on December 17, 2023.

11 American Medical Association (2021). Organizational strategic plan to embed racial justice and advance health equity 2021–2023. Retrieved from https://www.ama-assn.org/system/files/ama-equity-strategic-plan.pdf on December 17, 2023.

Part 2

Ritual

Chapter 4

Indigeneity

Introduction

This is not a chapter that offers a critical review of the concept of indigeneity. I am not an American Indian Studies scholar. Nor am I of Native American descent. The purpose of this chapter is to answer the question: how do experiences with local, personal, and diaspora indigeneity blunt the impact of cultural deprivation? Further, how do they support cultural security? The chapter answers "how" theoretically with rationale and explanation; and practically with narratives and activities.

As with other chapters, this chapter begins with critical family history, in this instance to illuminate themes concerning Indigenous fetishization by people who are not native to the North American continent. Excessive or irrational devotion can lead to exploitation and misinformation. It can also be born out of empathy and regret, especially among minoritized communities who have their own experience with colonization. Further, it can mean we occupy a different relational space. Or simply that we want to act differently—in ways that are not exploitive. We can. Now. With new understanding about our relationship to the indigeneity of this land, and to our own indigeneity.

This section is directed to Black Indigenous People of Color (BIPOC) professionals and allied health professionals broadly speaking. It is not specifically directed to American Indians. I humbly defer to the Indigenous communities of North America—sometimes called Turtle Island—to lead their people on connecting to their indigeneity. The broader message of this chapter is for allied health professionals and educators to acknowledge and honor indigeneity where we are, on multiple levels for psychic orientation; for connecting to a thread of our individual and collective human history and answering perennial questions, such as Where am I? What happened in the place we are standing or sitting? How am I connected to what happened? How can we be whole again after what has happened on this land?

DOI: 10.4324/9781003177500-7

Figure 4.1 The Muskingum River viewed from the Putnam Hill Park overlook in Zanesville, Ohio. The river used to separate Putnam—an anti-slavery town with an organized culture of assisting fugitive slaves—from Zanesville—an antagonistic pro-slavery town. Zanesville annexed Putnam in 1876.

These questions are not frivolous. Answering specific orienting questions related to historic and material realities, these orientation frames are neurobiological (Lakeoff, 2008). Again—where I am standing? What is behind me? What is below me? What is in the cardinal directions? Where have I moved away from? Where am I moving toward? etc. Nearly all humans have eyes that face forward, feet that face forward, and palms that fall inward to the sides. Deep structure frames influence the metaphors and syntax of our language and thinking, and the expression of our deep structure frames is impacted by the answers to these questions (Figure 4.1).

Critical Family History

"You Are a Nigger!"

"You are a Nigger! You got that, boy." My father growled at me, seemingly frustrated, almost cringing, perhaps even almost shameful. He had been looking at another one of my drawings. My adolescent identity development faculties emerged from historic, intergenerational, institutional and family cultural deprivation, strategies, pathways, and assaults. My father's escape from prison and our family's subsequent fugitive lifestyle caused my parents to limit what they shared with me, and my brother and sisters about our roots, our family history, and culture. The less we knew about where we came from, the less we might say at school to teachers, social workers, administrators, or the police. These activities didn't stop our identity development process, but they limited the availability of fundamental tools or resources—such as family stories, rituals, and connection to land or location for healthy ethnic and racial identity development.

Even deeper than that, colorism that spread across both sides of the family often caused dissociation with aunties and uncles, first cousins, and beyond. Only a few descendants of George Allender, who immigrated from central Ireland in the early 1800s, maintained relationships with my father and grandmother after William Allender, her husband, died. They were all light-complected Black Appalachian people, some with skin shades pushing into Black and others into white. Connections to the Allenders further dwindled as our family fugitivity increased. Connections dwindled with the Webbs, Turners, and Adams as well. By middle school and even further into high school, the conditions created a kind of "vacant identity."

Sometimes I experienced a false sense of freedom in developing into who I was becoming because of my unwieldy interests in art, mythology, mysticism, etc. I also often engaged in naively cliché colonial tropes. No matter who I thought I was, I always had people pressing me about my wide nose, dusty skin, and dark hair.

From Magical Thinking to Critical Consciousness

I gravitated toward indigenous cultural images. I mimicked images depicting Native American portraits I found in *Southwest Art* magazine with professional-level oil-based crayons on five-by-four-foot butcher paper all junior year. I grew my hair long. I tried to straighten it. I spent 45 minutes working on my hair one day. I blow-dried it and tied it tightly behind my head with multiple tiny rubber bands to try and prevent my coarse curls from escaping back into their own tune. After sitting for several hours with bounded hair, I clipped the bands and released it into what I hoped would be a loose, thin flow beneath my shoulders. I walked outside, headed to the beach along Lake Michigan during a humid Milwaukee afternoon. My hair responded by circling back into a soft wavy Afro around my head. Frustrated, I recalled my father taking me to the barber before a rare visit with my grandfather in Cleveland. I thought the barber had taken too much hair off. My grandfather looked down at me and simply said, "I thought you got that nap cut." It was not going to flow like that.

I had a small group of friends who identified as Native American: a young man who referred to himself as Ojibwa, rather than Chippewa—a weightlifter, a foster care child, and a fighter; a young woman from the Oneida Nation constantly moving back to the reservation near the Door County Peninsula only to return to Milwaukee a few weeks later.

Another young woman in this loose, often transient group said she was Native American, but that she did not know from what tribe her people belonged. She lived alone with her mother. Everyone said she was Mexican or Italian because she had a Latin surname. I'll never know, but perhaps she was among the Indigenous diaspora of Mexico. Another young man in this group referred to himself as Chippewa—or just an Indian person. He had been adopted by white parents who were divorced. The custodial parent was a gay male whose partner lived in the home. One day when I went to visit him, they told me that he had been taken to a youth home for treatment. They told me that he was white and that he was delusional about being Native American.

I had another friend who was not part of this group. He identified as bi-racial, Black and Chippewa. His older brother was a photographer. My relationship with him lasted the longest because it overlapped with other Black friends, but we eventually fell out of touch as well. I remember him reading a yearbook entry from a young woman whom we both knew. She wrote that she wishes she had spent more time with him. She explained that she never really figured him out. He felt particularly incensed by this.

I also established a relationship with a Mohican man, named Steve, and his elderly white woman benefactor. Together, they owned a small gift store selling Native American art and jewelry on Milwaukee's eastside. I learned how to differentiate plastic jewelry from glass beadwork, and hand-sewn vs. mass-produced leatherwork. I also learned to notice popular culture styles that were largely a co-opting of mostly Central and North American Indigenous cultural dress. There were several boutiques and clothing stores selling these items in this area of the city that was once the primary home of hippie culture. There was no shortage of long leather fringes, even in the early 1980s.

The boutique also carried independently published Indigenous literature, poetry, and political books. I was especially intrigued by the Indigenous journalism. I read *Awkesanse Notes* and *Indian Country Today* every month. I had never had such direct exposure to news about Native Americans, especially not written by Indian reporters.

Although my grandfather was not happy with my haircut, he mailed newspaper articles from the *Cleveland Plain Dealer* about Native American issues to me. He always sent me something to read, no matter how obscure my family's hiding place. Reading the *Plain Dealer* alongside Steve's source material sharpened my understanding of multiple perspectives and the need for critical representations. This was especially the case after I started reading Vine Deloria Jr's books at Steve's suggestion.

I learned about blood quantum and tribal rolls. I learned about state vs. federally recognized tribes. I learned about natural vs. forced migrations. And I reflected that the little I did know of my family culture, all references to indigenous heritage were vague, and without reference to tribal relationships.

I also attended the Annual Autumn Pow Wow at the University of Wisconsin–Milwaukee and the Spring Pow Wow at the Wisconsin Armory. The powwows were cultural and social events. I always enjoyed attending, but it was clear that I was not part of the community. I was not a dancer, an artist, a vendor, nor a family member or friend of anyone who traveled the powwow circuit for cultural sustenance and livelihood. My loose group of high school friends never came with me. Occasionally my mother and or my little sister went, but we participated as outsiders. I almost always attended alone.

And no one ever verbally mistook me for Oneida, Potawatomi, Chippewa, or Menominee, or any of the other local tribal communities—despite all my efforts to grow out and straighten my hair. I was used to being called a Puerto Rican, Palestinian, or "that light-skinned dude" sometimes a "light skin brotha." Phenotype is not a stable container to hold identity, especially not alone. Not all Native Americans have long, straight hair. They don't all look like Iron Eyes Cody, "the actor who played an Indian shedding a tear at the sight of a littered American landscape in one of television's best-known and most-honored television commercials" (Waldman, 1999). I was processing all of this as alongside my father's crude pronouncement.

Spearfishing against Beer Bottles and Rocks

In 1983, after nine years of litigation, the U.S. Court of Appeals had upheld the Wisconsn's Band's (Lac du Flambeau band of Lake Superior Chippewa Indians) rights to hunt, fish, and gather on the lands and lakes of the northern third of the state, the area ceded in the treaties of 1837 and 1842. The court decision upheld the Native American right to use traditional methods to harvest fish. No one had been permitted to spear game fish in Wisconsin for over a century before that decision. The court case focused on the Lac du Flambeau band's harvesting of spawning walleye pike, a species of game fish that the state had been cultivating in the northern lakes for over a century.

Many non–Native Americans living in the politically conservative and rural, north-central area of Wisconsin saw themselves as dependent on tourism and feared that spearfishing would destroy the economy over time. Non–Native American groups, such as Equal Rights for Everyone, Protect America's Rights and Resources (PARR), and Stop Treaty Abuse/ Wisconsin (STA/A) emerged and became allied with national anti–Native American organizations in order to oppose the local Native American exercise of treaty rights and hundreds of non–Native Americans protested at the lakes where Native Americans spearfished (Nesper, 2002).

Shortly after the appeals court decision, the nightly news covered the non–Native American demonstrators marching to the lakes to throw beer bottles and rocks, and hurl insults and racial epithets at the Lac du Flambeau attempting to engage in cultural practices for sustenance. I watched white sport fishers harass Chippewa on the nightly news repeatedly. It made me angry and it made me sick. It made me want to fight with my mind, words, and fists. At the same time, no one in my family seemed the slightest bit moved by the news. This made me even more angry. Tribal leaders report that the harassment persists—40 years after the court decision (Seo, 2021).

* * *

I met Suzanne Zipperer picking up my son from daycare while she was picking up her daughter. Suzanne published *The Key,* an adult literacy magazine and I was a student at Milwaukee Area Technical College. When I was in middle and high school processing local indigeneity, personal indigeneity, and indigenous diasporas, Suzanne was in the Republic of Rhodesia, located in south-central Africa. She saw the transition from white majority rule by settler colonists from England to a Black Nationalist government, after nearly a decade of guerilla warfare. Rhodesia became Zimbabwe, and Suzanne eventually moved to Milwaukee.

Back in Milwaukee, while working with *The Key*, Suzanne received a grant to publish an adult literacy reader. The reader included stories about immigrants to Milwaukee since 1970. Suzanne gathered a team of writers to go out into the neighborhoods and interview Nicaraguans and Salvadorans from Central America, Hmong from Laos, and Vietnam, Palestinians from Gaza, etc.

I joined the group and volunteered to write about the Palestinian immigrant community. There were three small Palestinian-owned grocery stores each within two blocks of my apartment. Although I completed the interviews and wrote the chapter, I didn't really understand it as a story about indigeneity until years later. I was watching the local news in Sacramento describe the November 2023 Annual Indigenous Sunrise Gathering on Alcatraz Island. In 2023, the Indian Treaty Council, the sponsoring organization, invited a contingent of Palestinians to surface their struggle.

Imaginary Native Americans Aren't Real

After joining an ancestry database service and purchasing a DNA kit, I quietly confirmed my father's pronouncement. My family had no real connection to Native American ancestry from North or South America. And, despite phenotypic stereotypes, as I had already known there was no Arab, Puerto Rican, Persian, Indian, or Pakistani. Further, as Alexandra Finley's (2010) Ohio State honors thesis attests, many pioneering families—including some on my father's side—who migrated into Chestnut Ridge in West Virginia and then spread into Stark County, Ohio, who occasionally identified as Native American often did so to hide their mixed Irish/African American heritage.

Indigeneity

In an attempt to rationalize, gloss over or hide genocide of Indigenous people living in what is now the United States, and the enslavement and subsequent genocide of Africans, accurate stories of this reign of terror enacted upon countless families and communities have been suppressed, rewritten, and reframed. This is the dual nature of inhumanity: first, there is the original violation. Next, there is the act to cover up and justify it. And the act to conceal takes on varied forms such as lies, disinformation campaigns, propaganda, stereotypes, omissions, erasure, etc. The cover-up then becomes part of the cultural deprivation process. The cover-up prevents people from accessing their history, and it can skew their orientation faculties.

While the narratives above explore some of my personal and professional experiences with Indigenous peoples and with Indigenous struggles, the following sections explore how I've come to understand those experiences.

Local Indigeneity and Land Theft

Reflecting on my evolving experiences with indigeneity helps me understand that wherever I am, I need to reconcile my relationship to the land: the land I am standing on and the land surrounding me. This is the most immediate way that I can honor Indigenous communities who have been stewarding the land long before my arrival. We need to take care of the land.

However, we cannot take care of the land if we don't know how. We have to know the land. And while this may include contemporary knowledge and information about the best ways to care for whatever land we are living, working, playing, and praying on, caring for the land can be therapeutic. There is ample evidence to support the health benefits from working in the natural environment. Whether we work in a garden, tree-trimming or participating in a larger scale restoration project, working with the land is good for everyone involved.

Much of the world's population lives on or is dependent on stolen land. Because the theft is never not benign, but violent in nature and deed, we are all living in post-genocidal geographies. Prior to the theft and genocidal practices, there were communities who cultivated the land.

We can ask ourselves: who are the indigenous people where you live and work? This question is either preceded by or simultaneously with the question Where are we? And what happened here? What happened to the land and what happened to the people who were on the land? How did we get to the place where we are now? And what are we doing with this land?

Who are the Indigenous people where you vacation or where you traverse?

As educators and allied health professionals, we need to care more for the land; deepen our knowledge about and facilitate personal relationships and political alliances with local indigenous communities.

Personal Indigeneity: We Come from the Land

Exploring local and diaspora indigeneity may be a more obvious path toward solidarity than personal indigeneity, but identifying where we come from is important. Far from being a "new age" effort proclaiming, "we are all Indian now" it is an ontological and epistemological necessity for building cultural security.

There is a documented history of intergroup relations among enslaved Africans and the Seminole, Cherokee, and some other Indigenous communities. And there are examples of contemporary political alliances (Mays, 2021) social relationships among Black and Indigenous people, sometimes leading to bi-racial and multiracial families and children. And there are an increasing number of African Americans who have identified this history and in some cases DNA connections. Some are actively seeking tribal memberships to validate these historic connections.

However, Rick Kittles—geneticist and owner of the DNA company African Ancestry—reviewed African American genetic ancestry and can identify only small amounts of Indigenous DNA percentages mixed with a small number of Black African Americans living in the United States. Like Finley's findings noted above, Kittles suggests there is not as much mixing between African Americans and Indigenous folks as there is lore about Indigenous ancestry among Black communities. R. L'Heureux Lewis-McCoy (2018) concurs with Kittles' research. African Americans are not alone in this often over-identification, but the focus of this text is on cultural security for BIPOC.

We can consider overidentification with Native Americans, at least for some of us as an effort to establish connection with our Indigenous roots, which often extend much farther back than the history we reach for to establish cultural security. Kyle Mays (2021) challenges us to think about Africans, especially enslaved Africans as Indigenous folk—Indigenous to the lands on the continent of Africa. While he chides "Hotepers"—some followers of Kemetic philosophies that point to Africa as the birthplace of psychic and spiritual templates for world culture—this tradition is one place that answers his challenge.

In addition to Kemetic traditions, Wade Nobles' life work to establish an authentic African psychology—which is inclusive of African Americans—includes a deep exploration and identification with Bantu Congo culture. In many lectures and interviews, Nobles' asserts "we are all Bantu" when referring to African American descendants of enslaved Africans. Relatedly, many of the West African-derived spiritual systems migrated to the Western Hemisphere during the transatlantic slave trade, and later through contemporary immigration of West Africans to the United States and other parts of the world. These traditions include Santeria, Lucumi, Vodou, Hoodoo, Relga Congo, etc. Finally, perhaps more controversial, African Americans can also turn to land stewardship and cultivation, such as planting and farming traditions. The chart below presents this paradigm in condensed form, but there is much to unpack.

Approaches to Indigeneity for African Americans

Kemet	East Africa, Egypt
West Africa	Nigeria, Senegal, Ghana
Bantu Congo	Central and Southern Africa
Black Farmers, Diaspora Root Traditions, Urban Farmers	Southern United States, The Caribbean, Parts of Central and South America

Ethnic Studies and Indigeneity

After advocating for an ethnic studies education high school graduation requirement; creating curriculum materials; and providing teacher professional development for a northern California public school district, administrators were interested in evaluating the work. They wanted to know if they could measure the promised academic and social value in their district, that was reported in San Francisco and Tucson school districts might be in the works for them. Superintendents at the district directed their evaluation office to create a survey and send it to the approximately 300 ninth-grade students taking an entry-level ethnic studies class.

The results of the survey were impressive. Ninety to ninety-eight percent of the 300 students reported Agree or Strongly Agree to such statements as "I learned more about my history" "I learned more about my community." "I learned more about my classmate's history." "I want to learn more about my community's history." The results suggested we were addressing cultural deprivation in education.

As excited as we were with these responses, we could not use the results in publication or evaluation. Upon closer look at the data, I noticed that the district neglected to list Latinx, Latine, Hispanic or any similar category as demographic information alongside the other ethnic and racial categories for the students to fill in. I was sure it was an oversight, but it was still problematic.

In addition to noticing that this community was missing on the survey, we noticed that there was an overrepresentation amongst the students listing Native American as their ethnicity. In a district with 0.5% American Indian or Alaskan Native and 41.3% Hispanic/Latino, seventy percent of the students listed themselves as Native American—and 0% Hispanic.

The textbook the class used explores indigeneity in several ways: first, we worked with Rose Borunda, former director of California Indian Curriculum Commission and Crystal Martinez Alire–Chair of the Ione Band of Miwok. They wrote the opening chapter of California Indian History with a focus on the Sacramento Region and Northern California.

Next, we worked with Brian Baker, professor of Native American studies and enrolled member of the Chippewa. Dr. Baker wrote a chapter on contemporary images in popular culture and consumer culture, focusing mostly on North American Indian tribes. He also referred two additional writers, one who write about Ishi, and another who write about on Danza Azteca. In addition, we worked with a member of Danza to facilitate a photo essay of a Danza dance rehearsal.

Could the students have listed themselves as Indigenous because the new learning they had about Danza and their geographic connection to Mexico? Could there have been an unrecognized population of indigenous students in the room, perhaps having come with a recent population from the Oaxacan region of Mexico? The truth is we don't know why, and this is why the evaluation is not valid, but the scenario itself is very important in terms of how the students view themselves. Were they taught this identity by the course? Were they taught this identity at home or amongst their peer group?

This is not only worth exploring, it underlines the importance of acknowledging and clarifying our relationships to indigeneity in pedagogical and therapeutic spaces.

Indigenous Diaspora-Forced Removal

Diaspora refers to groups of people living on land other than their homeland, but who maintain their traditions and culture. Who are the Indigenous diasporas? Indigenous people displaced nationally and internationally? They have experienced forced migration, removal, and avoidance migration. While some aspects of North American Indigenous migration, such as the trail of tears occurring between 1830 and 1850, where Chickasaw, Cherokee, Choctaw, Creek, and Seminole tribes were marched from South Carolina and Florida to Oklahoma are more widely discussed, many other instances of rounding Indian people up and marching them en masse to a new location have also occurred. Consider the Winnebago of Wisconsin, who were removed to Nebraska before they migrated back in small groups of their own accord. Also consider the Oneida who left their ancestral lands in New York after illegal land transactions with the state left them with very little to live on. The Oneida purchased land from the Winnebago and Menominee tribes in Wisconsin before statehood. The relocation was ratified in a treaty between the tribes and the state in 1838.

Virtually every state in the United States includes Indigenous diasporas. For example, according to the UCLA project Mapping Indigenous LA, the city:
"… includes layered, sedimented cultural geographies of Indigenous Los Angeles that includes the

• Gabrielino/Tongva and Tataviam who struggle for recognition of their sacred spaces and recognition as nations,
• American Indians who were removed from their lands and displaced through governmental policies of settler colonialism, and
• indigenous diasporas from Latin America and Oceania where people have been displaced by militarism, neoliberal economic policies, and overlapping colonial histories.

When we consider Pacific Islander and Latin American Indigenous Diasporas, Los Angeles has the largest indigenous population of any city in the United States. While many would argue that there is not one Los Angeles but multiple LAs, what is less known is that there are multiple indigenous LAs whose histories are layered into the fabric of the city." These populations have similar and unique experiences with cultural deprivation and cultural security needs.

Summary

This chapter begins with critical family history narrative about the author's personal experiences processing local indigeneity, personal indigeneity, and diaspora indigeneity. The chapter continues with a reflection on these three categories. Connecting to local indigeneity includes caring for the land, studying the history and culture of the local Indigenous communities, and building personal relationships and political alliances with these communities. One paradigm for African Americans to enter dialogue with their personal Indigenous identity includes exploring kemetic traditions, Bantu Congo culture, West African traditions and culture, and Black farming traditions. Last, Indigenous diaspora is described as layered and complex.

Activities

Addressing indigeneity offers us the opportunity to reorient our relationship with ourselves and with Native people toward solidarity. It can help us orient or understand our relationship, our extended family's relationship; and our ancestors' relationship with the Indigenous communities on the land we currently occupy and the land we occupied in history. Rituals of Indigeneity ask the perennial question—Where am I from? Where are we from? Or where do I come from?

Land Acknowledgment Activities

Land Acknowledgment and the Sacramento State University College of Education Multicultural Education Conference

During my first year as co-chair of the College of Education Annual Multicultural Education Conference at Sac State University, the conference committee decided to issue a Land Acknowledgment at the opening session. Soon thereafter, Sacramento State University released a formal acknowledgment developed in partnership with local Indigenous communities. Sacramento State's effort became part of a national effort to change the orientation of individuals and institutions about where they were and what the location and the very land itself afforded. Land acknowledgments are now widely available for review online, simply by searching with these search terms.

Years after our university's land acknowledgment was institutionalized as a ritual at all major events on campus, the practice became routinized, mechanized, and no longer meaningful on a few occasions. Groups of faculty came together to dialogue about the importance of engaing in land acknowledgments with mindfulness and attention. We committed to sticking to the script because it spoke to specific American Indian tribal communities relevant to

our location, rather than simply saying "We acknowledge the Native American communities ..." or something similarly vague.
We also committed to learning more about the Land Back movement.

Where Am I on Native Land?

NativeLands is a website that allows visitors to type in a full or partial address to identify traditional territories, languages, and treaties of tribal nations, but also the treaties that governed their removal. This tool can be used as an opening land acknowledgment ritual or a catalyst to a larger and deeper conversation.

Personal land acknowledgment grounds us as individuals in our social and historical identity, locating our proximity to Indigenous genocide and land theft. The following website was developed by Native Land Digital, a Canadian not-for-profit organization, incorporated in December 2018. Native Land Digital is Indigenous-led, with an Indigenous executive director and board of directors who oversee and direct the organization.

1 Visit the website: https://native-land.ca
2 Make sure the "Territories," "Languages," and "Treaties" buttons are enabled.
3 Type in the address for

- where you live
- where you were born
- where you grew up
- where you work
- where you frequent for leisure, entertainment, or family gatherings.

4 Record the results for the "Territories," "Languages," and "Treaties" for each of the bulleted categories in number 3 above. Be sure to write down the exact name of the tribal community for each location.
5 Discuss what you found with others. Note any common experiences, directions, discoveries, thoughts, or feelings.

Land Acknowledgment at Language Academy

Language Academy is a K–8 Spanish emersion school. The faculty and staff at the school are over 95% native Spanish speakers. Many are from Mexico, and a few are from Central America.

I provided anti-racist teacher professional development workshops at the school during the 2020–2021 school year in response to the national cry for more anti-racist education in the wake of the murders of George Floyd and Breonna Taylor. At the workshop, I shared the Native Lands website activity above. After reviewing where the school was located, many of the participants began asking questions about the Indigenous communities from where they had come. The participants' research on the website led to a rich conversation about Indian populations in Mexico and the United States.

Travels on Indigenous Land

We live in a mobile world and many people travel or move to take up residency in different locations. Wherever we go we are on Indigenous land. We might be on land that our Indigenous ancestors have occupied, or that of other Indigenous peoples. Or we may be a guest or a trespasser on lands that do not belong to our ancestors. In this activity, we account for our travel by identifying whose land we have moved through.

1   Begin by creating a timeline. List the locations of several places you have lived, visited, or spent time at for significant purposes.
2   Record some details from memory about the location and your time there. Write your recollections under the timeline entries.
3   Enter those locations in the Native Lands search engine.
4   Add the additional information gained from the search to your timeline.

"Tracing Ancestral Travels on Indigenous Land" in the box below provides an example of this activity in progress.

Tracing Ancestral Travels on Indigenous Land

The following narrative uses the website https://native-land.ca as the initial source to identify which indigenous communities made their traditional homes in locations where I had pivotal life experiences, and to try and determine where those communities call home today; lastly, to reflect on my relationship with the land and tribes. In some cases, I use additional sources, such as tribal websites, and state departments.

My enslaved paternal ancestors referenced in the first chapter were held in bondage by Robert Carter on the Nomini Hall and Leo Plantations in Westmoreland County, Virginia. Westmoreland is the traditional homelands of the Onawmanient, Cuttatawomen, Pissaseck, and Rappahannock. Descendants of these tribal communities do not have tribal land in common, and only the Rppahannock are recognized by the state of Virginia.

My maternal second grandfather was named George Washington Turner. The farm he purchased on Coopermill Road in Zanesville, Ohio, was located on the land of the ancient Hopewell Culture, which later became the homelands of the Osage and the Shawnee. Today, these tribes are located on reservations in Oklahoma. While the Osage migrated from this area further West initially, they were then removed repeatedly after the Louisiana Purchase. The Shawnee were forced out of Ohio altogether, and into Kansas after the War of 1812. And they were removed from Kansas into Oklahoma after squatters took over their homes during their forced participation in the United States Civil War.

My maternal grandfather Ralph Turner's home at 9909 Columbia Avenue in Cleveland, Ohio, was on the traditional homeland of the Erie. Descendants of the Erie were moved onto the lands of the Seneca in Oklahoma, after they had been removed from their homelands. I never saw any sign of these communities when I was growing up and visiting my grandfather.

The University of Wisconsin–Milwaukee, where I earned my bachelor's degree in English Education, studied African dance. And attended Pan-Indian Pow Wows, is located on the traditional homeland of the Eastern Dakota, Western Dakota, Ho-Chunk, Pottawatami, Menominee, Kickapoo, Myaami, And Peoria. Today, these tribes are located on reservations in Wisconsin, Minnesota, and Oklahoma.

The College of Education at the University of Iowa in Iowa City, Iowa, where I went to graduate school and earned a master's degree in developmental reading; and where the Iowa Test of Basic Skills and the ACT test was created are located on the traditional homelands of the Western and Eastern Dakota, Iowa, Kickapoo, Ioway, Sauk, Fox. Today, these tribal communities are located on reservations in Oklahoma.

The apartment on Lake Merritt in Oakland, California where I lived for ten years, was located on the traditional homelandsof the Muwekma Ohlone. Today, members of the Ohlone live throughout the San Francisco Bay Area and the state of California without a formal reservation.

The University of Queensland, Australia, in the state of Brisbane and the city of St. Lucia, where I earned my PhD, is located on the traditional homelands of the Turrbal Aboriginal communities. In the 1890s, after near total genocide they were forcibly removed by the

British to the Barambah Aboriginal Reserve just northwest of Brisbane. Today the Turrbal are fighting the Australian government to reacquire their homelands under the Native Title Act of 1993.

California State University Sacramento, where I work as a professor, is located on the traditional homelands of the Nisenan, specifically, the Nissim Paewenan, and the Miwok people. Today, the Nisenan are fighting the United States government to restore their status as a federally recognized tribe, which was terminated by United States Congress in 1964. The Miwok, regained their Federal Recognition in 2009, after years of fighting.

Land Back

Podcast Review: Madonna Thunder Hawk: Matriarch of the Movement LANDBACK For the Prople NDN Collective https://podcasts.apple.com/us/podcast/madonna-thunder-hawk-a-matriarch-of-the-movement/id1684349697?i=1000610465060 delves into past and present LANDBACK struggles across Turtle Island and the Indigenous world. LANDBACK FOR THE PEOPLE is dedicated to lifting up the revolutionary strides within the liberation movement for Indigenous peoples and our homelands.

Podcast Elements

Speaker	Biography	Quotes
Nick Tilsen (Oglala Lakota)	Host, president, and CEO of NDN Collective	
Madonna Thunder Hawk (Oohenumpa Lakota)	Madonna Thunder hawk, often referred to as "Matriarch" of the [Red Power] Movement.	

Podcast Structure

LANDBACK Podcast episode teaser (0:00–0:31)
Madonna Thunder Hawk situates Land Back as the central ideology of all American Indian resistance movements.

Intro to Podcast (0:41–6:30)
Nick Tilsen introduces himself in Lakota and English. He introduces the podcast, recognizing not only the ongoing struggle for American Indian liberation but also the particular zeitgeist that names land Back.

In the first segment (6:31–17:00)
Nick Tilsen introduces Madonna Thunder Hawk. Thunder Hawk reflects on the moment and shares stories of resistance from her childhood and early years. Tilsen probes Thunder hawk to reflect on the meaning of Land Back.

In the second segment (17:01–24:45)
Tilsan and Thuder Hawk discuss specific demonstrations in the Black Hills, South Dakota, as an orienting point to understand the American Indian Movement. The conversation transitions to a discussion of movement across time.

In the third segment (24:46–30:35)
After announcements from the podcast producer, Tilsen returns to the discussion of the Black Hills as the longest legal battles in U.S. history. Tilsen recounts specific court cases and findings.

Closing segment (30:36–48:35)
Tilsan asks Thunder Hawk to share "war stories" of her activism.

Podcast Listening Prompts

The following questions below can help surface thoughts related to the content discussed in the podcast, promoting deeper processing. Answer the question in writing and then discuss them with others before listening.

a Pre-listening prompts

   i How do you steward the land you walk on?
   ii Imagine what you can do now to convey tangible land back to those communities.

b Listening prompts

   i What is the significance of the Black Hills to the Land Back Movement?
   ii What are some common stories discussed in the podcast?
   iii What are some counter stories discussed in the podcast?

c Post-listening prompts

   i How will you steward the land you walk on?
   ii How will you live differently on the earth knowing that it has not been ceded, others are benefiting from land, and the original stewards are often suffering for their lack of land?

Suggestions for Further Reading

The additional readings and resources below are intended to deepen understanding of local and personal indigeneity, and the Indigenous diaspora.

1 Preserving the Desert with NALC | Tending Nature | Season 3, Episode 2 | KCET. https://www.youtube.com/watch?v=0J-V_w44haA&t=83s

This film documents a collaborative group of desert tribes, concerned citizens, and funders who have formed the Native American Land Conservancy to acquire, preserve, and protect Native American sacred lands through protective land management, educational programs, and scientific study.

2 Native American Land Conservancy. https://www.nativeamericanland. org/

This URL links to the organization described above in the first resource.

3 Mays, K. (2021). A provocation of the modes of Black Indigeneity: Culture, language, possibilities. *Ethnic Studies Review* (2021) 44 (2): 41–50. Retrieved from https://doi.org/10.1525/esr.2021.44.2.41 on December 13, 2023.

4 Nobles, W. (1986). *African Psychology: Toward Its Reclamation, Reascension, and Revitalization*. A Black Family Institute Publication.

5 Mays, K. (2021). *An Afro-Indigenous History of the United States.*

Mays book explores moments in U.S. history when African Americans and various American Indian tribes crossed into each other's culture and established relationships and alliances. One example included narrates the relationship between the Black Panther Party and the American Indian Movement.

6 https://www.teenvogue.com/story/indigenous-land-acknowledgement-explained

Teen Vogue provides an excellent primer on the purposes and practices of land acknowledgment.

7 Mapping Indigenous LA. https://mila.ss.ucla.edu

Mapping Indigenous Los Angeles is a story mapping project with the goal of uncovering and highlighting the multiple layers of Indigenous Los Angeles. The project involves you, community leaders, and elders from Indigenous communities throughout the city.

Chapter 5

Ancestry

Introduction

The purpose of this chapter is to amplify ancestor veneration practices for allied health professionals and educators beyond current corporate DNA kits and document databases and into our professional practice spaces. While the ancestry companies provide a way for us to learn about our ancestry—and there is often an awe upon discovering ancestors and their possible narratives—this chapter offers a paradigm for veneration. The chapter is also an effort to expand our understanding of the idea of ancestor. In addition to the paradigm serving that goal, the chapter offers many examples of personal and professional ancestor acknowledgment and veneration. Many cultural groups have ritualized interaction with a deceased family member or members of the community, but not all groups engage their ancestors in the same way (Dennison & Powell-Watts, 2021). As with the other chapters, this content is still rooted in an African, African American, and African diaspora perspective (Figure 5.1).

Ancestor acknowledgment and veneration is an important building block of Chiek Anta Diop's concept of cultural security discussed in Chapter 2. Ancestry helps us get hold of Diop's "thread of history" concept. This chapter also includes a discussion of personal narratives of ancestral dreaming. While ancestral dreaming and other aspects of the chapter may seem overly mystical, recall the American Medical Association's (AMA's) strategic plan in Chapter 3 that formally acknowledges ancestors. More to the point, the chapter cites research and professional practice from anthropology, psychology, clinical psychotherapy, and education applying or addressing the role of this important area of cultural knowledge and practice.

DOI: 10.4324/9781003177500-8

Figure 5.1 Ralph Turner in Cleveland, Ohio.

Critical Family History: Ancestral Dreaming

I was haunted after reading Angela Davis' words. I put the book down and stared into space: *"After her burial the old country lands took on for me an ineffable, awe-inspiring dimension: they became the stage on which the history of my people had been acted out. And my grandmother, in death, became more heroic. I felt a strange kind of unbreakable bond, vaguely religious, with her in that new world she had entered"* (p. 73).

I struggled over selecting a college major. I dropped out of college at least three times and changed my major repeatedly. I couldn't handle the disciplined pace of creating and producing in the commercial art program. The nursing program required me to cut, puncture, and squeeze things I was not prepared to cut, puncture, and squeeze. I excelled in the social work program at Milwaukee Area Technical College, but ultimately, I decided upon a teaching credential. It wasn't an easy decision. One evening while alone on the couch, I went deep inside myself and asked "Where am I supposed to be? And what am I best suited to do, professionally? I did not believe I had stable professional models in my family. Although I decided to become a high school teacher, after completing my undergraduate education and earning a credential enabling me to teach English, I went directly into graduate school. I fell in love with literacy studies, so I entered the Developmental Reading MA program at the University of Iowa during my first year of teaching.

During the humid, endless Iowa summer, I spent between the end of one-degree program and the start of another, I found a discussion listserv online sponsored by the National Council of Teachers of English. I jumped right into the dialogue about teaching multicultural literature. I championed the teaching of diverse works of literature that challenged the content and the positioning of canonized works. I probed the contexts under which Mark Twain is taught and how the N word is addressed pedagogically. While some teachers pushed back, most members of the list lurked in silence.

One afternoon, a content developer from the standardized testing company ACT who had been observing the discussion reached out to me to help craft test items for the English and reading tests. For the English test, I would write a three-paragraph essay on almost any topic I wanted, and craft 30 questions about the writing. I decided to write a test item analyzing Countee Cullen's classic poem from the Harlem Renaissance era entitled "Yet Do I Marvel." I loved this poem's triumphant irony embedded in Cullen's wondering, but I struggled to write in this new genre. My passage was returned to me several times by the editors for corrections. I lost the cocky feeling I communicated on the listserv several months earlier. I was struggling. I went to bed one night and dreamt of my maternal grandfather, Ralph William Turner.

The dreamscape set a scene reminiscent of a 1940s era private detective film. Achromatic grayscale colored the entire scene. Ralph Turner sat at a large desk behind an office door with an etched, frosted glass window. He wore his customary fully buttoned white shirt, suit, and tie tied tight at the neck. He spoke to me on the phone. "I can't help you. But you are doing exactly what you are supposed to be doing." End of dream. Fade to black.

I didn't understand the significance of this dream at the time. I knew my grandfather had come to me. I knew I was doing right by him in terms of being literate and writing about literature. After all, I learned to read largely due to his books. He was not only an avid reader, he was a collector of book sets and single volumes, magazines, newspapers, theater programs, ticket stubs from sports, entertainment, and theater productions. He sent books and other reading material to me and all his grandchildren; however he could get them to us, even when we were fugitives from the law, hiding in hotels and halfway houses.

But I did not know at the time that the ancestral impulse was not only to read but also to teach. My grandfather and grandmother—my mother's parents—tied me to a Black teacher lineage extending back to the 1800s, and through Wilberforce University and Central State in Dayton, Ohio, and Tuskegee University in Alabama. I was not close to my maternal grandmother. She was mostly a mystery to me, spending most of her time behind dark glasses in the kitchen and dining room. I didn't know that her father was the chair of the Engineering Department at Tuskegee or that her mother was an administrator at Wilberforce. My grandfather related to me through books, and I respected that, but I didn't know that his sister, aunt, and multiple uncles were teachers, either. While he was a fixture in my earliest years, our time together would be increasingly fleeting as my father's experience with incarceration, fugitivity, and false identity took center stage.

. . . .

I went to New York for the first time to work at a National Council of Teachers of English annual convention. I left a day earlier to visit my friend Julia at her apartment, near where she grew up in the Bronx. She encouraged me to take some time during my trip to visit her brother, Robert. Robert lived all the way downtown in "Do or Die" Bedstuy. He was an elementary school teacher and a graduate student at New York University's newly established Education Theater MA program. Robert was also a Lucumi priest. Lucumi is a Cuban variation of a West African religion commonly associated with the Yoruba ethnic group originating mainly in the countries of Nigeria, Togo, and the Republic of Benin (Brandon, 2012). Julia suggested I see Robert because of my interest in African mythology.

Robert met me outside the NYU library on 4th Avenue. He was wearing a white parka, white sweatpants, white sneakers, and a thick white knit cap. We walked down 4th for a couple of blocks and then cut over onto West 3rd past the Blue Note Café to the West 4th Street subway station. Once we were above ground on Thompkins in Brooklyn, we stopped at a Chinese restaurant. Robert sipped on oxtail soup. He looked up at the ceiling and brought his voice crashing down proclaiming, "My ancestors are right here with me, right now. In this room. And that's exactly what I want you to feel and know, Dale Allender!" My chest rumbled when he spoke.

Before I left Brooklyn, he told me to set out food for my grandfather when I get home. He said to put the plate aside for him when I eat. He said that I could eat the food later because it shouldn't go to waste. He said it was the act of making the offering that was important. He told me that the ancestors would take the nourishment from the food through the offering.

Inviting Ancestors into Our Professional Practice

Currently, companies like Ancestry, AfricanAncestry, 23andMe, FamilySearch, and others are offering various subscription fees for people the world over to research documentation on networked databases and DNA connections related to their ancestry. Sometimes documents and newly discovered relations lead to personal social enrichment and sometimes not. More importantly, many ethnic communities and cultures have held their ancestors in special regard (Asante & Mazama, 2005; Dennison & Powell-Wats 2021), long before the advent of networked databases and AI search tools. Vega (1999), for example, examines and traces ancestor worship—espiritismo—in the Puerto Rican community as a probable legacy of African cultural traditions with specific focus on the African Kongo cultures brought to the island by enslaved Africans. Ancestor veneration has been part of Black African American and African diaspora culture (Asante & Mazama, 2005; Fairley, 2003; White, 2014) for centuries.

African Classical Religion (ACR) defines ancestors in three ways initially. Ancestors must be deceased—this factor provides the continuity from the living family members into the metaphysical ...; ancestors they must have children who will venerate them ritualistically, or who will remember them and thereby keep their energy salient; and they must have led a noble life—in order to give the descendant the desire, need, respect, or awe motivating memory and veneration practices (Asante & Mazama 2005). Among African and African-centered or derived religious practices, not all deceased are considered ancestors (Asante, 2005). This is an important point, as many have had unhealthy, harmful, toxic, or destructive relationships with deceased family members when they were alive. The idea of venerating these individuals can counter the intent of healing the person is seeking in therapy, social work, medicine, and education.

Hood outlines five reasons why ancestors are venerated in Africa: (a) ancestorship and parenthood are highly prized in African social status; (b) veneration of the ancestors is really the "ritualization of filial piety"; (c) observing the ancestors maintains communal living between the living, as well as between the living and the dead; (d) ancestors are safe guardians of communal ethics, family traditions, and community customs; and (e) ancestors are also spirits that communicate with their survivors through dreams, reincarnation, and visions (Asante, 2005). The form and intensity of veneration changed over the centuries, from a pivotal to a secondary role in religious life (White, 2014). For African Americans, ancestor veneration is often depicted as a way for maintaining communal living between the living, as well as between the living and the dead.

It may be true as White observes, that contemporary African American churches do not practice ancestral veneration as much as they did in their inception, or in pre-colonial Africa. However, in secular life ancestor veneration enjoys a robust presence. This is evident in the inclusion of ancestor reverence and veneration rituals in Black popular culture. Consider the film *Don't be a Menace to South Central while Drinking Your Juice in the Hood,* a 1993 parody of several U.S. film about living in Black, urban, impoverished communities. The scene from the film where the actor Shawn Wayans pours some of his beer from a 40-ounce bottle onto the ground as an offering to ancestors but instead hits several men sleeping on the other side of the fence highlights the frequency of this ritual in media and in daily living. Parodies called attention to the widespread or even overuse of a style, act, expression, or ritual with exaggeration. This parody could be calling attention to a need to take the ritual more seriously or question the ritual, or to take life more seriously, or simply to bring levity to the real trauma narrated in the films.

This movie clip was posted on YouTube in December 2022. Note that @mathewsalazar4553 comments: "About to post on Instagram for my brothers passing anniversary today. Some might see it as disrespectful, but I know he would find it funny." The comment includes the face with tears of joy emoji. The comment suggests that the poster recalls a specific characteristic of his brother—he has a sense of humor. Further, he believes that posting something funny on the anniversary of his death would honor his brother. He explains that he knows others might find this parody of a sacred ritual, and the posting of the parody disrespectful; he knows his ancestor would feel honored with this ritual veneration.

In her research exploring relationships among the practice of ancestral dreams among African Americans in two eastern North Carolina Communities, Fairley (2003) describes the ancestral dream as a historically consistent element of ancestor veneration. Further, she explains that the ancestor dream is a form of continuous revelation, often shared only with close friends and family. Thus, while attention to ancestors in formal professional spaces may help address cultural deprivation, this should be done with culturally sustaining care and skill.

Clinical psychologist Edward Bruce Bynum (2021) has compiled and categorized family dreams as part of his clinical family therapy practice and for the Family Dream Research Project. Bynum describes dreams collected about family members, and dreams among members of the same family with shared themes, ideas, or images. Dr. Bynum asserts that "sometimes there is even apparently direct communication of information in dreams between family members" (p. 1). Individual and family dream-work therapy is one way to experience our ancestors. Additionally, Dennison and Powell-Watts (2021) explain that cultures who participate in ancestral worship as part of their spiritual practices often understand and believe that current healing practices can liberate the departed souls or spirits of family members from trauma going backward through prior generations and forward to future generations.

Dimensions of Ancestral Veneration

The paradigm above can create its own set of issues and challenges beyond the mentioning of family dysfunction and intergenerational trauma. For example, what if one does not know their ancestors due to foster care, adoption, refugee experiences, or other scenarios. There are different dimensions of ancetorship that are practiced that perhaps expand Classical African Religion (CAR) understandings.

Ancestors	• Deceased people. • Who had children. • Who led a noble life.
Personal	Important people in our families who have led noble lives and who have had a positive impact on us as individuals.
Unknown Ancestors	Important people in our families who we do not know for whatever reason who have led noble lives that we do not know about.
Communal	Important people in the community who have led noble lives and who have had a positive impact on the community.
Historic	Important people from historic times who have led noble lives and whose actions have had a positive impact on many for a very long time.
Mitochondrial Eve	The most recent ancestor of all humans traced through the maternal line.
Nature	The elements in the natural world.

Personal

As noted above, personal ancestors usually refer to descent and family line, blood or adoption. On December 9, 2023, a young man posts on Facebook "Happy heavenly 24th birthday son. We celebrate you on this day. Today I wear purple and I cook your favorite foods and we get your favorite red velvet ice cream cake, and we enjoy you. We shout your name in happiness not in sorrow as we thank God that he gave us the time we had with you."

Fabianna

Fabianna was born in Managua, Nicaragua. She immigrated to the United States with her family during the Nicaraguan Civil War in 1985. She lived in San Francisco's Mission District, a historically Mexican American, later Central American area of the city. She attended UC Berkeley, and later received a master's degree and credential in teaching English as a Second Language from Columbia Teachers College. After completing her MA, she attended the Universidad de Salamanca, in Spain. She spent the next 20 years traveling the world, mostly in Latin America. She traveled to El Salvador, Brazil, Guatemala, Nicaragua, Mexico, Belize, Puerto Rico, and Dominican Republic. Many of these places she visited multiple times.

Fabianna keeps an altar in an alcove off the hallway in her home. On top of an old dark wood bookshelf, she has a cluster of tealight candles, palo santo wood, and sage for incense; clusters of photographs of her grandparents; a trinket or two that belonged to one of them, such as a cross; and cards for the Catholic Church service from their funeral services adorn the shelves. She keeps the candles lit as often as she can.

When she went on a road trip, she took a picture of her grandmother as she always does. Sitting in the car before pulling out, she made a gesture and whispered something about bendiciones. "My grandmother will keep us safe on the trip," she said.

Several years ago, when she first heard of her younger sister having seizures, she ran home to her altar and prayed feverishly to her grandmother for her to intervene and heal her sister. She maintained her candle lighting and appeals through the surgery.

Unknown

While the various companies noted above make it possible to discover ancestors, for many there are still barriers to knowing exactly who some of our ancestors are by name, history, and personality. In these instances, we can always acknowledge ancestors unknown to us with an affirmation in writing or said aloud that makes clear that you care for the deceased who were helpful to others in life, although unknown to us in their death.

Communal

Asanti asserts that while ancestors most often refer to blood relatives, there are also political leaders, village heads, and so forth; people who have become leaders of the community.

Liberated Model Ethnic Studies Curriculum Consortium (LMESCC): Acknowledging Communal and Historic Ancestors

LMESCC emerged as the state of California was transitioning to a statewide law requiring all students to attend an ethnic studies class to graduate high school. The first step in this process was to craft an optional model curriculum for school districts around the state to use to create their ethnic studies course. Highly respected K–12 ethnic studies educators and higher education faculty from ethnic studies departments and Colleges of Education were selected by the community, and by the state agency managing the model curriculum development process. After the public comment process was disrupted by an organized effort to prevent the graduation requirement from being enacted, the State of California assumed management of the curriculum development process. In addition, they replaced all the authors of the initial draft of the model curriculum.

The initial writers established themselves as the *Liberated Model Ethnic Studies Curriculum Consortium.* They write curriculum and provide professional development for school districts around the state—despite their organization and individual members being targeted with lawsuits and other acts of cultural deprivation.

LMESCC frequently organizes their workshops with some of the same elements presented at the front of the American Medical Association's anti-racism strategic plan; especially land acknowledgments, ancestor veneration rituals. Theresa Montaño began one workshop by venerating Bobbi Ceriza-Houtchens, a Latina English and English language development teacher, and student advocate who taught at Arroyo Valley High School in San Bernardino City Unified School District. Bobbi had a national reputation for fighting on many fronts: She was an organizer for the National Council of Teachers of English Latino Caucus for decades and a Teacher Ambassador Fellow at the U.S. Department of Education during Barak Obama's presidency. This is an example of venerating a communal ancestor.

We all have access to communal ancestors. We can all learn about them or learn more about them. We can all appreciate them.

On another occasion, the speaker at an LESMCC opened by venerating bell hooks. This is another communal answer. On another occasion, a workshop leader venerated Carter G. Woodson, author of the 1934 classic, *The Mis-education of the Negro*. Dr. Woodson died decades ago and almost no one alive has even an indirect personal connection to him. Veneration of Dr. Woodson is veneration of a historic ancestor. Communal and historic are very similar. The difference is in degrees of separation over time.

Historic

Historic ancestors are ancestors from history. While communal and historic ancestors have a blood lineage of their own, they are important to the community for what they did during their lifetime. Thus, we call out names from history as the Jamaican poet Mutubaruka in his poem entitled "Dis Poem":

"dis poem shall say nothin' new
dis poem shall speak of time
time unlimited time undefined
dis poem shall call names
names like lumumba kenyatta nkrumah
hannibal akenaton malcolm garvey
haile selassie"

In this portion of the opening stanza, names from ancient Egypt, the decolonization era in East and West Africa, and the Black nationalist era. Historic figures are venerated for helping see new possibilities and changing the culture in enduring ways.

Mitochondrial Eve

Mitochondrial Eve is a term used for the most recent common ancestor of all living humans traced through the maternal line. Much of the mitochondria is passed down from the mother without recombination with other DNA. Based on genetic analysis, in 1987, scientists Allan Wilson, Mark Stoneking, and Rebecca Cann have been able to trace the lineage of all living humans to a single woman living in the Kalahari Desert in Southeast Africa approximately 150,000–200,000 years ago. All living humans can trace their lineage back to her. There is also a Y-Chromosome

Adam, equivalent to Mitochondrial Eve from West Africa. Genetics is a complex science. There is much more to know about Mitochondrial Eve and Y-Chromosome Adam. For the purposes of this entry, it is enough to know that based on evidence from numerous scientific fields, we can say with confidence that all humans descend from common ancestors and those ancestors came from Africa. Whether we know the names and personalities of our personal ancestors, we can venerate our common African ancestors.

Nature

Traditional Akan belief systems understand that ancestors can dwell in various aspects of the natural environment, including hills, forests, rocks, trees, mountains, and animals (Morgan & Okyere-Manu, 2020). This understanding is not limited to the Akan of Ghana, Togo, and the Ivory Coast. Resmaa Menakem has also talked about nature as ancestor. While there are ancestral veneration rituals and offerings that can be performed in nature, all we really need to do is go out in nature and listen. More details about the role of nature and natural objects in ancestral veneration follows in the next section as part of the interview with Mama C.

Ancestor Acknowledgment and Veneration with Charlotte Hill O'Neal AKA Mama C AKA A Panther in Africa

Charlotte Hill O'Neal, Mama C, was co-chair of the Kansas City Chapter of the Black Panther Party along with her husband Pete O'Neal. She has lived with her husband who is in exile in Tanzania since 1971. Arrests and imprisonment became two cultural deprivation tools or weapons the FBI used against the Black Panther Party, other Civil Rights leaders through the COINTELPRO program, and by extension the Black community as a whole. Of course, co-founders Huey Newton and Bobby Seal were targeted in this way. But many other leaders, such as Angela Davis, Asata Shakur, Erica Higgins, and David Hilliard, were also targeted. After being charged with carrying a gun across state lines, Pete and Charlotte O'Neal escaped for Algeria, where many other freedom fighters fled. This was a Black Panther Party International Headquarters (Farmsworth, 1970). Eventually, they left Algeria for Tanzania.

Fleeing the United States and landing in Tanzania afforded both the opportunity to live the true life of Black Panther service and cultural revolution. Very specifically, they built the United

African Alliance Community Center from the ground up into a flourishing place where they care for village children and host art and music education workshops, and teach about community service political theory for international travelers. Mama C developed her poetry. She studied African music. She also began practicing African spirituality. She enrolled in Ifa University to learn about the Orisha traditions. And she became a member of the Ancestor Society. Now she travels through the African continent, the Caribbean, and the U.S. counseling, teaching, and sharing her poetry and music.

The interview below occurred in May 2022 over Zoom while I was in California, and she was still in Tanzania. We were planning for a three-day workshop so I could deepen my understanding of ancestral veneration rituals, such as the ring shout and ancestor altars.

The transcript has been lightly edited to retain the wholistic conversation between the two of us as opposed to rendering Mama C as a citation in an academic paper.

Mama C is a woman of the African diaspora in a literal sense. She is a revolutionary. A homesteader. An educator. A healer. An artist and a priest whom I am honored to talk with about the role of the ancestors in Black Indigenous People of Color (BIPOC) lives (Figure 5.2).

Figure 5.2 Charlotte Hill O'Neal AKA Mama C at the Ring Shout.

00:00:00.719 → 00:00:21.419
Dale Allender: I would love to hear you say any of that again, because you were once you started, I knew, you were in a place, I said to myself I gotta record.

Mama C: Yeah, I was in a place, so I gotta get back to that place. Sometimes it's hard to back to the right moment.

00:00:21.420 → 00:00:23.820
Dale Allender: Yes, I know. You were in a zone. It was all intuitive.

00:00:24.180 → 00:01:33.030
Mama C: But hey! I'ma say it again because you know, this is something that's so close to my heart, you know: people understanding the importance of connecting with our ancestors! And you have done that brother, you are so blessed to have experienced that. You know you are so blessed to have walked on the soil that your ancestors walked on. Even if you were in the vicinity, you know you, I just—that just makes me have chills and one of the things.

That causes me to know when my ancestors are speaking to me or some of the experiences that I've had is when my flesh crawls. I call it goosebumps, I don't know if that's what you call it, but that's what I call it is goosebumps. And also, when my hair feels like electricity lifting it up. You know I used to have really long locks down my waist right.

00:01:33.150 → 00:01:33.570
Dale Allender: All right. No, I didn't know.

00:01:36.540 → 00:03:33.150
Mama C: Yes, I did yeah I had locks for like 30 years actually.

You know, when my when my mom passed in 1997, I cut them and I kept them like wrapped up like a little baby. Some I used in my artwork. And then I immediately store them again. and then, when I was initiated into Osun in 2014 I cut them again. I didn't have to, but I felt like it. But I'm mentioning that because, even when I would have these experiences with my ancestors when I add my heavy locks, I could still feel them, you know, raising up. It will feel like electricity, you know. And even now, even with you telling me what you were experiencing, it was making me have goosebumps. This means that either my ancestors approve what you were saying, or the Asé that I'm covered with, much of this from my ancestors and some are from the Orisa, they are approving of that.

You know you might know this thing called Egbe. Egbe, yes, that's the community that we chose before we came to earth, we chose that community in Orun. Which is, I guess, you could say that we can describe that as heaven. And I meet many people who I feel, are part of my Egbe. I feel you are part of my Egbe too, and I think that's why I was getting these goosebumps and all that we knew each other before. You know a lot of people don't believe in things like that, but it's true brother is not like. It's not like it's just talk, it's true.

00:03:33.630 → 00:03:34.080
Dale Allender: I believe.

00:03:34.110 00:06:27.090
Mama C: You know how sometimes you can meet somebody you say "Dang I must know you. I've seen you before. I felt you before," or whatever. When you actually might not have seen them with the eyes that you're carrying now, but you know them from when y'all were in the same Egbe. You see what I mean. And you feel it. And you don't lose that feeling. You don't lose that feeling. you can even have that feeling with with young young children, you know and.

It's it's magic to me. Magic kind of diminishes I think what I'm saying, but it is magical it's a different realm that we are honored and blessed to be in. You know what I mean. In the parlance of the 60s, we might say "man, that's a trip." You know. You know I mean? It is like you trippin'. But it's real. Even the scientists have discovered these different planes, you know. These different, dimensions, you know. They might refer to it as something else, but we who walk in our spiritual reality and embrace our spirituality, we know that those different planes are real.

You know they're real and some people can just access those very, very easily. Many people have to meditate, sit in front of your altar, hold some of the things that your ancestors love, you know, to reach that kind of a plane, or that kind of dimension.

But I think the more and more that you practice that; the more and more that you are comfortable with those feelings and are comfortable with letting that, that being inside of you. It gets really, really easy, you know. It does. It really does. Sometimes music can make me feel it. You know, like right before my dad passed away. For a few weeks, we discovered this song, and it was one day at a time. Even just saying it, that is giving me goosebumps, you know. It was [singing] "One day at a time, Dear Jesus. That's all I'm asking of you." Do you know that song? I didn't know that song.

00:06:31.110 → 00:06:31.980
Yes. My grandmother used to listen to it. On my father's side. I mean it was just like in the background, sometimes when I was really young.

00:07:03.180
Mama C: Yes, yes, yes, and so once he discovered that you know, and I'm sitting at the table, we would say at every day when he would have his dinner and everything. He would play that ev—er—y day! And you know. It is just a beautiful thing. It's just a beautiful, beautiful thing.

I'm trying to think of your questions, brother.

00:07:03.540 → 00:07:39.570
Dale Allender: So the next question was– and you really answered the one question, about just you know "How do we distinguish?" Right, How do we know? But then there were other questions, one question was "How do we acknowledge ancestors, who we know may have hurt others or who have hurt us?"

00:07:39.630 → 00:08:44.700
Mama C: And let me say one more thing about what we were just talking about, because you know everybody feels their ancestors in their own personal way. It might not be goosebumps for some people, you know it might be feeling cold; it might be feeling hot or whatever, but the important thing is that we open ourselves up to receiving these messages, you know. It might be in dreams. It might be in songs. it might be in smells, you know, but we have to open ourselves up and be comfortable with receiving those messages. You know sometimes this happens to me too.

I don't know how much time we have on here.

00:08:44.760 → 00:08:46.800
Dale Allender: We're OK. We have time.

00:08:46.890 → 00:12:05.460
Good, because I really feel like we need to have this conversation. Sometimes I see something out of the corner of my eye, you know. And I look like that. And it's almost like a shadow. It's like something that's real quick.

I'm gonna tell you something that I haven't shared with maybe a couple of people. After my dad passed, you know, and he's buried right here in our front yard there—I don't know if you know that.

After he passed, brother—and I had never experienced nothing like this. I actually saw him; it was almost like he was swimming. He was, he was in my room here, and he was up above, he was close to where the ceiling was. And I mean I could see. It wasn't like no smoke it wasn't like no, what do you call it? Steam or nothing like that, which I've experienced with one of my dogs when he passed. It was a steam that came up. But this was his whole form. I mean this was him, brother. Yeah, it didn't scare me, or anything. I was like wow. It was like he was floating like this, you know. Just floating. And then he just disappeared.

You know, and I don't tell people things like that, because sometimes people, "This mother must be off her rocker." But I think that you are experienced enough in your spirituality to know that things like that are possible, even if you haven't experienced it yourself.

You know something else that happened to me? I was at my—I mean this probably way off our topic! But you, I want to share it to you. You know, I think you know Nedra T. Williams. Maybe you don't. She is one of my Eas and I belong to her or Ele. Her spiritual house. And most of the members of that spiritual house are artists. You know so that's one thing that falls together. But I was in her house playing my instrument. And all the sudden, brother—this still blows my mind. I was way up past the ceiling, you know, and I can see myself playing that instrument. And it scared me till I screamed, you know. And I apologized to her, and this other Ea that was there. I said your neighbors are going to think I think something is going on in here, whatever because I was like "aagghh." It, it, it frightened me, but I felt like that's just how I had to respond to it. To see myself, there?! Talk about blowing my mind! You know, so I experienced things like that. You know and other people do, and some people don't. But they're still walking in their spirituality. All of us are different. All of us.

Now what was that question you brought up?

00:12:33.000 → 00:12:42.090
Dale Allender: You know. You were answering that question, you were really. I really feel like you were answering two questions at the same time, what you just said.

00:12:42.300 → 00:12:43.710
Mama C: Oh, I know what it was. Yes, said, "What if the ancestor who has, has done something terrible or was abusive or was this or was that?" Well, you know, in Orisha spirituality those people are not ancestors. You know, they just go on.

You know, our ancestors are the ones who have lived the life of what we term Ewa Pwele, which means a life of good character; a life of doing something in community: helping people; doing something positive. And those who have done atrocities, you know, for whatever reason—maybe, maybe it happened to them too, maybe they had a brutalized life. But, those kind of people are not accepted as ancestors.

I was in class one time—you know I go to Ifa University. And one of the things that they taught was we have good ancestors, who can be reincarnated, for lack of a better word. And we have bad ancestors, who unfortunately—maybe I shouldn't say unfortunately—who can't come back, you know. And because I mean that's just the law of the universe. You know those are not ancestors, they just aren't. And we can't embrace them like that. That would make me feel kind of bad, and I would say "isn't there some kind of way, we can rehabilitate them or whatever?" but apparently that's the way it is, you know. Apparently, that's the way it is.

You know, I was talking about how we can, you know, speak to our ancestors in dreams. I mean we can get messages from them from our dreams. But there's something called you're Ori, Dale. And your Ori—we choose that already before we come to earth. And your Ori Is your personal Ori—sha! That is your first Orisha. Before Osun. Before Eshu, even. Before all the orisha that you know. That is your ORI-sha! And that's where you are able to channel and touch your instincts. That's what lets you know what's right and what's wrong. And your Ori is your most important aspect of your life. And that's something that we should honor and give thanks to every day. That's what I do every day when I wake up.

Everybody got their consciousness and knows what's right or wrong, right? So that's coming from your Ori. The space that we term our Ori is at the top of our head, you know. It can be kind of where your third eye is. And that's why I like to mark here because that's not only the mark and my third eye, that's also a daily blessing. And that's also letting people know that I'm a knower. You know, I'm a knower.

Sometimes that can be dangerous letting people know that. You know, because in Orisha spirituality we understand that there are good forces in the world and they're evil forces in the world. Everything has to be balanced, you know. And those evil forces can sometimes cause you problems, right. And that's why it's important to open ourselves up to the messages that our ancestors give us because they can help us overcome these evil forces. I mean, it's just true. What can I say, you know? It is. It's really, really true.

But the point that I was making, you know, is the people who have lived immoral lives, they're not ancestors. And sometimes you might not even know that; people might be one way around their families and they might be another way when they're in public. You know what I mean? So sometimes you don't know. Sometimes you don't actually know if your relatives were living a moral life and that they went on to the ancestor realm, you know.

That's really a question that I haven't fully answered for myself, you know. I know one thing: if I have pictures of some of my, I'll call them ancestors, for lack of a better word, and they don't like me, I don't get no feeling from them, you know? They don't speak to me. I feel, like, I have to almost avert my eyes, you know. I say, "Uh oh, they must have been doing stuff that we didn't know about." You know what I mean?

So that's why it's very important for us to walk in Ewa Pwele; to live our life in Ewa Pwele, and to be surrounded by goodness that we can put back into the universe, put back into other people; because the way we live our life is the way we're going to experience our journey to the ancestral realm—or our journey to whatever ain't the ancestral realm.

And we don't really believe in hell so much. But there are different layers. You know I mean? There are different layers of Orun, I guess. Orun is actually translated as heaven. Let me think about it, brother. Let me think about that a little bit more.

Another question that you had was "How can you tell If someone was your ancestor if you were adopted or, or, you know, raised by someone else, or whatever?" You know, I think that, again, it is that feeling that your Ori gives you, you know. But it might be good to go to a Babalow who can do a divination, you know. You know before I was initiated into the Ancestors Society—did I tell you this? And you have to get a roots reading?

00:20:48.480 → 00:20:52.080
Dale Allender: No, no, no. See I didn't even know about this, the Ancestor Society.

00:20:52.410 → 00:25:32.580
Mama C: Yes, yes, you have to get what's called roots reading, right. And it's a Babalow who does it. It could be done by a Ewonefa also, but I went to a Babalow. And, you know, when he did the divination—of course, you know when a Babalow is speaking to you or an Ewonefa is speaking to you, that's not really them speaking to you. That is Ifa. Or the Orisha speaking to him if they

really are the real deal. You know, some of them try to trick you or whatever. I've never experienced that. But, what happened was, I found out that, you know, through DNA testing, I thought all my ancestry came from West Africa, right, from Cameroon, Congo, Mali, Ghana, and Nigeria. Like many of us, our ancestors come from West Africa.

But this Bablow, he said, "You think that you came to Tanzania because of the Socialist policies; because they welcomed y'all as freedom fighters"—y'all meaning me and Brother Pete—"And all that, and that you felt immediately at home." He said, "No. That was your ancestors calling you." And he ran down so much about my ancestry. That is what I carry. And not just East Africa, brother, Tanzania! Where Tanzania is now. Of course, it wasn't Tanzania back in the day, you know. But it's that same area. And I remember when I got off that plane. I got this goosebumps thing. I got the hair standing on end; my locks standing on end.

And come to find out my ancestors were artists. They were community workers. They were soothsayers. They were fishermen. Osun was our orisha. I mean this is generations ago, right. And the royalty—the royals used to come to us and ask us to, you know do divination, and tell them whatever. And apparently, you know, some of these royals weren't living a moral life and we called them out. And we have much respect in the community. We called them out, and they didn't like that. And they sold us into slavery.

And that's how, yes—oh that makes me just wanna ... (Pauses for a moment. Bows and shakes her head slowly from side to side.) And you know, so we were shipped down round the Cape of Good Hope and in South Africa and then we're taking to, either the Caribbean or somewhere in South America. I don't know if it was Brazil, maybe—I don't know where it was. And then eventually we went to North America. And that's where my ancestors who were captured from and enslaved from West Africa, they went also, of course to North Africa, and you, I mean North America.

And because of that experience, you know, of my ancestors calling out these royals which caused us to be sold into slavery, I didn't want to learn divination at all, you know. I'm learning it now. I mean I'm learning Sixteen Cowries, you know. "Sixteen cowries" or owo mçrindinlogun—that's the name given to a form of divination used by the Yoruba. The Yoruba from Nigeria are the founders of the Orisha spirituality. Sixteen Cowries is a simpler divination practice than the full Ifa divination system. It involves throwing sixteen cowrie shells onto a basketry tray and counting the number of shells which fall mouth upwards. The pattern of the fall represents one of the many stories of the Orisha that are then discussed in relation to the person seeking divination. Yes, yes and I've accepted that.

And you know what else? I'm also a daughter of Oshun, which involves bodies of water. But. I don't like to get into the ocean. I don't like to get into those kinds of big bodies of water. Why? Because I still carry that experience of our ancestors who crossed that water. And I have a fear of the water. That's something that I have to work on. You know what I mean? It really is. But you know, I feel my ancestors so strongly, brother Dale, that I could not only feel them when they were chained in the bottoms of those ships, but I can see it, you know? I can actually see it. And it's just so terrible. It's so, so terrible.

I think that's why I had claustrophobia for so many years too, you know. But I don't have that now. So far, I don't. You know I've been able to elevate myself from having claustrophobia. But that water [shakes her head from far left to far right, rocking back and forth in a long "no" gesture.]. I can get in a river. Because, you know I've been initiated. And when you've been initiated you had to get in the river, you know. And there's different rituals that have to happen. And I'm cool with that, but don't put me in nobody's ocean [laughs out loud and sighs]. It's funny how we have these ancestral memories like that. I mean they are embedded in our DNA. There's no doubt about that, you know. And again I keep harping on scientists because some people have to have empirical evidence.

00:27:49.080 → 00:27:49.860
Dale Allender: For sure right.

00:27:50.340 → 00:28:46.440
Mama C: One scientific experiment that can help us shed some light or better understand this idea of how we pass along memories, especially traumatic memories into different bodies was done with caterpillars and moths (Suri, 2014). They did a study where they gave caterpillars a whiff of nail polish remover and shocked them with electricity at the same time. Apparently, caterpillars and moths are indifferent to the smell of nail polish remover normally. But in this case, eventually, the moths avoided the odor even though there were no longer any shocks happening. And you know what, when the caterpillars metamorphosed into moths, most of them still avoided the odor as well.

From that study, they determined that even though when the caterpillars are becoming moths they break down and they reconstruct most of their tissues, traumatic memories from earlier in their life continue throughout that process and remain even after the caterpillar is a full-grown adult moth. Isn't that something? Those caterpillar memories continue to impact the moth.

And you and you know what? I got a mark here, on my head that shouldn't be there. And it's been there for so long. At one point, I said to myself, "I wonder if that mark is maybe from a time when I got hit with a machete or something, you know, generations ago." I don't know. That's awful. I know I have this here.

00:28:47.730 → 00:31:21.840

Dale Allender: What you're saying, though, I'm aware of other scientific studies that speak about epigenetic memory.

When you started talking about that mark on your head ... I know that I have had a pain right here on my right side for as long as I can remember. And one day I went to a woman who was a massage therapist at the recommendation of one of my friends. And before I got there, they told me that she was a psychic, but I learned later that she was either a practitioner of Santeria, Condomblé, Lucumi, or Ifa, but she was in that mix. But I just thought she was a psychic now. While I am getting the massage, she says, "Oh you've got some real tightness on your right side around your shoulder blade. What is that about?" I wasn't really trying to be a belligerent, but I thought, "If she's a psychic she's supposed to know some things I don't know." I replied, "I don't know what it is. Can you tell me?" "It has something to do with your dad," she said.

I had heard so many stories from when I was growing up about a time when my dad's desk stepfather shot him. The bullet lodged in his right side, somewhere near his shoulder blade. The storytellers always told a tale about a country doctor at the hospital who didn't want to take the bullet all of the way out because it was too close to his heart. The doctor said he didn't want to cause further injury to a vulnerable part of his body, this is how the story was told, but now I probably understand it differently. It's probably racism. But whatever the reason was, my father always had something lodged in him from that incident: shrapnel or buckshot or something. I would see him periodically shift his right shoulder up and back when he walked. He didn't walk like that all the time; just every now and again, as if it was causing him discomfort, an itch he couldn't scratch or a sharp point poking from inside.

And so, when she said that to me, I knew she was onto something. Because that was when he was 18 years old. I wasn't around at that time. I didn't get shot. I didn't see him get shot. I didn't hear any of the arguing, the screams. The sirens. I wasn't there. So that trauma was conveyed to me and localized in a constant knotty muscle mass between my spine and shoulder through the union of my parents. Physically. Psychically.

I've since read about those epigenetic studies we have these memories that cause us to

00:31:21.840 → 00:31:22.620
Mama C: behave.

00:31:23.400 → 00:31:37.710
Dale Allender: ... in ways, and we don't know, we don't know why we have a temperament or gesture, or what have you. But yeah. So I feel you. Feel you.

00:31:38.790 → 00:32:55.770
Mama C: I do, yes, there's so much we don't know. You know, so much we don't know. But I feel like if we just leave ourselves open to experience these things, you know. Then we will know.

It's just so much and it's so interesting and so fantastic and so magical to experience, all this, you know. And knowing that many people never will. They never will. They maybe want to experience what you, what you lived carrying that clock from your great-aunt Mae through the airport. They'll never experience it because they just can't believe. Maybe belief isn't really a part of it. It is just feeling it: instinctively knowing that those are the ancestors.

You know, I was talking about how you know our ancestors who have been able to move on to the ancestral room. They don't have to be like elders, of course. You know that, because there can be children who have passed on, who might be five years old or eight years or whatever, but they embody the wisdom of an ancestor who lived a good life, you know. And it was just part of their destiny to pass on at a young age, you know. Do you ever look at children in their face and can tell their old spirits? Have you ever experienced it?

00:35:26.730 → 00:35:32.910
Dale Allender: That was what people always said about me going up—I was older.

00:35:33.450 → 00:35:34.680
Mama C: Older yeah.

00:35:36.210 → 00:35:41.640

Dale Allender: I had a reading once from a Babalawo out in Brooklyn, Bedstuy. He was Lucumi. He was a child of Obatala. I believe his wife was a child of Obatala, as well. I am the middle child among my siblings. I have two older siblings and two younger siblings. But he said to me that I was actually at the head of the table. And the head of the family. He told me that at a really important time. My father had been re-incarcerated.

Throughout the years, I was the one that took care of my family in different ways on and off. Well, of all of my brothers and sisters, I became more stable in many ways.

00:36:57.540 → 00:36:58.860

Mama C: Wow. There is so much we don't understand you know we just gotta like swimming (Figure 5.3).

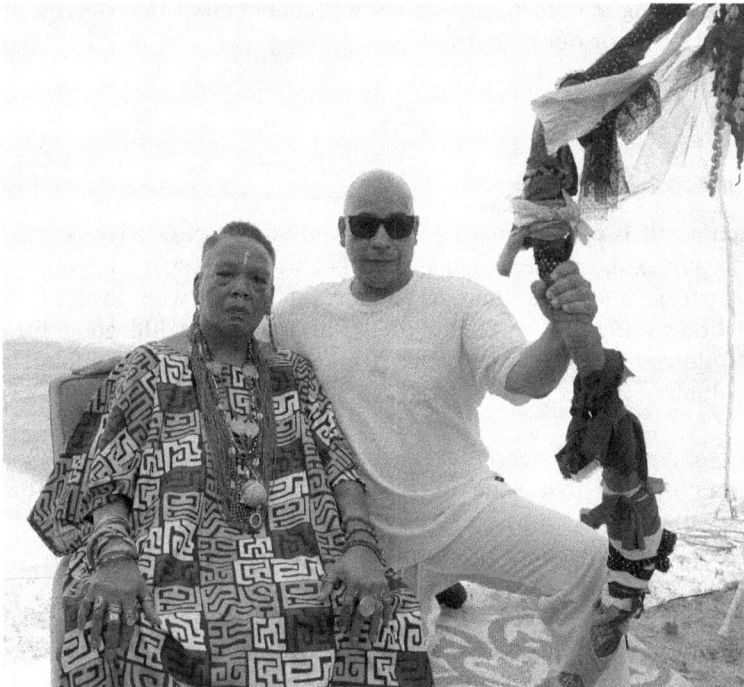

Figure 5.3 Dale Allender with Charlotte O'Neal Hill AKA Mama C after the Ring Shout.

Summary

Chapter 5 begins with a critical family history narrative that embeds an ancestor dream—a psychic-spiritual phenomenon described by psychiatrist Bruce Bynum in the Dreamlife of Families. The dimensions for thinking about and working with ancestry in professional spaces discussed include personal or family ancestors; unknown ancestors from our family; communal ancestors known and respected by many for their support and contribution to their lives; historic ancestors; Mitochondria Eve, the most recent living ancestor of all human beings traced through the maternal line; and nature, the building blocks of life and the spirit that animates life. The chapter includes the full transcript of an interview with Charlotte Hill O'Neal, former co-chair of the Kansas City chapter of the Black Panther Party with Pete O'Neal, and co-founder—also with Pete O'Neal—of the United African Alliance Community Center, a non-profit, community-based NGO, formally established in 1991 in Tanzania. O'Neal shared concepts from West African psycho-spiritual traditions, such as *Egbé,* meaning chosen family or chosen community, and *Orí,* meaning personal deity, or our conscience.

Activities

Ritual Acknowledgment

Sometimes it is enough just to understand and acknowledge personally and in public and professional spaces that we have personal, communal, and historic ancestors that are important to us, who love us, who have done things to take care of us, and to make life good for us. The following are a few steps that I take when working in groups and individuals.

1   I often begin by sharing a photo of one of my ancestors. Sometimes on the first slide of a slideshow before class or before a presentation.
2   I follow up by telling a brief story or anecdote about this ancestor, and explanation of why I am acknowledging or honoring that specific ancestor on that specific day or occasion. I keep in mind the classic African religion qualities—especially having lived a noble life or a life of service when I talk about my ancestor. I also clarify what my relationship is to that ancestor (personal, communal, historic ...).
3   I give thanks to that ancestor for the role they played in helping make me who I am on the day I am speaking.

4   I empathize with the pain my ancestor may have experienced on my behalf. I sometimes note that I too carry some of the pain from those events. And I explain to the ancestor that I am on a healing journey for myself and for them.

5   I welcome that ancestor in, to share their learning and healing with me and I pledge to listen. And I invite them to take anything from our gathering that they think will heal them.

6   I then invite others with me to acknowledge their ancestors silently or aloud.

7   I wait a few moments to allow others to process and follow suit or not. But also to be aware of the ancestral energy that is being let into the space.

Acknowledging Communal and Historic Ancestors

I see communal ancestors venerated most often in large educational or spiritual events. As noted above, LESMCC opens their professional development session by acknowledging communal ancestors to open their professional development workshops for ethnic studies teachers. I have also seen elaborate acknowledgments at the Dia de los Muertos Community Celebration at the Oakland Museum of California.

The most empowering historic ancestor veneration I experienced happened during an impromptu Black affinity gathering at a Paulo Freire and Augusto Boal workshop in Omaha, Nebraska. The workshop location called everyone to gather in a circle and call out the name of Al-Hajj Malik El-Shabazz: Malcolm X, born as Malcolm Little in Omaha, Nebraska, May 5, 1925. Suggestions for communal and historic ancestor acknowledgment follow below.

1   Identify who you need to acknowledge—be clear and be affirming. Say the name or names of the ancestor. You can say the many names that the ancestor was known by, such as nicknames, born names, chosen names, names by reputation, etc. Or you can use just one name appropriate for the occasion.

2   Identify why—sometimes when someone important to the community passes, we are compelled to honor them immediately at the opening of our events, classes, or healing sessions. Sometimes because of an anniversary date of their death or an event where they took a stand for others out loud or quietly in some way. Sometimes at the opening of a school or a clinic, there is cause to name communal or historic ancestors.

3   Recite/Read—if you are in a group, form the group into a circle. Call the ancestor's name out loud three times on your own or in unison with the group. Say something significant about the ancestor. Consider some kind of percussive music accompaniment if it feels celebratory and affirming.
4   Personalize—tell a story about why this communal or historic ancestor is important to you specifically. Again, invite others to do the same.
5   Close by calling out the ancestor's name three times again.

Ancestral Altars

Just as there are many BIPOC cultures with ancestral veneration traditions, many veneration traditions include altars as a holder of artifacts of cultural production. As such, altars are places of cultural security.

My first exploration with altars was with the Dia de los Muertos celebrations at the Oakland Museum of California, and later, through the work of African Art historian Robert Ferris Thompson's extensive work on African altars. And eventually through training with Charlotte O'Neal on African ancestral altars. Dr. Margarita berta-Avila's Participatory Action Research (PAR) and PAR Entre Mundos workshops demonstrate an instance of the incorporating altars into formal instruction.

Some common elements:

1   Objects from nature
2   Pictures
3   Artifacts
4   Favorite items
5   Stories
6   Poems
7   Memories

Critical Family History

"This work generated a research process I call Critical Family History, which involves locating ancestors within historical contexts shaped by membership in sociocultural groups and by conflict over power and resources. It includes genealogical research drawing on sources such as family stories and documents, vital statistical records, military records, digital newspapers, and property records ..."

Sleeter, C. (2019). Critical family history. In Cuauhtin, R. T., Zavala, M., Sleeter, C., & Au, W. (Eds.) (2019). *Rethinking Ethnic Studies.* Rethinking Schools Publications (p. 126).

The following activity has been adapted from the article by Christine Sleeter, quoted and cited above. I facilitate this activity in my master's level ethnic studies course for educators, and in professional development in services for teachers, school counselors, social workers, and administrators. The goal of this assignment is to participate in, evaluate, and analyze a model K–12 ethnic studies assignment.

Recall	Think of a family memory or story, ideally something about your grandparents, or great grandparents. Ask other family members to help you recall details. Consider using one of the genealogy websites, such as FamilySearch or Ancestry.com.
Record	Write it down. Focus on the story itself. Ask others to review your initial draft to determine if there are any details missing and add new details if needed. Don't be concerned about contradictory details from others. Incorporate alternatives where relevant. Add your text, artifact images, or other illustrations to a PowerPoint slideshow to share with others.
Relate	Connect your story to the daily lives of other communities ethnically and/or racially different from your own during that time and/or in that location. Use the questions below from Sleeter as a guide: 1 What laws and other processes that benefit white people (such as Jim Crow laws, union membership, voting, banking, schooling, etc.), shaped opportunities for my ancestors? 2 What kind of relationships did my ancestors have with members of other groups around them? 3 What role did my ancestors play in the colonization of Indigenous people? 4 What was my ancestors' location to the growing capitalist economy, and how did that location impact them? 5 Did any of my ancestors work for equity and justice? 6 How did patriarchal systems and norms play out in my family's history?
Reflect	Think about how your story can help you answer or speculate about answers to the following questions: 1 How much of my family history was forgotten or suppressed? 2 How and why was it forgotten or suppressed? 3 What happened to the diverse culture and languages my ancestors brought?

(Continued)

Review	Review your critical family history with others. Notice their reactions.
Rewrite	Update your family story with new information and insight, and credit all sources (human, print, digital, archival, etc.) in APA format.

Suggestions for Further Study

The resources below are presented as a critical annotation so as to provide readers with context for their review of the resource ... identifies specific aspects ...

1 Podcasts:

   Podcasts are an increasingly valuable platform for the dissemination of and engagement with professional expertise, traditional and Westernized. Below is a list of podcasts that I have used personally and professionally. These podcasts are located on Apple, Spotify, YouTube, and other platforms.

   a The Ancestors First, Period. A Little Ju Ju Podcast Episode 1 November 4, 2018. https://podcasts.apple.com/us/podcast/ep-1-ancestors-first-periodt/id1444197888?i=1000424317076

      In this episode, the host describes African American and African-based practices for ancestor veneration.

   b Ancestors. Beyond Belief BBC Radio 4 Episode May 29, 2017. https://podcasts.apple.com/us/podcast/ancestors/id261779770?i=1000385930663

      This episode facilitates a discussion among a geneticist, a genealogist, and an archeologist about the universal and culturally specific interest in ancestry.

   c Honoring my enslaved ancestors parts 1 and 2. Code Switch. National Public Radio. https://podcasts.apple.com/us/podcast/code-switch/id1112190608?i=1000617766775

   d Ancestor Demons? Hoodoo Plant Mamas Episode 1 October 15, 2020. https://podcasts.apple.com/us/podcast/ep-1-ancestor-demons/id1536994730?i=1000495695875

      This podcast is similar to "A Little Ju Ju," but not repetitive. Both offer important insights and reinforce each other. This podcast highlights everyday ancestry veneration practices within African American culture and challenges the culture to embrace a more African-based understanding of those practices. This podcast provides instruction on creating ancestors' altars.

e Ancestors: Our Psychological Inheritance. This Jungian Life Episode 105 April 1, 2020. https://podcasts.apple.com/us/podcast/ancestors-our-psychological-inheritance/id1376929139?i=1000470263658

Three European and Euro-American Jungian analysts explore ancestry and ancestor veneration from Universalist Jungian lens. As a student of Sigmund Freud, Jung was seeking unconscious motivation for conscious behavior while bound to his own cultural context. They were both seeking something deeper than surface culture. The expansion of awareness of ancestry beyond even the sacred seven generations.

f Ancestor Veneration and How to Connect with Your Spirits. Sage Yo Soul Podcast. Episode 6 August 7, 2021. https://podcasts.apple.com/us/podcast/6-ancestor-veneration-and-how-to-connect-with-your-spirits/id1562953833?i=1000530858483

This podcast episode begins with a personal narrative of ancestor veneration.

2 Music

a Ndegiocelo, M. (199_) Akel Dama. Cookie the anthropological mixtape.

Blends communal and heritage ancestors. Invokes Eldridge Clever and Langston Hughes. Narrates a story of bloodline.

b Sister Sledge (CITE) We are Family.

3 Books
4 Video Series: Who is Nicka Smith (BlackProGen Live) https://www.youtube.com/channel/UCDfGEwZ7P8kHvvr-9iChExA

A practical conversation about genealogy methods, tools, and experiences in a witty, intelligent presentation from a group of professional genealogist who are mostly Black and Latinx women.

a Researching while Black
b Probate

5 DNA Services

a African Ancestry https://africanancestry.com

African Ancestry is a for-profit corporation boasting one of the largest, if not the largest collection of DNA samples from people of African descent living on the African continent. This company specializes in identifying the specific African ethnic group with whom diaspora Africans are related.

6   Genealogy Services

   a   Family Search https://www.familysearch.org/en/

Family Search offers a free genealogy site similar to other commercial sites in that it connects to a range of databases, such as the National Archives for vital records. This is not a DNA database.

Chapter 6

Mindfulness

Introduction

Dr. Bynum identifies Kemetic cultures from Ancient Egypt as the source of meditative sciences often associated solely with India. His argument for Kemetic culture as the source is laid out in a full, rich trans-disciplinary text on par with Cheik Anta Diop's work that precedes Bynum, and whose work Bynum references. A primary purpose of this chapter is to return mind/body awareness disciplines as cultural practices to BIPOC communities. And to encourage all allied health professionals to punctuate and initiate their activities for themselves and with their clients and patients with mindfulness transitions and activities. Embracing mindfulness meditation practices supports cultural security at a deep structure level.

First, I will continue to share critical family history vignettes; in this instance, focusing on my lifelong exploration of mind, body, and spirit relationships through sitting and moving meditation practices such as chi gong exercises, walking meditation, and drumming, on my own and with groups. The narratives contextualize and foreshadow selected research describing cognitive and social value of meditation practices.

Critical Family History

My grandmother took care of our family off and on throughout my young life during the 1970s and early 1980s. She always lived nearby so I visited her to eat grits and eggs on Sunday morning. She let my father drive her car. And sometimes me and my four brothers and sisters, along with our parents would live with my grandmother and her husband in their two-bedroom apartment in Cleveland, or Milwaukee, or Waukesha. If we were at grandmother's house on Saturday afternoon, I would hide in her bedroom and watch Kathleen Hitchcock teach Hatha yoga on channel 10 or 36. I had never seen or heard anything like it before on television.

DOI: 10.4324/9781003177500-9

My grandmother's bedroom became a fleeting sanctuary with alcohol and arguments in the other rooms. It became a place not simply to hide and eat, but by happenstance healing.

I remember hearing the hypnotic flute and watching Hitchcock's posture and flowing arms; and the trailing duplicates of her body that the producer, H. Jon Miller, created for the opening credits. Kathleen Hitchcock's steady, melodious flow expressed insight about our body, breathing, and their relationship to the mind. I mostly watched her explain and demonstrate yoga postures, especially at first. But eventually, I tried a few stretches. I was especially attracted to the breathing exercises. My body felt like the calm I heard in Kathleen's voice after I would follow her directions, breathing in as I raised my arms shoulder level, breathing in again as I opened my arms wide, then exhaling as I bent forward. My lungs were charged with energy, but my body was stable and calm.

The summer after eighth grade, I found a magazine hidden on my grandfather's bookshelf back in Cleveland, during a now-rare road trip to his house with my parents. The magazine had directions for meditation and progressive relaxation exercises. I was intrigued. My grandfather told me to take it home, along with the other *Time Life* book collections he managed to squeeze into our car before getting on Interstate 90 West and heading back to our home in Waukegan, Illinois.

When we were home, I laid in bed at night, tightening and loosening groups of muscles according to the directions in the magazine article: face and neck; shoulders, biceps, and fists; and so on. After tightening, I would observe the warm flow into the relaxed muscle group. And I observed my breathing, finding a deep and slow rhythm on its own as I progressed through each muscle group. I felt relaxed, my adolescent angst soothed. I continued to practice over the next several weeks.

Sometimes I would lay in bed and just listen to my breathing without doing the progressive relation. The more I listened, the lighter my feet and legs began to feel. I had never known such peacefulness being with myself. Then my hands would lose their heaviness as well. I stopped as the lightness moved into my hands. I didn't know where I would "go" if I kept observing and the lightness moved into my whole body. I needed more reading or a mentor to guide my mindfulness practices.

I took up the study of yoga and meditation in earnest after high school and throughout my undergraduate schooling. I first studied with Nina Johnson at the Himalayan Institute of Milwaukee. Nina taught classes in joints and glands exercises, beginning hatha yoga, and meditation classes. She also initiated me with a seed mantra, a single-syllable sound in the Sanskrit language to repeat in my mind as a focal point for meditation. I read books, attended lectures, and discussed the content of my reading with others. Most importantly, I practiced a full range of deep breathing exercises, mantra meditation practices, and chanting out loud. I practiced meditation on my own, with friends, at retreats, and regular monthly meetings.

Nina also introduced me to Dr. Usharbudh Arya (who later changed his name to Swami Veda Bharati), and Swami Rama—their teacher. In addition to his lifelong work as a meditation teacher, Dr. Arya was a professor of Sanskrit language at the University of Minnesota in Minneapolis.

I studied under Dr. Arya for several years after Nina first introduced us at a gathering in northern Illinois. I studied perception, motivation, sensation, and personality. I learned about the role of the breath in facilitating and regulating my thinking, feelings, and behavior. I wasn't dealing directly with racialized trauma, but I was releasing some of the tension. I was opening "resource." I was tapping into creativity and agency. I was able to stop and reflect and not just live in the cycles of dysfunction resulting from the racialized trauma.

Most of my reading and reflection at the time was mystical and philosophical. The bulk of reading material available at the time had a spiritual bent, being associated directly or indirectly with ancient Hindu or Buddhist scriptures. As with all religions, there was also a psychological paradigm out of which the practices evolved, and which the practices impacted. There were some efforts at the time to substantiate the psychological and physical benefits of mindfulness practices, such as Rudolph Balentine's studies on diet and nutrition and Swami Ajaya's book on yoga psychology. Today, there is extensive research on the impact of meditation practices on our neurobiology, physiology, social behaviors, and individual cognition.

One of the ways that these practices were benefiting me at that time was reducing my stress hormone, cortisol. My body must have been flooded with it. I was also releasing tension held in my body. The time I took to engage with Kathleen Hitchcock, lay in my bed and breathe, or study deeply was reducing that fight, flight, or freeze response.

I reflected on my practice while doing an internship at a residential treatment center for boys while studying to be a social worker in the 1980s. We were not taught any grounding rituals or mindfulness practices in our coursework during that time, but I was sure the residents at the treatment center could benefit from reduced stress after doing some deep breathing or other meditation practices. I felt the same way about the students I was teaching in my teaching observation and student teaching placements. I wanted to incorporate mindfulness practices into the classroom when I taught high school, but there was still too much negative attention and vocal critiques equating visualization and relaxation practices with witchcraft and satanism.

Ethnic Studies: A History of Gangs Class at Oakland Unified School District

However, nearly 20 years later I was asked to teach a pilot Ethic Studies class at a K–12 full-service grade 7 through 12 high school. The school had a medical clinic, counseling services, public health services, social workers, and other support systems for students. The school was in East Oakland, California—a vibrant and beautiful community with some of the highest concentrations of poverty in the city, especially before the gentrification the increase after 2014. Although I never observed violence at the school, the area was carefully cut up by rival gangs. And the school was put on frequent lockdowns due to the violence just outside the school doors at bus stops, crosswalks, and street corners.

This was nearly six years before California legislators voted to make ethnic studies a high school graduation requirement. The school's administration constructed the pilot class to serve as a course in transition from an after-school program sponsored by the school and run by a gang interventionist non-profit, into a formal ethnic studies class. As the instructional lead, I had to adapt the non-profit's curriculum to fit an ethnic studies paradigm and integrate the program's founders: a recently retired critically minded Black male prison guard and a recently released Peruvian inmate as co-instructors.

In addition to examining ethnic-specific voices, critical analysis of socio-historic structures and events that gave rise to different gangs in California and critical resistance strategies to constructs such as disproportionate minority contact, I designed an opening ritual with at least three different mind-body awareness practices, including breath awareness, Kinin, or some other form of walking or moving meditation and a few moments of drumming and other percussion music. We committed to beginning every class in this way.

In addition to the practices, we talked about taking opportunities to slow down, look, and listen to overserve as often as possible. And we reflected on how our physiology changes and what that feels like when we have encounters with the police. As instructors, we were working to help students understand the importance of being in touch with themselves in all high-stress situations, so they are better able to make the most life-preserving and affirming decisions for everyone involved.

One day while driving to the school for class, the school secretary sent me a text message, telling me to wait for the latest lockdown to end before I came in. When I arrived, I sat in my car outside the school looking up at the turquoise sky through the palm trees. Police helicopters circled, searching for shooting suspects on the move through the neighborhood. I waited for what seemed like half the class period.

When all clear was called, I rushed into class, visibly thankful for the close of the lockdown. I worked frantically to set up my PowerPoints, hoping to salvage what I had left of the now-shortened class period. I decided to jump right into the content since we had missed a chunk of class time by the threat of violence. The students were not having it. They were unattentive, overly animated, occasionally disruptive, and once or twice combative. Lockdowns can be triggering to students who are used to having people in the community or their family as a target of police search, interrogation, or arrest regardless of the reason. Even if not triggering, prolonged "shelter-in-place" orders or lockdowns can be stressful in a variety of ways.

I called out to the class, "What is going on? Why is it so difficult to focus today?" It was a lame question. I was equally off after sitting in the car and losing class time. And I wondered what was happening in the neighborhood. "We didn't do our breathing, sir." A few of the students responded. I said, "You're right. We didn't." And so I stopped everything I was doing, gathered everyone together, and moved through our normal opening class rituals.

Qi Gong in the Twin Cities' Outer Rung

I have worked as a consultant for the National Urban Alliance, teaching teachers in Minneapolis St. Paul area schools aspects of The Pedagogy of Confidence since 2012. For one year, I worked with a middle school in Little Canada, MN, a town in the outer rung suburbs where a voluntary desegregation order had been in effect for the public schools; ten miles from Falcon Heights, where Philando Castille was shot by the police; and five miles from St. Anthony where Philando Castille worked in a school cafeteria.

I met with the teachers, counselors, and district diversity officer for the second time in late September 2016. In between then and my first visit during the spring, Castille had been shot. Black Lives Matter led demonstrations in the middle school; students marched to the school-district building headquarters calling for ethnic studies education. And between that first visit in May and January 2017, eight hours drive west, thousands of water protectors representing 300 American Indian tribes and many non–Native American activists gathered near the Standing Rock Sioux reservation in North Dakota to protest against the oil pipeline development known as the Dakota Access Pipeline. Finally, on my fourth visit to Little Canada, Donald Trump had been elected the 45th U.S. president.

Four years later, of course the tensions from increased police violence erupted. But during the morning of my last visit, the principal assigned me to spend time with a group of about 200 students in the school's theater. Most of the seventh and eighth graders were in the cafeteria, having a pancake breakfast and participating in the end-of-the-year award ceremony. My group did not win any awards. Most were with me for disciplinary reasons. They were not being fed or celebrated. They were nonetheless amused enough to follow me through a few qi-going exercises after they had all shuffled into the theater. During the exercise and for a few moments after, the noise subsided and the students' facial tension settled. I told them from the stage that they were beautiful.

I continued to include mindfulness practices in my professional development and youth work in Minneapolis; Buffalo, New York; and Redwood City, California. Now, in 2023, the California Faculty Association includes a grounding activity as a regular part of their meetings. Thus, many people are incorporating mind/body awareness activities into their professional spaces. At the same time, we are also experiencing decreased mental health across a range of age categories and demographic groups. And we have a shortage of mental health care workers. We cannot say enough about mindfulness practices, especially for the most marginalized and minoritized communities. The following review of selected studies should deepen or reinforce knowledge about mindfulness practices as a regular discipline.

African American and Latinx

Although there is a growing body of quantitative and qualitative, medical and social science research on meditation and mindfulness practices, there is limited research specifically looking at mindfulness practices with minoritized and marginalized communities, such as African Americans and Latinx individual or families. In her review of literature, Kimberly Alline Davis (2019) notes, "the summary of results included limited research regarding the use of mindfulness-based interventions with at-risk African American youth; however, the studies that utilized mindfulness with this population demonstrated positive outcomes. Themes in Davis' review included decreases in depressive and anxiety symptoms and increases in focus and attention, self-awareness, and emotional regulation." While Davis' review included studies that demonstrated cultural relevance in utilizing interventions specific to the needs of at risk African American youth, recommendations from her full study suggest a need for more attention to cultural relevance in designing and recruiting for mindfulness interventions.

Based on their findings correlating high mindfulness to lower rates of perceived stress among African American students, Wright et al. (2018) recommends student health center providers (doctors, nurse practitioners, nurses, counselors, and psychologists) screen students for perceived stress levels and offer mindfulness as a technique to relieve stress, anxiety, and stress-related health conditions. In their study on the *Effects of Qigong Exercise on Physical and Psychological Health among African Americans,* Chang et al. found that qi-gong exercises have the potential to improve the physical ability and function, and spiritual well-being of African Americans and needs further testing in a randomized clinical trial. And Quinn Thomas (2016) reveals that mindfulness practice has a significant effect in reducing the stress of racism.

In an earlier study, Zayda Vallejo and Hortensia Amaro (2009) adapted their Mindfulness-Based Stress Reduction (MBSR) program for a community-based addiction treatment setting serving highly marginalized and poor African American and Latina women with histories of trauma. They taught the class to contribute to skills the women were being taught to help prevent relapse. Specific strategies included body scan, seated meditation, Hatha yoga, and walking meditation. Adaptations included avoiding traumatized areas of the body during the mental scans, decreasing length of time for seated meditation, and beginning walking meditations at a faster pace and then gradually slowing down. Each class was divided into five segments comprising (a) a welcome meditation, (b) setting out the objectives of the class, (c) a brief didactic psychoeducational presentation based on each theme of the class, (d) experiential and formal practices, and (e) readings of recovery literature and poems by the participants and setting assignments for the next class. With appropriate adaptations, mindfulness can be implemented successfully for relapse prevention in early recovery. The women in the study rated the class high on exit surveys indicated high levels of acceptability and satisfaction.

In another more recent study measuring the feasibility and acceptability of a community-based mindfulness practice with Latinx families, Tobin et al. found that while several adolescents in the study struggled with distractions from peers, overall responses suggest that parents and children found the program convenient and enjoyable, and perceived benefits from the curriculum (Tobin et al., 2021).

Marginalization and Other Stressors

In addition, the following studies can illuminate the potential of mind/body awareness practices as supportive of cultural security.

Another study conducted four sessions of a brief mindfulness intervention training for a cohort of college students with histories in foster care. Researchers found that the brief sessions resulted in significant short-term reductions in stress levels and increases in sleep quality for the cohort.

They concluded that mindfulness and similar interventions can help other vulnerable college student populations, as well (Gray et al., 2018).

In a randomized controlled experimental study, Chang et al. sought to determine the effects of a meditation program for nurses. They found that the experimental group receiving an eight-week meditation program reported that the quality of their life improved significantly after the experiment, compared with the control group. Chang determined, therefore, that meditation allows nurses to become aware of changes during life, make choices, behave freely as intended, get involved in the changes, and ultimately maintain a more positive emotional state and quality of life (Chang et al., 2016).

Lee et al. (2017) found in their study that meditation practice, with its intentions to cultivate a mindful existence and positive emotions, can be beneficial for women trauma survivors with co-occurring disorders. Meditation can enhance their capacity to attend to the present, to stay calm, and to better regulate their emotions. Further, meditation can increase the chances of benefiting from treatment, and integrating their trauma experiences.

Queen Sugar *Season 6 Episode 4*

Queen Sugar is a television series produced by Oprah Winfrey and Ava DuVernay based on the novel written by Natalie Baszile. The novel tells the stories of an intergenerational and blended Black family from St. Joseph, Louisiana. The series explores the legacy of slavery, Black farming, miscegenation, professional sports, white supremacy, police violence, and local political corruption. The series frequently depicts relational struggles toward integrity, solidarity, and self-respect. In the scene illustrated in the script below, Micah is learning how to practice meditation from his friend, Isaiah, in Micah's room at a Black fraternity house, where they are students at Xavier University.

(Knocking at door)

Isaiah:	Yo.
	You wanna roll to that Delta party?
Micah:	I don't know, really.
Isaiah:	What's good with you, man?
Micah:	Jordana kicked me to the curb.
Isaiah:	Oh, for flowers?
	Damn! That's cold.
Micah:	Wasn't over flowers. I think she's just not that into me.
Isaiah:	You were just hitting. Wasn't love, right?

Micah: I don't know. I'm not a love and leave 'em kinda guy.
           Can't really separate my mind and body like that.
Isaiah: I'm same.
           Well, it just makes us human.
           There's no shame in that.
Micah: Yeah, I don't think I'm gonna go.
           Feel really like, out of it.
Isaiah: You got a lot going on.
           All right, your parents hooked up again, you're worried about your family back home, you got midterms coming up and you just got kicked to the curb.
           Your life's a little extra right now.
Micah: No, my life is crazy right now.
Isaiah: All right.
           Come on.
           Sit.
           Close your eyes.
           Just be still.
Micah: (Scoffs) What's that supposed to do?
Isaiah: Chill your tense ass out.
           It's meditation.
           All right, it works for me, and it could work for you.
Micah: I don't know I'm from Cali and everything, but I don't know about …
Isaiah: Look, it gives your mind a chance to pause.
           And you can choose what you wanna focus on.
Micah: (Exhales) All right.
Isaiah: Pay attention to how you breathe.
           You remain present in the here and now.
           (Chuckles)
           And you can release everything else.
           What's the worst it could do?
Micah: (Exhales)

Later in the episode, Micah shares insights with his mother about how he is dealing with his anxiety. He shares that he has been able to choose how to respond to stressors. Soon after, in another scene, Isaiah comes back to Micah's room and asks if he is still meditating. Micah shares that he is trying. Isaiah informs him that if he practices daily, it is easier to let things go and get into a meditative state. Micah shares that this is what he is experiencing, and that he likes it. In the next episode, he shares with his mother that has learned that he can't prevent trouble that has happened in the past or that may come up for him in the future, but that he can control how he responds to it. Micah's realization is the goal of mindfulness practices.

Two episodes later, Micah is still referencing his meditation practice. The extended storyline is important because it keeps this practice in the mind of the viewer. It models that he engaged this practice over time and that it impacted him positively. It is also not an isolated storyline. For seven seasons, the series demonstrated action, reflection, and communication on efforts to improve mental health and relationships through African Indigenous spiritual practices, communal therapy, and meditation. This narrative is also a critical amplification of themes that the executive producer, Oprah Winfrey, has expressed in other productions.

Summary

Chapter 6 began with a quote from Dr. Bruce Bynum about ancient African meditation traditions, followed by a critical family history vignette focusing on my lifelong exploration of mind, body, and spirit relationships through sitting and moving meditation practices such as qi-gong exercises, walking meditation, and drumming, on my own and with groups. The narrative described instances of mindfulness practices in unique teaching and treatment contexts. The narratives were followed by research describing cognitive and social value of meditation practices with trauma treatment, addiction relapse prevention for low socioeconomic African American and Latinx women, stress related to racism among African American college students, perceived stress by African American college students, and qi-gong practice among African American women college students. The chapter closes with a reflection on a 2021 scene from a television adaptation of a novel depicting two African American men in college learning to meditate together.

Activities

Chocolate, Skittle, or Mint on the Mouth

I learned this practice from my sister, who is a middle school teacher. It is a good low-risk, fun activity to begin with.

1 Unwrap candy.
2 Look at it. Notice its colors, shape, size, and texture.
3 Smell it to see what scent it carries. Fruity? Coffee? Milky?
4 Place the candy in your mouth.
5 Hold on the candy on your tongue.
6 Observe the candy on the tongue.

7   Observe the body's reaction to the candy just sitting there. What happens to the flavor? What happens to the jaw? What happens to the inside of the mouth? What thoughts come into the mind while you are holding the candy?
8   Hold for as long as you can.
9   Slowly start eating.
10 Observe.
11 Share your experiences either by writing them down or talking with someone.

Counting Breathing

This simple breathing exercise can be done anywhere with very little effort. Jennifer Sweeton (2019) identifies five research studies whose findings state that this exercise can reduce stress and anxiety, increase quality of life, reduce blood pressure, and improve self-regulation, reduce inflammation, and intrusive memories. It is a good activity for beginning mindfulness practice.

This is a good practice to incorporate right before routine labs, such as bloodwork. It is a good practice for technicians to do alongside their patients. It is similarly good in counseling, education, or any human communicative or service-oriented interaction.

1   Sit with your back against a chair.
2   Focus on the weight of your body in your seat.
3   Focus on where you are touching the chair with your back, arms, and legs.
4   Focus on the feeling of your feet against the floor.
5   Focus on your breathing without forcing yourself to breathe hard or to hold your breath.
6   Focus on the rise and fall of your stomach as you breathe in and out.
7   Now when you breathe in, count the number "one."
8   When you breathe out, count the number "two."
9   Repeat: when you breathe in "one," when you breathe out "two."
10 Continue counting your breathing for about five minutes or until you are ready to stop.

Joints and Glands Exercises

I first practiced these gentle exercises in an introductory Hatha yoga class in 1984. The first two weeks/two sessions of the yoga class consisted of these slow, gentle movements (Rama, 1977). I purchased the mimeographed book at the Yoga Society of Milwaukee, later the

Himalayan Institute of Milwaukee. I have been using that book to practice these light stretches on my own for over 30 years. And I incorporate them into my teaching and advising experiences frequently.

1   Head Rolls

   a   Stand with back straight, feet aligned with shoulders, and arms resting by the sides.
   b   Or sitting.
   c   Gently bend the head at the neck, causing it to lean forward.
   d   Gently lift the head and move it backward until you are looking at the ceiling.
   e   Slowly and gently repeat at least three times, increasing the bend forward and backward. You should feel gentle stretching.
   f   Pause in the center with your head upright so your eyes are looking forward.
   g   Turn your head slowly and gently all the way to the left; pause momentarily.
   h   Return your head to the front in one slow, graceful movement.
   i   Turn your head slowly and gently all the way to the right; pause momentarily.
   j   Slowly and gently repeat at least three times, increasing the turn to the left and to the right. You should feel gentle stretching.

2   Shoulder Raise

   a   Continue standing with feet aligned with shoulders, and arms resting by the sides.
   b   Or sit up straight, but comfortably, feet aligned with shoulders, and arms resting by your side.
   c   Gently raise shoulders straight up toward the ears, hold for three seconds, and then release.
   d   Pause for a moment and observe how your shoulders, arms, and hands feel.
   e   Repeat at least three times, raising your shoulders higher each time.

3   Outstretched Arms
   This practice is good for gathering energy and sharpening focus. I guide large groups through this practice before presentations.

   a   Continue standing, feet aligned with shoulders, and arms resting by the sides. Or sit in similar fashion.
   b   Raise arms to shoulder.
   c   Stretch out to the sides.
   d   Breathe in.

e   Slowly fold arms at the elbows.
f   Join palms.
g   Stretch arms in front.
h   Breathe out.
i   Repeat 3–5 times.
j   Observe the breath.

Kinin

There are many different types of walking meditation exercises. Jennifer Sweeton (2019) describes slow-walking and fast-walking mindfulness practices. I frequently begin my ninth-grade ethnic studies classes with this walking meditation practice. Walking meditation can be helpful in a group education, counseling, or advising sessions. Mindfulness walking practices can reduce stress and allostatic load (Streeter et al., 2012); increase ability to concentrate (Kerr et al., 2011); and increase the volume of several brain areas, such as the hippocampus (Hariprasad et al., 2013); dorsolateral prefrontal cortex (Wei et al., 2013); and insular (Villamure et al., 2015). Mindfulness walking exercises can be done by most as long as the person or people can stand and walk slowly for short distances.

1   Stand with head slightly bowed, eyes looking at the ground in front, and palms lightly clasped at the waist or bellybutton.
2   Slowly walk alone or as a single-file group in a clockwise circle.
3   Walk around the circle at least three times.
4   Slow your pace each time you go around the circle.

Progressive Relaxation

Progressive relaxation involves alternate tensing and relaxing of different muscle groups throughout the body, followed by tensing all muscle groups throughout the body all at the same time and ending by releasing. The process is often repeated two or three times with short pauses in between to observe the effect on breathing, thinking, and feeling. During the pauses, it is easier to see how closely the releasing of physical tension is associated with the release of mental tension. Clinical Trauma Psychologist and Neuroscientist Jennifer Sweenton (2019) says that this activity reduces cortisol levels, reduces depression, and reduces headaches.

1   Focus on the forehead. Tense and relax.
2   Focus on the Jaw. Tense and relax.
3   Focus on the eye. Gently tense and relax.

4   Focus on the neck. Tense and relax.
5   Focus on the arms: shoulders, biceps, forearm, wrists, and hands. Tense and relax.
6   Focus on the torso: chest, abdomen, and lower back. Tense and relax.
7   Focus on the legs: hips, thighs, knees, calves, and feet. Tense and relax.
8   Now observe your entire body.
9   Tense and relax every muscle all at once. Hold. Then relax.
10   Observe your breathing.
11   Repeat the process at least once or twice to deepen the relaxation.
12   Always pause and observe your breathing as often as possible.

Location, Location, Location

1   Sit with hands empty and placed loosely on the lap. Look straight ahead with eyes open or closed. Place the feet on the floor.
2   Feel your legs and back against the surface where you are sitting.
3   Feel your feet against the floor and inside of your shoes.
4   Feel your hands resting against your lap.
5   Listen to all of the sounds in the room, in your home, and anything you can hear outside.
6   Say to yourself:

   a   "My name is (say your full name)."
   b   "I live at (say your full address, including city and state)."
   c   "I was born in (say the name of the place you were born)."
   d   "I believe (say something about what you believe and how you demonstrate this belief)."
   e   "I can (say something about what you can do)."

7   Open your eyes.

Suggestions for Further Reading

1   Menakam, R. (2017). *My Grandmother's Hands: Racialized Trauma and the Pathway to Mending Our Hearts and Bodies.* Central Recovery Press.

   Although referenced several times throughout this book, Resmaa Menakem's two books are whole systems within themselves. He addresses racialized trauma through somatic abolitionism, a body practice with an accompanying long-term racial liberation project. *My Grandmother's Hands* and the *Quaking of America* listed below are not only books to read, but they also offer systematic practices that the author recommends should commit to practice with others for an extended period of time.

2 Menakam, R. (2022). *Quaking of America: An Embodied Guide to Navigating Our Nation's Upheaval and Racial Reckoning.* Central Recovery Press.

3 Parker, G. (2020). *Restorative Yoga for Ethnic and Race-Based Trauma.* Singing Dragon.

This book by psychologist and yoga therapist Dr. Gail Parker explains ethnic and race-based trauma for therapists and encourages the incorporation of specific restorative yoga practices for healing ethic and race-based trauma where it is lodged in the body. As president of the Black Yoga Teachers Alliance, Dr. Parker is also speaking to a growing multi-racial and multi-ethnic yoga students and teachers.

4 Balentine, R. Ed. (1977). *Joints and Glands Exercises as Taught by Sri Swami Rama.* Himalayan Institute Press.

Joints and glands exercises is the source of several mindfulness practices listed above. Sri Swami Rama was a monk from India who came to the United States in the 1960s. He established the Himalayan Institute, a worldwide educational and medical organization with centers in Europe, Asia, and the United States based on the science of yoga.

5 Hersey, T. (2022). *Rest Is Resistance: A Manifesto.* Little Brown Spark.

Chapter 7

Relationship

Introduction

In this chapter, I will discuss the importance of relationships in cultural security and the role of educators and allied health professionals as advocates and facilitators of relations within Black Indigenous People of Color (BIPOC) families and communities when children and families interact with social service agencies. This chapter will also discuss relationship-building considerations and activities for educators and allied health professionals working with BIPOC clients and students. As with each chapter, a critical family history narrative introduces concepts and practices identified and reflected upon later. The narrative is followed by highlights from the 2006 study by the NICHD and NCATE discussing the role of relationships in cognitive and social development, and a charge to teacher educators to apply this information in teacher training. Next, the chapter explores the role of social workers and allied health professionals in prioritizing placements within biological and cultural families to avoid separation where possible. The chapter concludes with reflections on embodied practices for promoting or antagonizing relationships, such as affinity groups, unconscious bias, language practices.

Critical Family History: Black Men Healers

The first time my father escaped police custody, he left Ohio altogether. Bail bondsmen paid the court for his release from jail in downtown Cleveland, pending a trial on felony charges. My mother went with him. My grandmother, and her ride-or-die boyfriend, Roland "Randy" Leroy Randleman, followed. My grandmother followed my father into fugitivity. She followed her son out of Ohio in 1973 just as she followed him out of Black Appalachia communities from northeastern Ohio and West Virginia and into Cleveland in 1959. Sometime after, my grandmother's sisters, Donna Jean and Eunice, moved to Cleveland, as well.

DOI: 10.4324/9781003177500-10

While they were all on the run, I lived with my aunt Donna, and her husband/partner Randolph Randleman. Everyone called Randolph "Bus." I don't know why. Maybe because he was built like a bus: high, square forehead, square jaw, and square fists. Maybe because he would bus' someone in the head if crossed. Bus and Randy were brothers dating sisters: my grandmother and my aunt. I don't have any memory of my brothers or sister's whereabouts during most of that time.

Bus was kind to me. He gave me crayons to color pictures of Superman at the kitchen table in the duplex apartment above my cousin, Carolyn, her husband, David Ross, and their children, Kelly and D. Bus let me wear his pants when mine got dirty because I didn't have many of my own with me. The plaid bell-bottoms bunched around my ankles. I wrapped the waist and held the excess fabric in my hands to keep from falling. In my first memory of meeting Bus's brother, Randy, who was riding with my grandmother and my father and mother, he tore the buttons off his brand-new navy-blue sweater for me to play with.

Donna's son, Bilbo, was released from jail during the time I stayed at her home. Bus was not home. Everyone held onto their tension, quietly waiting all day and into the night for him to come home after his release. When Bilbo arrived, he was angry. Incoherent. Violent. He stumbled and crashed into dining room chairs. Donna stood several feet from him, throwing water into his face as if to wash away the veil separating him from sanity. Someone later said he had ingested PCP. Others said he was drunk. Donna's daughter, Becky, overdosed during that time as well. Paramedics came out to the house to revive her. I learned the word "catatonic."

At some point, Aunt Donna drove me and my siblings to my mother's parents on Columbia Avenue. Aunt Donna referred to my grandfather as Mr. Turner during their brief drop-off exchange. I don't remember her getting out of the car or even looking in my grandfather's direction when he came out to collect us. This is the last time I would see her until her sister's funeral decades later.

Mr. Turner was Pop Pop or Poppy to me and my brothers and sister. He bought us pajamas, toffee-covered peanuts, and books to read. And he had us wash with Packers Pine Tar Soap just as he did. We learned a mix of my grandmother Turner's southern manners and the Black urban bourgeoise culture they cultivated in Cleveland. We lived in a stable and orderly home for the first time in memory.

Eventually, my parents came for us and wouldn't see my grandparents until middle school. We drove from Cleveland to Milwaukee, Wisconsin, to live with them again. We settled into an apartment above a house on the West Side. A long hallway connected our apartment to my grandmother and Randy's smaller unit. A month or so later, two bail bondsmen busted through our chain-locked living room door while we sat on the floor watching. The men took my father and held him until they somehow retrieved their money. After his release, we regrouped in a two-room kitchenette on the eighth floor at a Sydney High hotel. The Sydney was located on Milwaukee's lower Eastside overlooking Lake Michigan. The Sydney was full of hippies, pimps, "Jesus freaks," and drug dealers. We watched them mingle in the lobby on days when Randy brought me fudgesicles from the tiny hotel market.

For many years after, my father was always in and out of our lives. Evasion. Isolation. Arrest. Recidivism. A sociocultural karmic wheel of cause and effect across multiple states, different time zones, and ages. Impacting lives, relationships, and ambitions.

At 34, I felt like I had broken my father's cycle—or at least left it behind. I meditated my way through Milwaukee's crack cocaine epidemic while living in rival gang territory during the late 1980s and nurtured Chicago-born high schoolers navigating new dimensions of the dark trade during the 1990s. I earned a master's degree. I was an executive at an education association. I owned a home in Champagne, Illinois. All signs of stability, even when the 9-11 era saw declines in education association membership.

Although my parents' life consisted of continued transience, I believed that when I transitioned into middle-class lifestyle, we all left behind the deep crisis of my childhood. My father's collect call from a Los Angeles County Jail pay phone quickly reminded me that we had not. I needed grounding in my life's priorities and clarity about the best ways to support him, my mother, and older brother. All three had been living together for decades in desert towns and cities between Los Angeles and Las Vegas. I was not ready to be immersed, once again in cycles of family incarceration. Homelessness. Trauma response. The call triggered feelings of family separation from my childhood, even as I thought I had kept the experiences and related feelings at bay.

I reached out to Robert Harris, a Babalawo who lived in Brooklyn, New York. I needed help understanding the spiritual context unfolding around me. Robert was initiated in the Lucumi tradition—one of several West African–derived spiritual systems that survived the middle passage and has been revitalized among contemporary African diaspora. When I first met Robert, he was an elementary school teacher and an MA student at NYU's Theater Education program. He wore a white parka, sweats, Nikes, and knit cap in accord with his spiritual house.

Robert once helped me explore the relationship between Ogun—the West African force of iron, strength, and blind battle-rage—and John Henry—a West Virginia–based, Black folk hero who died of exhaustion in a steel driving competition against a machine, sponsored by an Appalachian railroad company. After Robert completed the reading, he sent me down to the railroad tracks for a ritual. I had to go to the subway station with a water offering. I had to pour the offering directly onto the subway train tracks three times, each time calling out the name "Ogun." When I reached out to him about my father's call, he quietly reminded me that I "sat at the head of the family table." My family needed me, so I had better be of sound mind when interacting with them.

I also connected with Sam Smith, a licensed MSW for help processing my emotions about this recurring experience during that time. Sam asked questions and listened. And guided me through a series of Kung Fu stretching, breathing, and flowing movements. We met several times. Sam not only helped me navigate the moment emotionally, but he also established a more holistic relationship with me.

I visited Sam several years later in Iowa City, Iowa, after I had moved to California. While we sat, talking over coffee at Prairie Lights Bookstore, I received a call on my cell phone from my mother. I announced the call to Sam. I reacted with alarm and excused myself. He was happy to hear that my mother was calling me. Even after I explained to Sam that the call was another crisis intervention moment, he still positioned my parents' role in the structure of my life positively. He balanced his awareness of my need for safety, with my need as a Black person for having a cognitive and social awareness of where I came from, and how I fit in the world historically and culturally.

Sam entrusted me with his son during his first trip out to California for a weekend. Kofi was traveling to visit his uncle and sort out his next moves in life. After I picked him up from his uncle's home in the East Bay, we went to visit my Grand Master Cedric Robinson's dojo on Florin Road in Sacramento for Tae Kwon Do practice.

Developing Cultural Security through Relationships

In 2005 and 2006, the National Institute of Child Health and Development (NICHD) and the National Council of Accreditation in Teacher Education (NCATE) partnered to host a series of roundtable discussions among teacher educators and experts in child and adolescent development. Created by the U.S. Congress in 1962, the NICHD is 1 of the 27 institutes and centers of the National Institutes of Health. The NICHD supports and conducts research on topics related to the health of children, adults, families, and populations. NCATE is an alliance of national professional organizations of the teaching profession and education policy community committed to quality teaching. NCATE member organizations include such groups as The National Council for Teachers of Mathematics, The National Council of Teachers of English, The International Literacy

Association, etc. It is recognized by the U.S. Department of Education and the Council on Higher Education Accreditation as a professional accrediting body for teacher preparation. These organizations represent some of the most accomplished professionals in their various fields of endeavor. Any utterance from such a gathering is worthy of our collective professional attention.

The purpose of the gathering was to articulate a consensus about what teachers should know about adolescent development and cognitive science, and how to apply that knowledge in their professional practice for optimal health and growth in school. Among the findings and conclusions arrived at during the talks: Relationships Matter (2007). The report from this convening explains that classrooms are active social systems, and children with positive relationships demonstrate positive behaviors. Further, the teacher–student relationship is central in this system. Knowing this, teacher education programs' curriculum and instruction should emphasize data demonstrating how emotional support and attention to the student–teacher relationship, in fact, enhance children's capacities to learn academic knowledge.

However, the report calls for more than promoting pleasant interpersonal interactions among students, and between students and teachers. James Comer, founder of the Yale Child Study Center School Development Program, and the chair of the roundtable discussions, offered a more encompassing and multidirectional understanding of the relationship dimensions that teachers need to know about and help foster. And that teacher education programs need to teach their credential students. Comer's paradigm, adopted in the report, identifies social, psychological, and ethical dimensions relationship development for teachers to learn about. Relationship development in classrooms is often limited to focusing on quietness and polite exchanges at best, and control and compliance at worst. But Comer's ideas, as outlined in the convening report, are notably anti-colonial.

To address the social dimension of Comer's paradigm, the report recommends that pre- and in-service teacher educators should create opportunities whereby teacher credential students can learn to increase youth's capacity to build healthy relationships across the range of human diversity. Healthy relationships with individuals from communities different from our own are undergirded by a healthy sense of self. Thus, teacher educators are advised to teach their credential students how to increase their future students' capacity for self-acceptance, self-reliance, self-confidence, and cultural identity formation. Last, pre- and in-service teacher educators need to teach their students how to increase youth's capacity to understand the importance of integrity and respect for self and others.

Culture is produced, transmitted, and co-constructed in relationships with parents, caregivers, and community members, including teachers, healthcare providers, social workers, etc. Under colonized conditions, community institutions often contribute to cultural deprivation. While not framed with this critical understanding, the convening and the report address a widespread disconnect between marginalized and minoritized populations and schools.

For teachers to increase youth capacity to build healthy relationships across the range of human diversity; develop self-acceptance, self-reliance, self-confidence, positive identity formation; and internalize the importance of integrity and respect for others, teachers need to learn to eliminate cultural deprivation practices in their curriculum and instruction. Curriculum and instruction should help students navigate various discoursal and bureaucratic processes to access often-blocked dominant cultural resources; identify or uncover their own communities' frequently stigmatized, ostracized, and minoritized cultural resources; and explore and interact with the broad variety of multicultural experiences. Relationships support students' cultural security.

The National Urban Alliance for Effective Education, referenced in Chapter 1 in relation to Feuerstein's conception of cultural deprivation, includes relationship development in their list of high operational practices (Jackson & Allender, 2016). And there are educational standards that have been developed, especially by Learning for Justice (formerly Teaching Tolerance) that present grade-level benchmarks for facilitating these three levels of relationship development. The three categories identified by Comer that teachers need to learn about, and the implications of teachers' application of their new learning to their curriculum and instruction, can be considered across the allied health professions as well. Relationship development is equally at the center of work between, for example, social workers, nurses, physical therapists, or dieticians, and their clients or patients. The fluctuating degree of healthy relationships clients have within their own community, including their family, and across different and diverse cultural groups, has been dynamically impacted by cultural deprivation and thus impacts professional practice.

Similarly, allied health professionals need to be concerned about the state of clients, healthy sense of self, and ethics of relationships. Comer's relationship development-learning paradigm presents one important avenue for these professions to promote cultural security. The following sections explore cultural deprivation and cultural security implications of a relationship development and facilitation practices by allied health professionals among BIPOC families, communities, and professional services.

Family Relationships

Chapter 4 explored the American Psychological Association's second definition of cultural deprivation, whereby marginalized and minoritized groups are prevented from having access to their own culture. *Cultural destruction* and one form of this definition was also discussed. *Cultural destruction* includes destruction in part or whole of real property, the place where culture is transmitted and co-constructed; mobile property, the tools or objects for transmission and co-construction; and humans, the instruments of cultural transmission.

Destruction of families is a long-term avenue of cultural deprivation by way of *cultural destruction*. Destruction by way of family separations is enacted through enslavement, human trafficking in general, incarceration, etc. Chapter 4 also referenced Joy De Gruy's assertions that this long-term form of cultural deprivation not only traumatized many BIPOC families over the past centuries, family separations have negative impacts on contemporary and future BIPOC family relationships as well. Thus, allied health professionals, social workers, and educators should frame their work as an opportunity to facilitate or reinforce family relationships and relationship-building in ways that are relevant to their specific employment focus and the needs of the family.

The following two examples demonstrate how allied health professionals and social workers working from ideological frames that actively prioritize BIPOC family relationships can combat cultural deprivation efforts within and outside their profession, or support it. The first example considers amicus briefs filed in support of the Indian Child Welfare Act (ICWA)—a federal law enacted in 1978 that governs state-level adoption and foster care cases involving Native American children. Among other provisions, the ICWA gives tribal governments jurisdiction over the adoption of Native American children who reside on a reservation or have certain tribal connections. The friend of the court briefs were filed as part of *Deb Haaland, Secretary of the Interior, et al., Petitioners v. Chad Everet Brackeen, et al.* The second example reviews the National Association of Black Social Workers position statements against the Multi-ethnic Placement Act (MEPA) and the Interethnic Placement Act (IEPA). MEPA prohibits child welfare agencies that receive federal funding from delaying or denying foster or adoptive placements because of a child or prospective foster or adoptive parent's race, color, or national origin and from using those factors as a basis for denying approval of a potential foster or adoptive parent. The law also requires agencies to recruit foster and adoptive parents that reflect the racial and ethnic diversity of children in out-of-home care, a process known as diligent recruitment. MEPA and ICWA are differentiated because Indigenous communities have a sovereign relationship with the U.S. government and African Americans do not. NABSW essentially argues for the spirit of ICWA to be upheld with regards to African American foster children.

The Brackeens

Deb Haaland, Secretary of the Interior, et al., Petitioners v. Chad Everet Brackeen, et al., known as the *Brackeens* or the *Brackeen* case, was a Supreme Court case that began when one white couple in Texas appealed to the court to prevent the transfer of a foster child of Navajo and Cherokee descent who they had hoped to adopt, from their home. The child had been ordered by the courts to be transferred to a Navajo couple living in New Mexico, in accordance with ICWA. With pro bono help from Gibson Dunn—a law firm whose past client list consisted of international corporations, such as Shell Oil Company—and the Texas Attorney General's office, the couple won their appeal and were granted adoption rights (Nagle, 2022).

Immediately after their victory, the couple joined a State of Texas lawsuit against the federal government to strike down ICWA altogether. The same law firm that assisted the couple in their appeal—Gibson Dunn—represented the State of Texas in this lawsuit. In addition, they were joined by a white foster family from Nevada with a child of Isleta del sur Pueblo citizenship; and a third white foster family from Minnesota fighting to keep an Ojibway child. Ohio, Indiana, and Louisiana later joined the State of Texas in this lawsuit.

The families were concerned with the checks and balances on what they perceived was a simple inter-ethnic adoption. But ICWA ranks their application to adopt as the last consideration after birth family members, and extended family members, tribal members, and other Native Americans from different tribes. The families understood this ranking as a race-based law. As such, they felt it was discriminatory to only be considered as a last resort for placement because they were neither biological family, tribally connected nor Indigenous to the United States. Thus, the lawsuit asserted that ICWA discriminates against non–Native Americans based on race. If this view of ICWA were true, it would be in violation of the equal protection clause of the Fourteenth Amendment, which holds "*No State shall make or enforce any law which shall abridge the privileges or immunities of citizens of the United States; nor shall any State deprive any person of life, liberty, or property, without due process of law; nor deny to any person within its jurisdiction the equal protection of the laws*" (Amdt14.S1.8 Equal Protection). The lawsuit's second argument claimed that Congress never had the constitutional authority to create ICWA in the first place. Finally, the lawsuit asserted that, even if Congress had the authority to create ICWA, the federal government can't tell states they have to carry out this federal law. This would be federal overreach. Further, it is burdensome to the states. For example, provisions of ICWA require notifications to tribes regarding identification, status, and process updates, etc., about their tribal citizens burden state agencies.

The initial lawsuit in the Fifth Circuit found in favor of the State of Texas, invalidating most of ICWA. The federal government appealed this decision. But the appeal resulted in a split decision, considered unwieldy and even inconsistent and thus, triggering a final appeal to reinstate ICWA to the U.S. Supreme Court. On Thursday, June 15, 2023, the Supreme Court issued its decision in the *Haaland v. Brackeen* case. In a 7-2 decision, the Court clarified and re-codified the state-to-state relationship between Indigenous people and the United States. On the overreach argument, the Court found that the parties had no standing, no legitimate grounds for bringing the case before the Court. Further, the record-keeping requirements were consistent with the Tenth Amendment and therefore constitutional and the active provisions requirement of ICWA was consistent with other statutes.

A critical review of this case is beyond the scope of this chapter. There are investigative reports, legal and cultural analysis from Indigenous communities that served as the source of the above summary. Two noteworthy examples include Nagle's podcast *This Land*, which is a multipart series of investigative reporting. However, it is instructive to the larger conversation about choices and actions among the professions that support cultural deprivation or foster cultural security to surface some of the findings from these voices.

In some of the cases with these families, social workers did not know about or did not understand ICWA. This is an educational and supervisory issue. Future confusion concerning ICWA adoption cases can be remedied with professional development and pre-service training. In other cases, social workers were hostile to ICWA. Nagle notes that in the Nevada case, Washoe County social workers not only did not understand ICWA, they didn't like it and would not enforce it.

For example, while placement with the father was denied due to his impoverishment and substance abuse; the grandmother and uncle were discouraged from completing the foster parent process and adoption application. Ysleta del Sur Pueblo social workers then identified 39 tribal families interested in the adoption. Again, according to Nagle's investigative report, Washoe County social workers did not call any of these potential adoptive families to determine their eligibility. Ysleta del Sur Pueblo social workers turned to the court. However, even when the court ordered Washoe County social workers to reach out to the Ysleta del Sur Pueblo families, during the calls, social workers attempted to convince them not to follow through with the child. And in the Minnesota case, social workers did not initially inquire about the tribal status of family members who had been caring for the child before social services organizations intervened and removed the child. The family's tribal status was only considered after great effort.

In contrast, as the case reached the Supreme Court, social workers familiar with the Brackeens filed amicus briefs in support of ICWA through various professional organizations representing the social work profession. For example, the *Brief of the Casey Family Programs and Ten Other Child Welfare and Adoption Organizations as Amici Curiae in Support of Petitioners:*

> *Amici* agree with the United States and the Tribal Defendants that ICWA is constitutional and serves vital interests in protecting Indian children specifically, as well as their families and their tribes ... ICWA is a context-specific application of child welfare practices that best serve *all* children, not only children who meet ICWA's definition of 'Indian child.'

> Experts now agree on one overriding and universally applicable principle: Children are best served by preserving and strengthening their family and community relationships to the fullest degree that safety allows. This principle encompasses all relationships that surround a child from birth, from the closest ties (birth parents, siblings), to extended family, and radiating out to the child's broader community and culture.

This is the gold standard protocol for placing children in need of protective services. The protocol supports cultural security.

NABSW Position Statement

ICWA was established in 1978 in response to a report that nearly one-third of all Native American children had been removed from their homes due to policies and practices by the U.S. government, individual states, religious and secular institutions, and individuals. Similarly, in enslavement, incarceration, and social work practices, Black children have been removed from their homes in high numbers (DeGruy, 2017). The Flemming Rule of 1960 and the Child Abuse Prevention and Treatment Act (CAPTA) of 1974 increased removal and overrepresentation of Black children in foster care, and the length of time in foster care over that of other racial and ethnic groups (Williams-Butler et al., 2020). Nearly 20 years later—in 1994—the U.S. Congress passed the Multiethnic

Placement Act (MEPA). The 1996 interethnic provisions were enacted as Title I, Subtitle H, Section 1808, Removal of Barriers to Interethnic Adoption, of the Small Business Job Protection Act of 1996 to remove any ambiguity about whether race, color, or national origin could be considered in making placement decisions for children. The ACT's provisions:

- Prohibit state child welfare agencies from refusing or delaying foster or adoptive placements because of a child's or foster/adoptive parent's race, color, or national origin.
- Prohibit state child welfare agencies from considering race, color, or national origin as a basis for denying approval of a potential foster or adoptive parent.
- Require state child welfare agencies to act diligently to recruit a diverse group of foster and adoptive parents who reflect the racial and ethnic makeup of children in out-of-home care.

MEPA was intended to prevent delays in placement of foster care youth into adoptive homes.

Twenty-five years after MEPA, and MEPA/IEP, overrepresentation and extended stays in foster care persist for Black children. The National Association of Black Social Workers' position statement calling for the repeal of MEPA asserts that "not once in its 25-year history has disproportionality of Black children decreased" (NABSW, 2021). Research for this assertion comes from a series of reports ordered by former U.S. President Donald Trump's *Executive Order 13930 on Strengthening the Child Welfare System for America's Children.* An analysis of Executive Order 13930 in the *University of Illinois Urbana Champagne Law Review* (Ryan et al., 2021) identified veiled efforts in the order to direct an increase in government funds to religious and private adoption organizations which often operate with fewer safeguard requirements than public agencies. However, the order also directs the HHS to conduct research on the effectiveness of MEPA. The research reports confirm the assertions from the NABSW.

Even before the executive order, NABSW members had taken a position against the spirit of MEPA/IEP. In between the Flemming Act of 1960 and CAPTA of 1974, NABSW members produced two position statements fighting transracial adoption and calling for legal recognition of extended family and fictive family as foster parents for Black children. The position calling for recognition acknowledged the African cultural practice of extended family care, and the social cultural research supporting these traditions. We now have neurobiological research that substantiates the importance of extended and fictive family care.

Equally important, this position statement highlighted the unequal support for extended family members fostering Black children. During the time the position statement was written and released, extended family supporting children either received no support or limited support in the form of temporary aid for needy families. In contrast, out-of-family placements received financial, medical, counseling, and other kinds of support for fostering the children. NABSW called for Title IV-E support for kin caregivers just as it was given to foster parents in out-of-family placements. NABSW member social workers were fighting a complex battle against cultural deprivation. They were not only fighting to keep families together, they were fighting for recognition of Black families. Further, they were fighting for Black families to have access to funds used to disrupt Black families in the name of care and best interests of children.

Black families do not have the legal or political status that Native Americans have in the United States. Nor is there a tribal government infrastructure enabling an ICWA-like process to ensue when seeking placement for a Black foster child. NABSW members understood that the same kinds of psychic and developmental harms from racial micro- and macroaggressions, unconscious bias, and general cultural disconnect and cultural destruction faced by Native American are present for Black people, regardless of the political class of the people. Political classes are colonial constructs. Further, since anti-blackness is so fundamental to white supremacist colonial thinking, ICWA-like protections for Black children are arguably even more crucial. Understanding this, NABSW wrote out policy recommendations that would take into consideration the same mental health and cultural needs for Black children that ICWA seeks to do for Native American children.

Several other complex considerations were addressed in the position statement, such as relaxed rules related to certifying extended family members as foster parents; increasing the length of time before parental rights are terminated; and greater consideration of the needs for the overall family: fostering extended family, birth family, and child or children; etc. This last consideration is the bottom line. BIPOC families as colonized people need greater supports in dealing with the legacies and ongoing practices of colonization, including all forms of cultural deprivation. Educators and allied health professions should practice their profession from a framework that affirms the importance of families and seeks to foster concrete and conceptual relationships among family members, extended families, and communities as a cultural security frame to work from.

While MEPA may make it legally difficult to attend to some aspects of cultural deprivation, professional standards of practice across the professions lead us toward operating from an understanding about whether our professional decisions support cultural deprivation or cultural security.

Cultural Security in Affinity Groups

The previous section explored educators and allied health professional's role in supporting cultural security by strengthening BIPOC families. This section explores the role of racial and cultural affinity groups. Racial affinity groups and racial caucuses broadly speaking provide another frame for thinking about how to promote cultural security. The idea is well known in many K–12, higher education, and allied health professional settings. However, there is still push-back on what can sometimes be called "neo-segregation spaces." In this instance, the concept of segregation—forced separation and substandard conditions—is weaponized and applied when BIPOC exercise choice to come together as people with a shared identity and sometimes a shared interest engaged in a common endeavor or a shared space. Affinity groups come together to discuss common experiences of cultural deprivation or other kinds of racialized experiences and to develop amongst themselves culturally affirming ways of being in oppressive or non-safe spaces.

Affinity groups can also be used to bridge disruptions in cultural continuities caused by cultural deprivation experiences in education and the media. Babalwa Kwanele, licensed social worker and trauma therapist from Berkeley, California, reflects on her facilitation of African diaspora affinity groups while attending college at Central State University in Ohio. Central State arose from Wilberforce University—the nation's oldest private historically Black college or university (HBCU) and a prominent stop on the Underground Railroad. Named for British abolitionist William Wilberforce, it was founded by the African Methodist Episcopal Church. Central State separated from Wilberforce in 1951. "The work started at Central State began because of my involvement with the All African People's Revolutionary Party as a young person. When I got to Central State, I began to work on campus around recruiting students for the party, trying to develop a new circle—a study circle." In the study circle, students did quite a bit of study of Africa in the plight of Africans in the United States. During the study experience, she learned that there was a divide between students who were African, born at home, and African American from the United States: "Meaning the two groups really didn't, from what I could see, didn't spend a lot of time with each other. And I couldn't understand that."

She would ask questions of both groups and found that there were many misunderstandings that both had about the other. For instance, she remembered "one of the African American students thought that the African students lived in a certain way from what they learned from American media. And the African students saw African American students in a different light, as well. They didn't really have a thoughtful under-standing of what our plight was, and our struggle with enslavement." And so, she thought,

"why not pull these two groups of people together? In addition to sort of like some of the party work. And so, I developed what was called the African Awareness Committee [for] students that were from home, from Africa and African American students where we would collaborate and do projects together, activities together. And then, and in so doing these community engagement activities and these programs that were mostly political in nature ... we would get to know each other in a different way. And it worked. So, it was really building relationships on campus with students who typically had not communicated with each other and didn't understand each other. We wound up, really getting to know people from different parts of Africa and developed these great relationships where we're communicating even after I graduated.

I learned why some of the ones that were from home use different names. They use American names and not their African names ... some of them were actually child soldiers that were you know, had had come out of that. [They were] recruited to come to Central State. And so when our students learned that as well ... It just changed the whole light in terms of how we knew each other, and how we learned from each other, and just the misperceptions that we have been taught by our own educational systems. [We learned our education system] kind of failed us all in terms of really getting to know one another for who we truly were, our histories, our cultures. We shared food. Did cooking together a lot of activities that just really brought us together."

Wilberforce University—the first Black-owned historically black college—and by extension Central State—has a history of welcoming students from several different African countries. Babalwa Kwanele supported this tradition based on her work with the All African Peoples Revolutionary Party and deepened the connections among these students. By hosting dialogues, academic extra-curricular presentations, group cooking parties, and political events for African and African American students attending an HBCU, Sister Babalwa fostered cultural security.

Sister Babalwa's affinity group at Central State served a different function than workplace racial affinity groups rooted in or focused on experiences of employment. Trauma therapist Resmaa Menakem offers another purpose and structure for affinity grouping. Menakem's work focuses on facilitating healing from racial trauma. First, he emphasizes the importance of being in the body. Next, he structures group-therapeutic spaces. Cultural deprivation didn't happen to individuals only; it happened to specific marginalized and minoritized communities, groups, ethnic groups, racially constructed groups, and racially intersectional groups. Next, he recommends affinity groupings. Affinity-based groupings in this context are important because of the unconscious process that will play out cross-racially for folks who have not tempered their bodies enough to be aware of these unconscious behaviors, images, and feelings; and the awareness that they will likely cause new harm and substantiate the responses to old harm.

Resmaa Menakem's work has been referenced in different places throughout this book. His work deserves engagement on its own terms and much more robustly than these references. This section highlights the role of racial and cultural affinity groups as one avenue for supporting cultural security through relationship-building in the workplace, at school, and in therapy. The next section offers insights about embodying relationship-oriented cultural security behaviors in professional practices.

Embodying Cultural Security

Allied health professionals have varying opportunities for relationship development during the encounter and over the duration of the professional engagement. As caseloads, patient loads, and class sizes increase, those opportunities may seem less. But attention to relationship development in the health professions, even in these fleeting moments, can be the difference not only between slow and more efficient recovery—it can be the difference between life and death for BIPOC patients (Washington, 2006). Some areas to consider in relationship development include the following.

Unconscious Behavior Guidance Systems

Much of our everyday emotional and physical behavior is in response to being primed—having internal frames cued or stimulated to surface and act or emote. When memories of our past experiences are primed by current experiences, we act to transmit or co-construct culture; or we struggle for cultural security in response to conditions of cultural deprivation. And for some, memories of past experiences prime them to enact or continue to enact cultural deprivation against others. (Bargh, 2017) Bargh says that unconscious motivations from the past concern evolutionary experiences from the human species and from our personal past. Menakem (2017) expands on these unconscious sources identifying historic, intergenerational, interpersonal, and familial influences, especially in relation to racial trauma. He explains that these deep structure attitudes and dispositions are experienced as vibes, emotions, images, meanings, behaviors, affect and sensations.

Menakem and Bargh articulated the unconscious mechanisms communicating to our wholistic selves that something or some things have happened and there may be residual hurt and the possibility of additional harm. Prior to their work, Steele desecribed the impact of that unconscious communication on our ability to perform a variety of tasks. Steele called them unconscious cues given off by another and read by the receiver, also unconsciously. These cues can cause a breakdown in performance and the amplification of stereotypes. What is the impact on people who experience these unconscious cues alerting them of danger when they are simply going to get blood drawn for labs; applying for housing assistance or veteren's benedits; an x-ray or a vaccination?

Stereotypes as unconscious motivators of behavior have been explored individually and socailly. For example, the Implicit Assumptions Test (IAT) is an indirect measure of the test-taker's associations between an attribute and a category. More specifically, the IAT focusing on race measures how fast the test-taker can put "good" and "black" together compared to how long it takes to put "bad" and "white" together. It calculates the difference in the amount of time and the number of mistakes the test-taker makse as a rough indicator of that idea in the test-taker's mind and their attitudes toward it. It is a measure of the stregnth of an associations the test-taker makes between attributes and categories of people. (Banaji 2014). 14 million people around the world have taken this test. Hehman, Flake, and Clanchini (2018) found that in communities where there is a high instance of white IAT-test-takers and their tests report a high instance of negative implicit assumptions against African American, there is a corrleational higher instance of police shootings of African American men. The authors of the study assert that the amount of anti-black bias in the community can help inform about the liklihood of police shootings of Black men. As explained earlier in this chapter, implicit and explicit assumptions are also responsible for higher instances of BIPOC charged with child neglect. The negative impact of anti-Black unconscious behavior guidance seen across the allied health professions have also been addressed earlier. Fortunatley, future events and experiences c an be primed by current experiences. Increasing awareness of our unconscious or implicit motivations through activities such as the IAT can help expand relationship-building capacity.

Language

Cultural security is reinforced or threatened by our language. The aesthetic and emotional quality of words formed by our tongues' shifting tension and relaxation and the choice of words we choose all deliver an impact. Beyond our daily speech acts that enact or shut down cultural transmission, and the professionalism present in our bedside manner, more ideosynchratic instances of our language impact can be surfaced. For example, Aasiyah, who was introduced in Part I, also shared an important exmple about confusing conversations with medical personell about medications that can cause frustration and difficulty in maintaining connections. Often, during medical checkups, Asiyah explained that doctors and nurses, and occassionally others will ask patients to list any medications they are taking. Sometimes they will review the list of medications in the patient's chart aloud with them for confirmation. Asiyah noted that there was often inconsitency in the medication names they choose to use when refering to the same drug. Sometimes they will use the drug name, generic name, or medication name, which is often related to its chemical structure or active ingrediant. Other times they will use brand names when reviewing medications. Brand names are often catchier or related to their intended use. For exmple, hydroxychlorquin, often used for patients with autoimmune conditions such as sytemic lupus. A common brand name for hydroxychloroquin is plaquenil. To the untrained ear they sound like different medications. To someone under duress from chronic illness and limited knowledge of medical terminology or pharmecuticles the confusion can cause anxiety. There are other examples, such as what to share with patients: sharing enough information, complete information, or need to know information only; or ensuring someone has had enough time to speak to process the medical infromation they are receiving.

Physical Space

Physical space can encourage or discourage cultural security through relationship-building. "Architecture sends a silent message to everyone walking into any place. It tells you what to expect and where the limits of behavior are" (Wall, 2016). Many large institutional architectural firms design everything—schools, libraries, hospitals, prisons—using similar Brutalist-style aesthetics (Latané, D'Aprile, 2021). And many people know this or feel this to be true, in large part, due to the impact of the Brutalist style.

Journalist and architect D'Aprile informally polled Twitter followers for examples of buildings that reminded them of prisons. Among the several dozen responses, he notes, "the overwhelming connecting thread was not material but purpose: most of the buildings people thought looked like prisons were educational facilities." The responses included high schools, middle schools, and college classrooms that included monolithic and menacing appearances from the outside, few windows and long corridors, and drab finishes, such as cinder block painted gray. D'Aprile says that several of the "responses included stories about rumors of their high schools or colleges being modeled after prisons or designed by architects who had also constructed prisons."

Facilities that conjure stories of perceived or actual connections between their public institutions of care and development and institutions of penalization, corruption, and dehumanizing and predatory practices can only facilitate relationship-building among client populations and between client populations and care providers with great effort and localized care. Changing the institutional paint color throughout a campus to pastel colors alone will not work (Tofle, Schwartz, Yoon, & Max-Royale 2004).

Summary

Chapter 7 emphasizes the importance of relationships as a pathway toward cultural security. After a critical family history vignette about family separation, and Black men nurturing within an extended family care framework, the chapter surfaces the 2006 report from a roundtable discussion between NICHD and NCATE enphasizing relationships. The report asserts teacher training should include explicit education about how to help youth build relationships across a wide array of communities. Next, the chapter explores the role of social workers and allied health professionals in prioritizing foster care and adoption placements within biological and cultural families to avoid separation wherever possible. The chapter concludes with reflections on embodied practices for promoting relationships in professional spaces, such as affinity groups, priming, language practices, and environment.

Activities

Courthouse Steps Decision: *Haaland v. Brackeen.* The Federalist Society June 30, 2023

On Thursday, June 15, 2023, the Supreme Court issued its decision in *Haaland v. Brackeen.* In a 7-2 decision, the Court affirmed the Fifth Circuit's finding that the ICWA is constitutional, rejected petitioners' Tenth Amendment argument, and found that petitioners lacked the standing required for other challenges. Sam Fendler and Jennifer Weddle joined us to discuss the Court's findings.

https://www.youtube.com/watch?v=985DEbtvpCg&t=2251

The Power of Affirmations

Read the following research-based statements:

Affirmations contribute to executive control and higher fluid intelligence, among lower socioeconomic populations.

Self-affirmations can boost adaptive functioning.

Self-affirmation is a "well-being" intervention.

Values affirmation can increase awareness of the needs of others and increase prosocial behavior.

After reviewing each statement, paraphrase the research-based statement below:

Affirmation appears to work best when it is delivered as a normal classroom activity and where identity threat co-occurs with resources for improvement and time to await cumulative benefits.

Share your paraphrase with others. Edit your paraphrase to incorporate additional ideas from others.

Create micro-affirmations in your workspace. Micro-affirmations are everyday acts that acknowledge, confirm, and complement cultural and ethnic identity ... and that counter often proactively racial microaggressions. Micro-affirmations can include the presence of BIPOC in the curriculum, in classroom decor, in aesthetics and symbols; culturally resonant gestures or identifying your students' community cultural wealth.

Affirmation Directionality

Teacher does		Students do
Affirms all students as a group and individually in sincere and specific ways every day all day.		Experience affirmation
Teaches students to affirm other classmates; schedules into the day moments when they affirm each other in writing and verbally; spontaneously directs students to affirm each other.		Affirm their classmates

(Continued)

Teaches students to affirm themselves; schedules into the day moments when they affirm each other in writing and verbally; spontaneously directs students to affirm each other.		Affirm themselves

Suggestions for Further Reading

1 Child and Adolescent Development Research and Teacher Education: Evidence-Based Pedagogy, Policy, and Practice Summary of Roundtable Meetings. (2007). National Institute of Child Health and Human Development (NICHD), National Institutes of Health, U.S. Department of Health and Human Services, and National Association for the Accreditation of Teacher Education.
2 Jackson Y. (2011). *The Pedagogy of Confidence: Inspiring High Intellectual Performance in Urban Schools.* Teachers College Press.
3 Jackson, Y., & Allender, D. (2016). Waiting to excel: Mediating 21st century teaching through the pedagogy of confidence. In Bellance, J. A. (Ed.), *Connecting the Dots: Teaching Effectiveness and Deeper Professional Learning.* Solution Tree Press.

References

African Union. (1981). African charter on human and peoples rights. Retrieved December 16, 2023, from https://au.int/en/treaties/african-charter-human-and-peoples-rights

Act (MEPA) and Inter-Ethnic Placement Act (IEPA). *The Guardian, NACC's Quarterly Law Journal, 43*(4). Retrieved November 21, 2023, from https://cdn.ymaws.com/www.nabsw.org/resource/resmgr/2021_position_papers/2021_4304_repeal_mepa_iepa.pdf

Abu-Jamal, M. (2012, February 26). The vision of fanon. Prison Radio. Retrieved August 14, 2022, from https://www.prisonradio.org/commentary/the-vision-of-fanon/

Alexander, M. (2020). *The New Jim Crow: Mass incarceration in the age of colorblindness.* 10th Edition. New York: New Press.

Amanpour, M. (2019, April 12). Traditional Chinese medicine and ayurvedic medicine. YouTube. Retrieved August 22, 2022, from https://www.youtube.com/watch?v=mgpWx--84nc

American Anthropological Association. (2020). 2020 statement on anthropology and human rights. Retrieved June 10, 2023, from https://www.americananthro.org/ParticipateAndAdvocate/AdvocacyDetail.aspx?ItemNumber=25769

American Medical Association. (2021). Organizational strategic plan to embed racial justice and advance health equity 2021–2023. Retrieved December 17, 2023, from https://www.ama-assn.org/system/files/ama-equity-strategic-plan.pdf

American Psychological Association. (2022). *APA dictionary of Psychology.* American Psychological Association. Retrieved March 14, 2022, from https://dictionary.apa.org/

Asante, M., & Mazama, A. (2005). The encyclAncestral healing in psychotherapyopedia of Black studies. Sage.

Baldwin, J. R., Faulkner, S. L., & Hecht, M. L. (2006). A moving target: The illusive definition of culture. In J. R. Baldwin, S. L. Faulkner, M. L. Hecht, & S. L. Lindsley (Eds.), *Redefining culture: Perspectives across the disciplines* (pp. 3–26). Lawrence Erlbaum Associates Publishers.

Ballentine R. (1984, 1977). *Joints and glands exercises: As taught by sri swami rama of the himalayas.* Himalayan International Institute.

Banaji, M. (2014). Implicit assumptions test. Serious Science. Retrieved March 11, 2024, from https://youtu.be/ABSeKU2qJoI?si=V_Ivsyt16FwO4oYX

Bargh, J. (2017). Before you know it: The unconscious reasons we do what we do. Touchstone.

Barret, K. (2022, March 10). Census Bureau releases estimates of undercount and overcount in the 2020 census. United States Census Bureau Press Release Number: CB22-CN.02. Retrieved March 15, 2022, from https://www.census.gov/newsroom/press-releases/2022/2020-census-estimates-of-undercount-and-overcount.html

Barnes, J., & Gottlieb, B. (2018 August 11). Equality under the law: The lost generation of Prince Edward County (1965). YouTube. Retrieved July 25, 2022, from https://www.youtube.com/watch?v=ah8gZu53V4A

Ben-Jochannan Y. (2004). *Cultural genocide in the Black and African studies curriculum.* Black Classic Press.

Bernheimer, L., O'Brien, R., & Barnes, R. (2017). Wellbeing in prison design A guide. Matter architecture. Retrieved October 25, 2023, from https://www.matterarchitecture.uk/wp-content/uploads/2018/05/421-op-02_Design-toolkit-report-online.pdf

Brandon, G. (2012). Lucumi divination, the mythic world and the management of misfortune. *Anthropologica, 54*(2), 167–188. http://www.jstor.org/stable/24467400

Brief for Casey Family Programs and Twenty-Six Other Child Welfare And Adoption Organizations AS *Amici Curiae* in Support of Federal and Tribal Defendants p. 8, Haaland, Secretary of the Interior, et al. *v.* Brackeen et al. 21–376, 21–377, 21–378, 21–380 US (2023).

Bynum, E. B. (2021). The African origin of familial consciousness and the dynamics of dreaming. *Dreaming, 31*(2), 91–99. 10.1037/drm0000171

Bynum E. B. (1999). *The african unconscious: Roots of ancient mysticism and modern psychology.* Teachers College Press.

Butchart, R. E. (2020, September 16). Freedmen's education during reconstruction. New Georgia Encyclopedia. Retrieved March 6, 2022, from https://www.georgiaencyclopedia.org/articles/history-archaeology/freedmens-education-during-reconstruction/

California Association of Realtors. (2021, February 17). Housing affordability for Black California households is half that of whites, illustrating persistent wide homeownership gap and wealth disparities, C.A.R. reports. Cision PR Newswire. Retrieved March 3, 2022, from https://www.prnewswire.com/news-releases/housing-affordability-for-black-california-households-is-half-that-of-whites-illustrating-persistent-wide-homeownership-gap-and-wealth-disparities-car-reports-301230161.html

California Indian Culture and Sovereignty Center & California State University San Marcos American Indian Studies. (2019). Land acknowledgement: You're on California Indian land, now what? Acknowledging relationships to space and place. A toolkit. California State University San Marcos. Retrieved March 12, 2022, from https://www.csusm.edu/cicsc/land.pdf

CASEL. (2020, October 1). CASEL'S SEL framework what are the core competence areas and where are they promoted? Retrieved March 3, 2022, from https://casel.org/casel-sel-framework-11-2020/

California Senate Bill No. 188 Chapter 58. Retrieved March 15, 2022, from https://leginfo.legislature.ca.gov/faces/billTextClient.xhtml?bill_id=201920200SB188

Chae, D., et al. (2019). Racial discrimination, disease activity, and organ damage: The Black women's experiences living with Lupus (BeWELL) Study. *American Journal of Epidemiology, 188*(8), 1434–1443. 10.1093/aje/kwz105

Chang, P., Lu, Y., Nguyen, C. M., Suh, Y., Luciani, M., Ofner, S., & Powell, S. (2021). Effects of qigong exercise on physical and psychological health among African Americans. *Western Journal of Nursing Research 2021, 43*(6), 551–562.

Chang, S. J., Kwak, E. Y., Hahm, B. J., Seo, S. H., Lee, W., & Jang, S. J. (2016). Effects of a meditation program on nurses' power and quality of life. *Nursing Science Quarterly*, *29*(3), 227–234. 10.1177/0894318416647778.

Chappell, B. (2022, February 15). Sha'Carri Richardson sees a double standard in allowing Kamila Valieva to compete. National Public Radio. Retrieved July 15, 2022, from https://www.npr.org/2022/02/15/1080694770/shacarri-richardson-kamila-valieva-doping

Click on Detroit. (2021, December 17). Detroit mayor says US Census Bureau undercounted residents. (Video). Youtube. https://youtu.be/eM8mXrSIaAk?si=4S4dZSejQGgm9j1w

Cooney, P., Farley, R., Jubaed, S., Metzger, K., Morenoff, J., Neidert, L., & Rodriguez-Washington, R. (2021). Analysis of the Census 2020 count in Detroit. Poverty Solutions University of Michigan. Retrieved July 16, 2022, from http://sites.fordschool.umich.edu/poverty2021/files/2021/12/PovertySolutions-Census-Undercount-in-Detroit-PolicyBrief-December2021.pdf

Crump, B. (2019). *Open season: Legalized genocide of colored people (First)*. Amistad.

D'Aprile, M. (2021). The architecture of prisons is everywhere we look. *Jacobin*. Retrieved on October 25, 2023 from https://jacobin.com/2021/11/prison-architecture-imaginary-brutalism-schools

Davis, K. A. (2019). Mindfulness-based interventions with at-risk African American youth: A comprehensive literature review (Order No. 27544516) [Doctoral Dissertation, Chicago School of Professional Psychology]. ProQuest Dissertations and Thesis Global.

Davis, A. (2022). *Angela Davis: An autobiography*. 3rd Edition. Haymarket Books.

DeGruy, J. (2017). *Post traumatic slave syndrome: Americas legacy of enduring injury and healing*. Dr. Joy DeGruy.

Demby, J. (2021). Code switch: Painting by numbers. National Public Radio. Retrieved July 12, 2022, from https://podcasts.apple.com/us/podcast/painting-by-numbers/id1112190608?i=1000539133327

Dennison, A., & Powell-Watts, L. (2021). Ancestral healing in psychotherapy. *Spirituality in Clinical Practice*, *8*(3), 188–194. 10.1037/scp0000254

Diop, C. A. (2012). *Civilization and barbarism: An authentic anthropology*. HBC Publications.

Doyle, J. (2009). State lawmakers tell UC: Return war dead bones. SF Gate. Retrieved March 8, 2022, from https://www.sfgate.com/world/article/State-lawmakers-tell-UC-Return-war-dead-bones-3289456.php

Dunbar-Ortiz, R. (2014). An indigenous peoples history of the United States (ReVisioning History). Beacon Press.

Education Law Center (2021, May 5). Tentative settlement reached in Minnesota school segregation case. Retrieved March 4, 2024 from https://edlawcenter.org/tentative-settlement-reached-in-minnesota-school-segregation-case/

Education Law Center. (2021, May 5). Tentative settlement reached in Minnesota school desegregation case. Education Law Center. Retrieved July 23. 2022, from https://edlawcenter.org/news/archives/other-states/tentative-settlement-reached-in-minnesota-school-segregation-case.html

El-Amin, E., & Dennis, A. (2023). What is black safety. Black in Appalachia, June 18 [Audio podcast episode]. https://podcasts.apple.com/us/podcast/the-black-in-appalachia-podcast-asks-what-is-black-safety/id1524089550?i=1000617502480.

Elliott, D., Martin, S., Shakespear, J., & Kelly, J. (2021). Simulating the 2020 census miscounts and the fairness of outcomes. The Urban Institute. Retrieved March 7, 2022, from https://www.urban.org/sites/default/files/publication/104961/simulating-the-2020-census_2.pdf

Encyclopedia of Cleveland History. (n.d.). "GILLESPIE, CHESTER K.". Case Western Reserve University. Retrieved June 10, 2022, from https://case.edu/ech/articles/g/gillespie-chester-k

Epperly, B., Witko, C., Strickler, R., & White, P. (2020). Rule by violence, rule by law: Lynching, Jim Crow, and the continuing evolution of voter suppression in the U.S. *Perspectives on Politics, 18*(3), 756–769. 10.1017/S1537592718003584

Eswarappa, K., & Gladis, M. S. (2019). *Ancestor worship. Encyclopedia of psychology and religion.* Springer. https://doi-org.proxy.lib.csus.edu/10.1007/978-3-030-24348-7_200237

Fairley, N. J. (2003). Dreaming ancestors in Eastern Carolina. *Journal of Black Studies, 33*(5), 545–561. http://www.jstor.org/stable/3180975

Falik, L. H. (2019). *Changing destinies: The extraordinary life and times of prof. Reuven Feuerstein.* Xlibris.

Farmsworth, C. H. (1970, September 14). Black panthers open office in Algiers. The New York Times. Retrieved August 7, 2022, from https://www.nytimes.com/1970/09/14/archives/black-panthers-open-office-in-algiers.html

Fensternwald, J. (2021, March 17). A final vote, after many rewrites, for California's controversial ethnic studies curriculum. EdSource. https://edsource.org/2021/a-final-vote-after-many-rewrites-for-californias-controversial-ethnic-studies-curriculum/651338

Feuerstein, R., Feuerstein, R., Falik, L. H., & Bransford, J. D. (2010). Beyond smarter: Mediated learning and the brain's capacity for change. Teachers College Press.

Feuerstein, R., Rand, Y., Hoffman, M., Hoffman, M., & Miller, R. (1979). Cognitive modifiability in retarded adolescents: Effects of instrumental enrichment. *American Journal of Mental Deficiency, 83*(6), 539–550.

Finley, A. (2010). *Founding Chestnut Ridge: The origins of Central West Virginia's multiracial community: a senior honors thesis.* The Ohio State University.

Flacks, M. (2023). The UDHR at 75: A conversation with UN high commissioner for Human Rights Volker Türk. The Center for Strategic & International Studies. Retrieved on May 12, 2023, from https://www.youtube.com/watch?v=OArEJ10FUC0

Flannery, M. E. (2015). The school-to-prison pipeline; time to shut it down: Suspensions and expulsions are doing more harm than good. Schools are getting better results by rejecting zero tolerance. National Education Association. Retrieved February 20, 2021, from https://www.nea.org/advocating-for-change/new-from-nea/school-prison-pipeline-time-shut-it-down

Foster, M. (1997). *Black teachers on teaching.* New York: The New Press.

Foster, T. A. (2011). The sexual abuse of black men under American slavery. *Journal of the History of Sexuality 20*(3), 445–464. 10.1353/sex.2011.0059.

Frawley, D. (2001). Ayurvedic healing: A comprehensive guide. Lotus Press.

Geertz, C. (1973). The interpretation of cultures: Selected essays. Basic Books.

Givens, J. (2021). *Fugitive pedagogy: Carter G. Woodson and the art of Black teaching.* Harvard.

Glass, A. (2015). United Nations adopts Universal Declaration of Human Rights, Dec, 10, 1948. Politico. Retrieved from https://www.politico.com/story/2015/12/united-nations-adopts-universal-declaration-of-human-rights-dec-10-1948-216489#:~:text=Roosevelt.,Turkey%2C%20a%20predominantly%20Muslim%20nation. on May 15, 2023.

Government Accounting Office. (May 2019). *Report to congressional requestors: 2020 Census Additional Actions needed to manage risk*. United States Government Accountability Office. (Retrieved March 16, 2022).

theGrio Politics. (2021, April 14). Penn Museum apologizes for collecting skulls of Black Americans (Black News Channel). Youtube. Retrieved May 1, 2022, from https://www.youtube.com/watch?v=mY0mK32tCWs.

theGrio Politics. (2021, April 6). Marc Lamont Hill talks Penn Museum apology for housing human remains from MOVE bombing (Black News Channel). YouTube. Retrieved May 1, 2022, from https://www.youtube.com/watch?v=qOVOByfMKtM.

Gray, L., Font, S., Unrau, Y., & Dawson, A. (2018). The effectiveness of a brief mindfulness-based intervention for college freshmen who have aged out of foster care. *Innovative Higher Education, 43*(5), 339–352. 10.1007/s10755-018-9433-3

Guetta, S. (2016). The Feuerstein approach to intercultural education and respect for human rights. Bulletin of the Transilvania University of Brasov, Series VII: Social Sciences and Law, *9*(1), 181–186. Retrieved March 18, 2024, from https://www.ceeol.com/search/article-detail?id=509958

Hariprasad, V.R. et al. (2013). Randomized clinical trial of yoga-based intervention in residents from elderly homes: Effects on cognitive function. Indian Journal of Psychiatry, *55*(Suppl 3), S357–S363. 10.4103/0019-5545.116308

Harper, S. (2022, October 17). Where is the $200 billion companies promised after George Floyd's murder? Forbes. Retrieved March 13, 2023, from https://www.forbes.com/sites/shaunharper/2022/10/17/where-is-the-200-billion-companies-promised-after-george-floyds-murder/?sh=58b3a5694507

Heppner, W. L., & Shirk, S. D. (2018). Mindful moments: A review of brief, low-intensity mindfulness meditation and induced mindful states. *Social and Personality Psychology Compass, 12*(12), 14. 10.1111/spc3.12424

Heilman, C. W. (1994). Booker v. Special School District No. 1: A history of school desegregation in Minneapolis, Minnesota. *Law and Inequality, 12*, 127.

Herskovits, M. (1990). *The myth of the negro past*. Beacon Press.

Hinrichs, E. (2018, August 21). As desegregation case proceeds, here's a look at what became of the metro's earlier effort. Minnpost. Retrieved July 23, 2022, from https://www.minnpost.com/education/2018/08/desegregation-case-proceeds-here-s-look-what-became-metros-earlier-effort/

Hobday, M. C., Finn, G., & Orfield, M. (2009). A missed opportunity: Minnesota's failed experiment with choice-based integration. *William Mitchell Law Review, 35*(3), Article 2.

Hoffman, K. M., Trawalter, S., Axt, J. R., & Oliver, M. N. (2016). Racial bias in pain assessment and treatment recommendations, and false beliefs about biological differences between blacks and whites. *Proceedings of the National Academy of Sciences of the United States of America, 113*(16), 4296–4301. 10.1073/pnas.1516047113

Holland, B. (2018, December 4). The 'Father of Modern Gynecology' performed shocking experiments on enslaved women: His use of Black bodies as medical test subjects falls into a history that includes the Tuskegee syphilis experiment and Henrietta Lacks. The History Channel. Retrieved October 2, 2022, from https://www.history.com/news/the-father-of-modern-gynecology-performed-shocking-experiments-on-slaves.

Howle, E. M. (2020). Native American Graves Protection and Repatriation Act: The University of California is not adequately overseeing its return of Native American remains and artifacts. Auditor of the State of California. Retrieved March 8, 2022, from http://auditor.ca.gov/pdfs/reports/2019-047.pdf

Hudetz, M. and Ngu, A. (2023, December 4). Tribes in Maine spent decades fighting to rebury ancestral remains. Harvard Resisted them at nearly every turn. ProPublia. Retrieved on March 4, 2024, from https://www.propublica.org/article/inside-wabanaki-tribes-struggle-to-reclaim-ancestral-remains-from-harvard

Humboldt State University Place Based Learning Communities. (2019, August 9). Indian tribal & educational personnel program, Department of Native American Studies, history of Native California. YouTube. Retrieved April 29, 2022, from https://www.youtube.com/watch?v=T-azcAugm Q&t=10s

Idang, G. E. (2015). African culture and values. *Phronimon, 16*(2), 97–111. 10.25159/2413-3086/3820

Ighodaro, E. (2021, January 4). Tragedy: The story of Dr. Susan Moore & Black Medical Disparities. Youtube. Retrieved September 20, 2022, from https://www.youtube.com/watch?v=dkGkLVgDfnw&t=2572s

Jackson, Y. (2011). *The pedagogy of confidence: Inspiring high intellectual performance in urban schools.* Teachers College Press.

Jackson, Y. and Allender, D. (2016). Waiting to excel: Mediating 21st century teaching through the pedagogy of confidence. In J. A. Bellance (Ed.), *Connecting the dots: Teaching effectiveness and deeper professional learning* (pp. 279–298). Solution Tree Press.

Jan, T., McGregor, J., & Hoyer, M. (2021, August 24). Corporate America's $50 billion promise. The Washington Post. Retrieved March 13, 2023, from https://www.washingtonpost.com/business/interactive/2021/george-floyd-corporate-america-racial-justice/

Jha, S. (2018). The purpose of the Bindi. Hindu American Foundation. Retrieved March 4, 2022, from https://www.hinduamerican.org/blog/the-purpose-of-the-bindi/

Jones, J. H. (1993). *Bad blood: The Tuskegee syphilis experiment.* Free Press.

Kaplan Medical. (2020, October 15). Black pain matters: How historical medical assumptions about black pain thresholds impact care. YouTube. Retrieved August 22, 2022, from https://www.youtube.com/watch?v=4IaiD11JJxM&t=2797s

Kendi, I. X. (2017). *Stamped from the beginning: The definitive history of racist ideas in America.* Bold Type Books.

Kennard, A. (2022, July 6). Supreme Court will hear Indian Child Welfare Act Cases this fall – What that means for Indian Country. Native News Online. Retrieved August 20, 2022, from https://nativenewsonline.net/sovereignty/supreme-court-will-hear-indian-child-welfare-act-cases-this-fall-what-that-means-for-indian-country

Kerr, C. E., Jones, S. R., Wan, Q., Pritchett, D. L., Wasserman, R. H., Wexler, A., Villanueva, J. J., Shaw, J. R., Lazar, S. W., Kaptchuk, T. J., Littenberg, R., Hämäläinen, M. S., & Moore, C. I. (2011). Effects of mindfulness meditation training on anticipatory alpha modulation in primary somatosensory cortex. *Brain Research Bulletin, 85*(3–4), 96–103. 10.1016/j.brainresbull.2011. 03.026

Kwenele, B. (2020). Quoted in Norris, A. (2020) Episode One: The time is now. With special guest Babalwa Kwenele. Unhidden Voices. https://podcasts.apple. com/us/podcast/episode-one-the-time-is-now-special-guest-babalwa-kwanele/ id1518645270?i=1000478058262.

Lakoff, G. (2008). *The political mind.* Penguine.

Lawyers Committee for Civil Rights Under Law. (2020). Census citizenship question. Lawyers Committee for Civil Rights Under Law. Retrieved March, 16, 2022, from https://www.lawyerscommittee.org/2020-census-citizenship-question/

Leary, J. D. (2005). *Post traumatic slave syndrome: America's legacy of enduring injury and healing.* Milwaukie, Oregon: Uptone Press.

Legal Defense Fund. (n.d.). The Southern Manifesto and "Massive Resistance" to Brown. Legal Defense Fund. Retrieved February 20, 2022, from https://www. naacpldf.org/ldf-celebrates-60th-anniversary-brown-v-board-education/southern-manifesto-massive-resistance-brown/

Lee, K. (2020, May 21). Skeletons in the closet: The Smithsonian's Native American remains and the NMAI. Boundary Stones: WETA's History Website. Retrieved April 11, 2020, from https://boundarystones.weta.org/2020/ 05/21/skeletons-closet-smithsonian's-native-american-remains-and-founding-national-museum

Lee, M. Y., Zaharlick, A., & Akers, D. (2017). Impact of meditation on mental health outcomes of female trauma survivors of interpersonal violence with co-occurring disorders: A randomized controlled trial. *Journal of Interpersonal Violence, 32*(14), 2139–2165. 10.1177/0886260515591277.

Lecker, W. (2018, July 15). Minnesota high court allows claim of unconstitutional segregation to move forward. Education Law Center. https://edlawcenter.org/news/ archives/other-states/minnesota-high-court-allows-claims-of-unconstitutional-segregation-to-move-forward.html

Lester, J. C., Jia, J. L., Zhang, L., Okoye, G. A., & Linos, E. (2020). Absence of images of skin of colour in publications of COVID-19 skin manifestations. *The British Journal of Dermatology, 183*(3), 593–595. 10.1111/bjd.19258

Leung, V., Mendoza, A., & Cobb, J., (2018). *Here to learn: Creating safe and supportive schools in Los Angeles Unified School District.* ACLU.

Levy, A. (2005). *The first emancipator: The forgotten story of Robert Carter, the founding father who freed his slaves.* New York: Random House.

Lewis-McCoy R. L. (2018 March 16). Ask a black history professor: Do all black people have Native American in them? (Video). Youtube. https://youtu.be/ kftztPa_d-A?si=zey-YTrdvy-sIp12

Lindert, J., & Priebe, S. (2006). Long-term health impact of genocide and organized violence. *Epidemiology 17*(6), S119.

Lindsey, S., Epperson, S., & Jacobson, L. (2023, January 21). How companies are fulfilling promises made following George Floyd's murder. CNBC. Retrieved March 13, 2023, from https://www.cnbc.com/2023/01/21/how-companies-are-fulfilling-promises-made-after-george-floyds-murder.html

Martin, R. S. (2022). 2020 census undercount; explaining copyright laws, HBCU funding, Colorectal Cancer Awareness Month. YouTube. Retrieved July 11, 2022, from https://www.youtube.com/watch?v=aZJZjiDwUOk&list= PLbsXPZPls2m-5LPmbxqYMPlXXKMX4130u&index=8

Martinez-Alire, C., Borunda, R., & Olsen, S. (2017). California history depth and breadth from original American Indian tribal nations: Beyond a mere 250 years. In D. Allender and G. Y. Mark (Eds.), *Our stories in our voices* (pp. 5–27). Kendallhunt.

Mays, K. T. (2021). An Afro Indigenous history of the United States. Beacon Press.

Menakem, R. (2017). *My grandmother's hands: Racialized trauma and the pathway to mending our hearts and bodies.* Central Recovery Press, LLC.

McDole, T., & Brixey, E. (2020, May 20). Counting all kids: How the census impacts education. EdNote: Your education policy blog. Retrieved July 21, 2022, from https://ednote.ecs.org/counting-all-kids-how-the-census-impacts-education/

Monteiro, L. (2023). Open access violence: Legacies of white supremacist data making at the Penn Museum, from the Morton Cranial Collection to the MOVE remains. International Journal of Cultural Property, 30(2), 105–137. 10.1017/s0940739123000127.

Morgan, S. N., & Okyere-Manu (2020). The belief in and veneration of ancestors in Akan traditional thought: Finding values for human well-being. Alternation (30), 11–31.

Nagle, R. (2022). The story of baby O—and the case that could gut native sovereignty. *The Nation.* Retrieved November 1, 2023, from https://www.thenation.com/article/society/icwa-supreme-court-libretti-custody-case/

National Association of Social Workers Code of Ethics. (2021). Retrieved December 16, 2023, from https://www.socialworkers.org/About/Ethics/Code-of-Ethics/Code-of-Ethics-English#purpose

National Association of Social Workers. (2015). standards and indicators for cultural competence. Retrieved December 17, 2023, from https://www.socialworkers.org/LinkClick.aspx?fileticket=7dVckZAYUmk%3d&portalid=0

National Institute of Child Health and Human Development, National Institutes of Health, U.S. Department of Health and Human Services, & National Association for the Accreditation of Teacher Education. (2007). *Child and adolescent development research and teacher education: Evidence-based pedagogy, policy, and practice.* Washington, DC: U.S. Government Printing Office. Retrieved November 23, 2023, from https://files.eric.ed.gov/fulltext/ED498392.pdf

National Associations of Black Social Workers. (Winter, 2021). The National Association of Black Social Workers (NABSW) calls for the repeal of the Multi-Ethnic Placement Act (MEPA) and Inter-Ethnic Placement Act (IEPA). The Guardian, 43(4), pp. 1–5. Retrieved March 18, 2024 from https://cdn.ymaws.com/www.nabsw.org/resource/resmgr/2021_position_papers/2021_4304_repeal_mepa_iepa.pdf.

National Association of Social Workers. (2015). Standards and indicators of cultural competence in social work practices. National Association of Social Workers. Retrieved February 25, 2022, from https://www.socialworkers.org/LinkClick.aspx?fileticket=7dVckZAYUmk%3d&portalid=0

Nelson, S. R. (2006). *Steel drivin' man-John Henry: The untold story of an American legend.* Oxford.

Nemeth, E. (2015). *Cultural security: Evaluating the power of culture in international affairs.* Imperial College Press.

Nesper, L. (2002). *The Walleye War: The struggle for Ojibwe spearfishing and treaty rights.* Lincoln: University of Nebraska Press.

Nittle, N. K. (2019, January 4). A review of cultural appropriation and how to spot it. ThoughtCo. Retrieved September 3, 2021 https://www.thoughtco.com/a-review-of-cultural-appropriation-2834563

Nobles, W. (2006). *Seeking the Sakhu: Foundational writings for an African psychology*. Third World Press Inc.

Office of Juvenile Justice and Delinquency Prevention. (2014). Disproportionate Minority Contact (DMC). Office of Juvenile Justice and Delinquency Prevention. Retrieved February 20, 2022, from https://ojjdp.ojp.gov/mpg/literature-review/disproportionate-minority-contact.pdf

Organization of Islamic Cooperation. (1990). The Cairo declaration of the organization of the Islamic cooperation on human rights. Retrieved from https://www.oic-oci.org/upload/pages/conventions/en/CDHRI_2021_ENG.pdf on December 16, 2023.

Ohito, E. & Brown, K. (2021). Feeling safe from the storm of anti-Blackness: Black affective networks and the im/possibility of safe classroom spaces in Predominantly White Institutions. *Curriculum Inquiry*, *51*(1), 135–160. 10.1080/03626784.2020.1843966

Orie, A. (2022, January 18). The creator of the viral Black fetus image will have his illustrations published in a book. CNN Health. Retrieved February 28, 2022, from https://www.cnn.com/2022/01/13/health/chidiebere-ibe-medical-illustrations-published-nigeria-spc-intl/index.html

Ortiz-Dunbar, R. (2014). *An indigenous peoples' history of the United States*. Beacon Press.

Owens, D. C. (2017). *Medical bondage: Race, gender, and the origins of American gynecology*. University of Georgia Press. 10.2307/j.ctt1pwt69x

Parker, R. B., Larkin, T. A., & Cockburn, J. P. (2017). A visual analysis of gender bias in contemporary anatomy textbooks. *Social Science & Medicine, 180*, 106–113.

Parkhill, M. (2022, April 1). Read the full text of the Pope's apology for Canada's residential schools. CTV News. Retrieved March 8, 2022, from https://www.ctvnews.ca/canada/read-the-full-text-of-the-pope-s-apology-for-canada-s-residential-schools-1.5844874?cache=%3FclipId%3D2097462

Patterson, W. (Ed.). *We charge genocide. The crime of government against the negro people*. International Publishers.

Quinn, T. (2016). The experience of mindfulness exercise and coping with racism in the African American community. (Publication No. 10149954) [Doctoral dissertation, Michigan School of Professional Psychology]. ProQuest Dissertations and Theses Global.

Raja, T. (2016). A long, complicated battle over 9,000-year-old bones is finally over. Codeswitch. Retrieved April 11, 2022, from https://www.npr.org/sections/codeswitch/2016/05/05/476631934/a-long-complicated-battle-over-9-000-year-old-bones-is-finally-over

Rama, S. (1977). Joints and glands exercises. Himalayan Institute.

Rand, Y., Tannenbaum, A. J., & Feuerstein, R. (1979). Effects of Instrumental Enrichment on the psychoeducational development of low-functioning adolescents. Journal of Educational Psychology, *71*(6), 751–763. 10.1037/0022-0663.71.6.751

Redman, S. (2016). *Bone rooms: From scientific racism to human prehistory in museums*. Harvard University Press.

Roldan, R. (2020). Indigenous tribe sees mission to reclaim remains from UT as a spiritual issue, not a legal one. Austin's NPR Station. Retrieved April 11, 2022, from   https://www.kut.org/texas/2020-09-14/indigenous-tribe-sees-mission-to-reclaim-remains-from-ut-as-a-spiritual-issue-not-a-legal-one.

Rosa, E., & Tudge, J. (2013). Uri Bronfenbrenner's theory of human development: Its evolution from ecology to biology. *Journal of Family Theory & Review*, 243–258. .10.1111/jftr.12022

Ryan, E., Escobar, B., Ferra, B., & Polyarskaya, K. (2021). The executive order: A comparative examination of scope, authority and influence in four case studies. *University of Illinois Urbana Champagne Law Review, 3*(1). Retrieved November 16, 2023, from https://www.uiucuglawreview.web.illinois.edu/wp/2021/05/24/vol-iii-no-1-the-executive-order-a-comparative-examination-of-scope-authority-and-influence-in-four-case-studies/

Seo, H. (2021, April 29). Indigenous harvest rights still under attack in the upper great lakes. Environmental Health News. Retrieved March 4, 2024 from https://www.ehn.org/indigenous-harvest-rights-2652632895.html

Sleeter, C. (2020). Critical family history: an introduction. Genealogy, *4*(2), 64. 10.3390/genealogy4020064. Retrieved March 18, 2024 from https://www.mdpi.com/2313-5778/4/2/64

Smith, L., & Brown, A. (2018). *Herskovitz at the heart of blackness*. California Newsreel.

Somé, M. P. (1993). *Ritual: Power, healing, and community*. Penguin Books.

Spievak, N. (2019). Can unions help close the black white wage gap? Urban Institute. Retrieved March 7, 2022, from https://www.urban.org/urban-wire/can-labor-unions-help-close-black-white-wage-gap. Urban Institute Retrieved 3/7/2022

Stewart, E. (2018, April 15). Two black men were arrested in a Philadelphia Starbucks did nothing wrong. Vox. Retrieved February 20, 2021, from https://www.vox.com/identities/2018/4/14/17238494/what-happened-at-starbucks-black-men-arrested-philadelphia (Retrieved February 20, 2021).

Stout, C., & Wilburn, T. (2022). CRT Map: Efforts to restrict teaching racism and bias have multiplied across the U.S. Chalkbeat. Retrieved February 25, 2022, from https://www.chalkbeat.org/22525983/map-critical-race-theory-legislation-teaching-racism

Seager, R. H. (2006). *Encountering the dharma: Daisaku Ikeda, Soka Gakkai, and the globalization of Buddhist humanism*. Universirty of California Press.

Streeter, C. C., Gerbarg, P. L., Saper, R. B., Ciraulo, D. A., & Brown, R. P. (2012). Effects of yoga on the autonomic nervous system, gamma-aminobutyric-acid, and allostasis in epilepsy, depression, and post-traumatic stress disorder. *Medical Hypotheses, 78*(5), 571–579. 10.1016/j.mehy.2012.01.021

Suri, S. (2014, August 1). *Despite metamorphosis, moths hold on to memories from their days as a Caterpillar*. The Conversation. Retrieved March 5, 2024, from https://theconversation.com/despite-metamorphosis-moths-hold-on-to-memories-from-their-days-as-a-caterpilla-29859

Sweeton, J. (2019). *Trauma treatment toolbox: 165 brain-changing tips, tools & handouts to move therapy forward*. PESI Publishing & Media.

The National Association of Black Social Workers (NABSW) Calls for the Repeal of the Multi-Ethnic Placement Act (MEPA) and Inter-Ethnic Placement Act (IEPA). *The Guardian*. National Association of Council for Children.

Tinkley, M. (2022). *African-Americans – slave population*. South Carolina's Information Highway. Retrieved March 7, 2022, from https://www.sciway.net/afam/slavery/population.html.

Tobin, J., Hardy, J., Calanche, M. L., Gonzalez, K. D., Baezconde-Garbanati, L., Contreras, R., & Bluthenthal, R. N. (2021). A community-based mindfulness intervention among Latino adolescents and their parents: a qualitative feasibility and acceptability study. *Journal of Immigrant and Minority Health, 23*(2), 344–352. 10.1007/s10903-020-00985-9

Tofle, R. B., Schwartz, B., Yoon, S.-Y. & Max-Royale, A. (2004). Color in healthcare A critical review of the research literature. *Coalition for Health Environments Research.* Retrieved on October 26, 2023, from https://www.healthdesign.org/knowledge-repository/color-healthcare-environments-critical-review-research-literature.

Tracey, M. D. (2022). California association of realtors apologizes for past discrimination. National Association of Realtors. Retrieved October 29, 2022, from https://www.nar.realtor/magazine/california-association-of-realtors-apologizes-for-past-discrimination.

Türk, V. (2023). The UDHR at 75: A conversation with UN High Commissioner for Human Rights Volker Türk. The Center for Strategic and International Studies. Retrieved June 10, 2023, from https://www.youtube.com/watch?v=OArEJ10FUC0

Tylor, E. B. (1889). *Primitive culture: Researches into the development of mythology, philosophy, religion, language, art and custom* (3rd American from 2nd English ed.). Henry Holt and Company. 10.1037/12987-000

UN General Assembly. (1956). Admission of Japan to membership the United Nations: Resolution/adopted by the General Assembly. Retrieved June 11, 2023, from https://digitallibrary.un.org/record/667226?ln=en

UN General Assembly, Convention on the Prevention and Punishment of the Crime of Genocide, 9 December 1948, United Nations, Treaty Series, *78*, 277. United Nations General. Retrieved May 15, 2023, from https://www.un.org/en/genocideprevention/documents/atrocity-crimes/Doc.1_Convention%20on%20the%20Prevention%20and%20Punishment%20of%20the%20Crime%20of%20Genocide.pdf

UN General Assembly 182nd Plenary Meeting, held on Friday, 10 December 1948: 10/12/1948. Retrieved June 10, 2023, from https://documents-dds-ny.un.org/doc/UNDOC/GEN/NL4/812/22/PDF/NL481222.pdf?OpenElement

United Nations General Assembly. (1948). *The Universal Declaration of Human Rights (UDHR)*. New York: United Nations General Assembly.

United Nations General Assembly. (2007). United Nations Declaration of the Rights of Indigenous Peoples. Retrieved December 16, 2023, from https://www.un.org/development/desa/indigenouspeoples/wp-content/uploads/sites/19/2018/11/UNDRIP_E_web.pdf

U.S. Food & Drug Administration. (2021, February 19). Pulse oximeter accuracy and limitations: FDA safety communication. Food and Drug Administration. Retrieved March 26, 2022, from https://www.fda.gov/medical-devices/safety-communications/pulse-oximeter-accuracy-and-limitations-fda-safety-communication

U.S. Government Accountability Office. (2020, August 27). Pulse oximeter accuracy and limitations: FDA safety communication. Food and Drug Administration. Retrieved March 16, 2022, from https://www.gao.gov/products/gao-20-671r

U.S. Government Accountability Office. (2020, December 3). 2020 Census: Census Bureau needs to assess data quality concerns stemming from recent design changes. U.S. Government Accountability Office. Retrieved March 16, 2022, from https://www.gao.gov/products/gao-21-142

Vallejo, Z., & Amaro, H. (2009). Adaptation of mindfulness-based stress reduction program for addiction relapse prevention. *The Humanistic Psychologist, 37*(2), 192–206. 10.1080/08873260902892287

Vega, M. M. (1999). Espiritismo in the Puerto Rican community: a new world recreation with the elements of Kongo ancestor worship. *Journal of Black Studies, 29*(3), 325–353. 10.1177/002193479902900301

Villamure, C. et al. (2015). Neuroprotective effects of yoga practice: age-, experience-, and frequency-dependent plasticity. Frontiers in Human Neuroscience (9). 10.33 89/fnhum.2015.00281

Waldman, A. (1999). Iron Eyes Cody, 94, an actor and tearful anti-littering icon. New York Times. Retrieved on April 5, 2022, from https://www.nytimes. com/1999/01/05/arts/iron-eyes-cody-94-an-actor-and-tearful-anti-littering-icon. html

Wall, I. (2016). Architecture and prisons: why design matters. *The Guardian.* Retrieved on October 26, 2023, from https://www.theguardian.com/global-development-professionals-network/2016/sep/28/architecture-and-prisons-why-design-matters.

Wall, L. L. (2006). The medical ethics of Dr J Marion Sims: A fresh look at the historical record. *Journal of Medical Ethics. 32*(6), 346–350. 10.1136/jme.2005 .012559. Retrieved October 2, 2022, from https://www.ncbi.nlm.nih.gov/pmc/ articles/PMC2563360/

Washington, H. (2006). Medical apartheid: The dark history of medical experimentation on Black Americans from colonial times to the present. Vintage.

Wei, G. et al. (2013). Can Taichi reshape the brain? A brain morphometry study. PLoS ONE, *8*(4), e61038. 10.1371/journal.pone.0061038.

Whitaker, A., & Walters, I. J. (2023). *Afro unidad: Culture, rebellion, across the diaspora.* KnuckleHead Publishing.

White, B. C. M. (2014). Death of the ring shout: African American ancestor veneration, Africana theology, and George Washington. *Black Theology, 12*(1), 44–57.

Williams-Butler, A., Golden, K. E., Mendez, A., & Stevens, B. (2020). Intersectionality and child welfare policy. *Child Welfare League of America, 98*(4), 75–96.

WPRI. (2022, May 19). RI overcounted population in 2020 census, federal study finds (Video). Youtube. https://youtu.be/0hjkIull3wo?si=hggw9r1FQVnqZhYK.

Woods, D., & Wang, H. L. (2022). The economic impact of the census miscount. The indicator from Planet Money. National Public Radio. Retrieved July 12, 2022, from https://podcasts.apple.com/us/podcast/the-economic-impacts-of-a-census-miscount/id1320118593?i=1000555527904

Woodson, C. G. (1934). *The mis-education of the negro.* Africa World Press.

Wright, R., Roberson, K., Onsomu, E. O., Johnson, Y., Dearman, C., Carr, L. T. B., Price, A. A., & Duren-Winfield, V. (2018). Examining the relationship between mindfulness, perceived stress, and blood pressure in African-American college students. *Journal of Best Practices in Health Professions Diversity: Research, Education and Policy, 11*(1), 13–30.

Yosso, T. (2005). Whose culture has capital? A critical race theory discussion of community cultural wealth. *Race, Ethnicity and Education, 8*, 69–91. 10.1080/ 1361332052000341006

Youtube. (2018, August 11). Barnes and Gotlieb (1965) Equality under the law: The lost Generation. Retrieved March 4, 2024, from https://www.youtube.com/ watch?v=ah8gZu53V4A&t=17s

Youtube. (2021, April 26). Hill, M. L. Marc Lamont Hill talks Penn Museum apology for housing human remains from MOVE bombing. Youtube. Retrieved March 4, 2024 from https://www.youtube.com/watch?v=qOVOByfMKtM&list=PLbsXPZPls2m_cVoXjeojt-q6eIR_AMiCC&index=7

YouTube. (2022, May 15). 2020 US Census Bureau understanding the count: a discussion on the latest 2020 post enumeration survey results. YouTube. Retrieved July 11, 2022, from https://www.youtube.com/watch?v=k8heXl TBSG8&list=PLbsXPZPls2m-5LPmbxqYMPlXXKMX4130u&index=19.

YouTube. (2020, December 15). *2020 US Census Bureau demographic online news conference.* YouTube. Retrieved July 10, 2022, from https://www.youtube.com/watch?v=XFBnnYmPIAk&t=1712s.

YouTube. (2022, March10). *2020 census data quality results news conference.* YouTube. Retrieved July 10, 2022, from https://www.youtube.com/watch?v=tl73H8JBuPU

Endmatter

Index

For Product Safety Concerns and Information please contact our EU
representative GPSR@taylorandfrancis.com
Taylor & Francis Verlag GmbH, Kaufingerstraße 24, 80331 München, Germany

9 781032 011707